Giorgio Caramanna has a Ph.D. in geology and over 25 years of experience as a professional scientific diver in Europe, Asia, and the USA. He is a consultant for the Diving Program of the Woods Hole Oceanographic Institution, Woods Hole, Massachusetts, USA.

He has published and reviewed scientific papers in international journals. He is also a guest writer for Ocean for Future. Giorgio has now distilled his experience as a scientific writer and diver into the "Risk Management for Diving Operations" book, developing an in-depth analysis of the main risks affecting divers and how to manage them.

Giorgio is a NAUI Instructor, Advanced European Scientific Diver, and American Academy of Underwater Sciences Diver. During his research activity, he used diving to collect the needed data in often challenging environments, including under the ice, caves, and volcanic areas.

In 2018 he was awarded the "Golden Trident" from the International Academy of Underwater Sciences and Techniques for his contribution to the progress of diving science and exploration.

When not underwater, Giorgio enjoys walks in the woods, bicycling, and running in the Cape Cod area where he lives. He is also passionate about books, mainly about the sea, diving medicine, and diving history.

RISK MANAGEMENT FOR DIVING OPERATIONS

How to Enhance the Safety and Proficiency of Diving Teams

GIORGIO CARAMANNA, PHD

With the collaboration of Brian Strickland, MD

International Academy of Underwater Sciences and Techniques

To my parents

CONTENTS

1. Hazard and risk

2. Human and organizational factors

3. Leadership

4. Situational awareness

5. Learning and overlearning

6. Stress and performance

7. Environmental and physiological hazards

7.1. Cold

7.2. Low visibility

7.3. Polluted water

7.4. Differential pressure

7.5. Depth

7.6. Hypoxia, hypoxemia and CO_2

7.7. Fatigue

8. Checklists

9. Fault tree analysis

10. Diving incidents and accidents

11. Case studies

12. Diving risk assessment structure

13. Medical fitness to dive

14. Planning for a successful dive

Appendices

FOREWORD

Dive Professionals that have dive planning, supervisory duties, or ascending the responsibilities of an underwater career have an ambitious trait. They seek knowledge in the aspects of this chosen discipline. It is always a journey that has no final Port of Call. The quest leads them into different venues of diving information, such as printed material, and learned and shared experiences, to name a few. The sum of these efforts is a comradery of opinionated strong-minded professionals that embrace an extreme environment for their daily labors.

The themes that resonate in any professional writing should contain information expressed in a pragmatic format that greatly assists the person in their vocation. Dr. Giorgio Caramanna's effort has achieved this at a high standard. *Risk Management for Dive Operations* is well-researched, easy to comprehend, and a most useful book for Dive Professionals. His method on the subject is academic in nature, with a bibliography, index, and footnotes at the end of the chapter for further investigation. The chapters' main points have bullet points that are both accurate and precise, along with professional examples that remind me of informational sea stories that an olde salt might tell someone in the pipeline. In this approach, Dr. Caramanna has crafted a book that gives substance to a topic to every type of reader based on their specific learning attitude.

Dr. Brian Strickland, a physician that deals with medicine in extreme environments, also has tremendous input. His chapters concerning fitness for diving and dive medicine subjects are essential for every Diver. A tremendous challenge to the Dive Professional is presented in a world where Divers' medical histories are diverse and complicated. These chapters give the Dive leader substance in determining the risks for his team in this regard.

Risk Management for Dive Operations should be read from front to back; once accomplished, if the Diver chooses to make it a handbook, reference book, or teaching abstract, that is their choice. The volume will undoubtedly be battered, dog-eared, and like some of my trusted books, held together with Duct tape. I suppose I am dating myself, however, as I am sure electronic copies will be the norm. Regardless, this information source will be utilized in many aspects of the Divers career.

I commend Dr. Caramanna and Dr. Strickland for their effort, and I am most thankful to them both for including me in reviewing vetting and even a few pictures at our Iselin Pier in Woods Hole. It has been a wonderful experience.

Ed O'Brien
Dive Operations Manager
Woods Hole Oceanographic Institution
Iselin Pier, Woods Hole, Mass
July 4th 2023

PREFACE

Diving operations are complex, often requiring the coordination of multiple teams working in potentially hazardous environments. Even if a "zero risk" approach is not possible, because there is always a degree of risk in any action we perform, a "zero accident" target should be the goal for safe and effective dives.

During my career as a professional scientific diver, I have been involved in various projects that required diving using multiple techniques and different gear, including snorkeling, open-circuit, rebreathers, surface supply, and even rigid normobaric suits. The operational environments have included lakes, rivers, karst springs, caves, open ocean, ice, and artificial structures. Each of these situations exposed the divers to specific risks that needed to be carefully considered and managed.

Throughout those years, I found much enjoyment in my career. Still, I was also saddened by the many fatal accidents that affected the diving community at large and which showed the same pattern of mistakes and bad decisions over and over again. We all make mistakes, but we should be able to learn from those mistakes and avoid repeating them. Errors are an integral part of human behavior and affect our daily lives. Still, while some have trivial consequences, others can be fatal, mainly when operating in hostile and unforgiving environments, such as when we dive.

From my experience, I have learned that planning, risk assessment, and reciprocal trust within the diving team are the cornerstone of safe and proficient operations.

This book aims to provide the reader with a good deal of information about sources of errors, human factors and their impact on safety, the importance of good situational awareness, what characteristics make a good dive leader, how we should learn essential diving skills, what kind of stress, both physical and psychological, affects our performance, and what specific hazards derive from the different diving environments and the effect of diving on human physiology. Some dive incidents are analyzed using a standard procedure so the reader can learn and apply it to their analysis. Finally, information and examples of risk assessment and management procedures are presented. The reader can use these examples to develop policies focused on specific needs.

In writing this book, I have followed a strictly scientific approach. References support the information; the reader can refer to them at the end of each chapter for further details.

The biomedical aspects of diving have been reviewed by Brian Strickland, MD, who completed his fellowship in wilderness medicine at Massachusetts General Hospital and is currently a practicing emergency medicine physician. He has also authored the chapter focused on medical fitness for diving, which seeks to understand the impact of underlying medical conditions on dive safety.

The book is divided into 14 "standalone" chapters; each has a summary of its main contents at the beginning and a "lessons learned" section at the end. You can read the book cover-to-cover or only focus on the chapters related to your diving operations – the decision is yours.

The following is a summary of the topics of each chapter:

Chapter 1: An introductory chapter to risk management. The concepts of hazard and risk are explained, and risk assessment outlines are provided.

Chapter 2: In this chapter, the reader can find an overview of human and organizational factors related to diving operations.

Chapter 3: This chapter focuses on leadership characteristics and related issues. The leader is a key figure in any team, primarily when the team is operating "in the field" of operations.

Chapter 4: In this chapter, the importance of good situational awareness for divers is explained with specific examples.

Chapter 5: Some key skills need to become almost "instinctive." This chapter will describe the essentials of the learning process and how we can "overlearn" the basics and emergency diving skills.

Chapter 6: A degree of stress is unavoidable when diving, and in this chapter, the reader will learn how to manage the stress to improve proficiency and safety.

Chapter 7: This is the longest chapter and describes several environmental and physiological hazards and how to reduce the associated risks. As environmental stressors, cold, low visibility, polluted waters, differential pressure, and depth will be described in detail. The risks related to hypoxia, hypoxemia, and CO_2 will also be addressed. Finally, fatigue will be considered as one of the most common, and underestimated, stressors for divers.

Chapter 8: This chapter deals with checklists, an essential tool for enhancing safety, mainly when operating under stressful conditions.

Chapter 9: Fault tree analysis (FTA) is a logical procedure that aims to identify the root causes of accidents. In this chapter, FTA will be applied to diving situations.

Chapter 10: This chapter overviews diving incidents and accidents, analyzing their leading causes and how such incidents can be avoided.

Chapter 11: In this chapter actual incidents are analyzed following a structured procedure. The aim is to provide the reader with knowledge and methods to perform their own analysis of potential mishaps.

Chapter 12: The structure of a diving risk assessment is presented in this chapter.

Chapter 13: Information about medical fitness for diving and its importance for risk management are provided here.

Chapter 14: In this final chapter, the reader will understand how to develop a sound and safe dive plan.

If you are diving as part of your profession or simply because you love it, this reading will make you a safer and more confident diver.

Reading this material without proper training and experience is not sufficient for safe diving. Failing to follow the correct procedures when diving may cause severe harm or even death. You must be adequately trained and certified for the diving level you intend to perform.

Giorgio Caramanna
Martha's Vineyard, MA, USA
June 2023

1. HAZARD AND RISK

Chapter highlights

Any action we perform exposes us to the risk of realizing an unwanted outcome.

Acting safely does not mean acting without risk; instead, it focuses on understanding the risk typology, assessing its potential impact on our actions, and developing adequate mitigating strategies.

The longer we are exposed to any given hazard, the more likely it is to cause some harm. Reducing exposure time is one of the most effective strategies for risk mitigation.

A risk assessment procedure is a logical analysis of the risks that may affect a given operation, starting with the correct identification of such risks, the likelihood of their happening, the degree of their impact, and finally, the definition of viable strategies for risk avoidance or mitigation.

Introduction

In any action we perform, the outcomes may not match the planned goals, and we may be exposed to some degree of harm. In other words, we have to accept a certain degree of risk. There are several strategies to manage and reduce the level of risk; however, even when we aim for the safest approach, we will still have to deal with some residual risk. "Safe" is not the same as "risk-free" (1). The more complex the procedure we have to perform and the more challenging the environment, the higher the risk will be (2), (3).

Diving is an inherently dangerous activity that exposes participants to the risk of injury or death in extreme circumstances. Developing a good knowledge of the risks associated with diving and learning appropriate risk-management strategies will reduce the likelihood of being hurt. Good training, physical and psychological fitness, mastering diving procedures, and using high-quality and well-maintained gear are the fundamentals for a safe approach to this fascinating activity.

Accidents, incidents, and near misses

Incidents and accidents are unexpected adverse events affecting operations but have different consequences (4).

Accident: An unexpected event that culminates in loss of or severe equipment damage or personnel injury.

Incident: An unexpected event that degrades safety and increases the probability of an accident.

For example, a weight belt becoming loose is an incident if the diver manages to reconnect it. If, instead, the weight belt is lost, and the diver becomes a victim of the consequences of an uncontrolled ascent (barotrauma, decompression sickness (DCS), arterial gas embolism (AGE)), then this is an accident.

It is possible to identify three components in the events leading up to an accident/incident (3):

- *Direct cause*: Faulty actions or lack of appropriate actions immediately preceding the error.
- *Contributing cause*: The root of the direct cause.
- *Compounding events*: Positive events can help to mitigate the error; adverse events can exacerbate it.

An example of a direct cause of a diving accident is the case of a diver holding their breath during the ascent, leading to barotrauma in the lungs. A contributing cause could be the poor knowledge of basic skills (always exhale when ascending) or panic that will impair such skills. A negative compounding effect could be an uncontrolled fast ascent exacerbating the change in pressure.

In many diving accidents, the contributing causes are multiple errors and negative attitudes, which start well before the diver enters the water (5).

For example, divers omitting pre-dive checks will be more exposed to not having essential dive gear or missing/forgetting to perform crucial procedures, such as opening the cylinder's valve or connecting low-pressure hoses to the BCD (Buoyancy Controlling Device) and drysuit inflator. This can lead to accidents/incidents where the contributing cause is to be found not underwater but on dry land before commencing the dive.

As an example of a compounding event, let's consider an error in gas usage calculation that may mean the air runs out at the end of a dive. This negative event might be mitigated by the fact that the dive was a shallow one, not requiring any decompression stop. On the other end of the scale, the same error could be aggravated and even have fatal outcomes if long decompression stops were omitted due to the lack of breathing gas availability.

Near misses are events that did not cause an accident but strongly reduce the safety of the operation. Near misses should prompt higher vigilance to avoid developing into actual incidents or accidents (6).

An honest analysis of any near miss should be included in the post-dive briefing so that the conditions leading to an unsafe situation can be analyzed and appropriate corrections can be implemented for future dives.

Only a fraction of unsafe situations will lead to an incident, and an even smaller fraction of incidents will cause an accident. Nevertheless, limiting the number of hazardous states will strongly reduce the risk of an accident (Fig. 1.1).

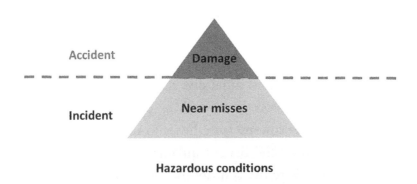

Fig. 1.1. Starting from hazardous conditions, increasing risk is represented by near misses and an accident where actual damage happens.

The concept of hazard and risk

A hazard is a potential source of harm or adverse effect that can impact people, materials, and activities. Risk is determined by the likelihood that a hazard can affect the action and the magnitude of its impact. Risk can be quantified as the product of the probability of a hazard causing harm and the severity of its consequences. The severity of a hazard is about the gravity of the resulting accident in terms of injuries to people and damage to materials. The probability of the hazard quantifies how likely it is for such an adverse event to occur during the considered timeframe (7):

Risk = P_h * C

P_h = Probability of the hazard

C = Severity of the consequences

Different combinations of probability and hazard can reach the same level of risk; a low-severity hazard with a high likelihood of happening may have the same risk level as a much more severe hazard with a lower probability of occurring. A risk with higher-severity consequences should induce more caution than a less severe one, even if both risks' numerical value (calculated above) is the same. Another important point in assessing the risk level is the considered timeframe: even low-probability hazards may happen if we consider very long timeframes. Generally, the longer the exposure to the hazard, the higher the risk will be.

Although it is possible to quantify risk numerically, its acceptance is still a question of personal decision (8). Are we willing to accept the risk of a hazard that has a very low probability of occurring, but if it does, it will have significant consequences – or are we more open to accepting a likely hazard with minor impacts? Our response will depend on various considerations, including our attitude toward risk, the importance of the goal we want to reach in performing our activity, former experience in similar situations, and social, professional, and environmental pressure.

The acceptable level of risk is correlated to the importance of the operation. For example, the US Navy will accept a much higher risk in war campaigns than peace operations. This means the same action could be considered acceptable under war conditions but forbidden in peacetime even if the risk remains the same (9). Professional divers may accept higher risks than recreational divers because risk-acceptance is part of their job and is needed to perform the required operations. On the other hand, a professional diver will likely perform a more careful risk analysis than a recreational diver and, under the same circumstances, may decline to dive if they identify unacceptable risks.

In a 1983 British Royal Society report entitled "Risk assessment," a distinction between objective and perceived risk was assessed. The same activity can be considered risky by some or safe by others with different skills, experience, and attitudes. Risk acceptance, as in the risk compensation model developed by G. Wilde in 1976 and modified by J. Adams in 1988, is influenced by potential rewards associated with the activity to be performed and by former experiences. For a given activity, some individuals are more exposed to the risk than others: the operators "in the field" are more exposed to the direct consequences of a hazard than managerial positions in the same organization. Therefore, operators' and managers' risk perceptions will differ (8). This can lead to some disagreement regarding the operations that can be safely performed. In uncertain situations, with limited objective information, the risk perception can be altered. In cases where clear evidence is limited cultural filters will create bias where only a limited number of the possible risks are considered. Experts have a better understanding of the risks and, therefore, a reduced bias. A reasonable estimate of the risk should be realistic, meaning that risks should not be overlooked, but also that an overestimation of the risk does not necessarily lead to safer practice and could cause reduced proficiency and an increase in costs (6).

Divers will have a different perception of the potential risks involved in underwater operations than people who do not dive because divers are routinely exposed to the unforgiving under-water environment, which allows them a better understanding and knowledge of the hazards that can be present. For this reason, when planning operations involving both diving teams and surface personnel, the divers, or the divers' supervisor, should be in charge of the diving risk assessment procedure.

Risk assessment matrix

Once the risk level has been assessed, adequate mitigation strat-egies should be applied to eliminate, reduce or control the risk. The combination of risk severity and probability makes it pos-sible to build a risk assessment matrix (RAM; see Table 1.1). Suppose no adequate mitigation procedure is possible, such as for events falling within the high-risk zone of the RAM. In that case, it may be necessary to refrain from proceeding further with the project to avoid exposing the participants to unacceptable dangers (10).

Probability	Severity			
	Catastrophic	Critical	Marginal	Negligible
Frequent	High	High	Serious	Medium
Probable	High	High	Serious	Medium
Occasional	High	Serious	Medium	Low
Remote	Serious	Medium	Medium	Low
Improbable	Medium	Medium	Medium	Low

Table 1.1. Risk assessment matrix.

For example, let's consider the risk of a total loss of breathing gas. In the RAM, the severity of such an event is catastrophic. It is, in fact, a life-threatening situation. To reduce the overall risk to an acceptable level (serious or medium in the RAM), the probability of total loss of breathing gas must be remote or improbable. To reduce the probability, the use of multiple redundant sources of breathing gas, such as two independent cylinders each connected to a regulator, and a conservative approach to gas usage, such as the rule of thirds, are enforced. Because the consequences are extreme, the overall risk will never be low, even with an improbable probability level. Is a medium risk acceptable? The decision is the diver's; the RAM helps assess the risk, but its acceptability remains a personal choice that cannot be delegated.

Qualitative hazard analysis

A qualitative hazard analysis aims to identify all the significant hazards and the mitigation strategies that can be applied so that the level of risk for each hazard is "as low as reasonably practicable" (ALARP), meaning that such risk cannot be further mitigated without incurring prohibitive costs and/or unreasonably complex procedures (11).

For example, we can consider the likelihood of incurring in DCS after shallow dives when a safety stop is performed. The risk is relatively low, but we could consider having a decompression chamber onsite to reduce this further moderate risk. This will require considerable cost, including the chamber, ancillary equipment, a larger vessel to host the chamber, medical and technical personnel, and more complex procedures. Under normal circumstances, such aggravation in expenditure and complexity is not justified by reducing a modest risk.

The US Navy defined its Risk Assessment Code (RAC; see Table 1.2) as a matrix of the severity of hazards and their probability of occurring based on the RAM model (12).

A: likely to occur		Probability			
B: probably will occur or expected to occur several times		A	B	C	D
C: may occur or can be reasonably expected to occur					
D: unlikely to occur					
Hazard severity	Diver fatality	1	1	2	3
1: Critical	Severe injury	1	2	3	4
2: Serious	Minor injury	2	3	4	5
3: Moderate	Very minor injury	3	4	5	5
4: Minor					
5: Negligible					

Table 1.2. Risk Assessment Code matrix

Of the 16 combinations of severity and probability, only three are considered negligible; this highlights that mishaps can easily lead to serious injury during diving operations. For the most severe events, such as fatality and severe injury, reducing the probability to "unlikely to occur" is mandatory to reduce the overall risk. This can be achieved by carefully evaluating all the realistic potential hazards and then identifying effective avoidance or mitigation procedures.

A qualitative risk analysis is often the only available and practical tool for a diver. To perform a reliable assessment, several pieces of information are required. This information will cover various aspects of the dive, including dive profile, dive environment, diving equipment, divers' experience, qualification, and familiarity with the tasks. Once this and any other relevant information has been collected, the divers can identify the potential risks and mitigation strategies that must be applied to reduce such risks to ALARP status. Once again, the acceptable level of risk is a personal choice; risk assessment is a helpful tool to identify the potential impact on the operation. However, the decision to proceed with the dive is left to the divers involved.

Risk assessment outlines

Making errors is almost unavoidable, but mitigating their impact is possible through a logical and consequential process defined as "risk assessment." The following is an example of this analytical process:

A dive is planned for tomorrow at 9:30 am, and from the tidal chart, we know the current will pick up by 10:30 am. This gives us a full hour of dive time before the environmental conditions deteriorate. Therefore, we plan accordingly for a 45-minute dive time to have a margin of safety. Some delays affect the setting-up of the diving gear, and we are ready to enter the water at 9:45 am. If we maintain the initially planned dive time, this will remove the safety margin. Should we reduce the dive time or not? It depends. Suppose we know that a strong current usually develops abruptly in the area, and we will have a long decompression time at the end of our dive. In that case, we should reduce our dive time to be safely within the margins in case of any delay. Risk is an objective value, but its acceptance or refusal is subjective. On the other hand, if we know that the current starts mildly, and that no decompression will be required, we may accept the risk of terminating the dive just at the beginning of the tidal current cycle. What should be noted is that the results of our risk assessment – reducing the dive time or not – may differ from those of other divers, even under the same circumstances.

The US Navy has developed a decision-making procedure (Operational Risk Management – ORM) that aims to identify, assess and manage risk, thus increasing the probability of a successful outcome. The following section will provide an outline of this procedure (9).

The ORM provides a systematic structure for reasoned and repeatable risk assessment. This helps develop effective risk control procedures, mostly when appropriate standards are unavailable. The operator is provided with enough data for an informed risk decision that is then checked by feedback through the planning, preparation, and execution phases.

The ORM is based on four principles:

1. *Risk acceptance*: Balancing risks vs. benefits requires knowledge and experience.

For example, an expert diver can correctly understand the risk involved in a given diving situation. In contrast, a novice diver could overlook critical aspects of dive safety, mostly if under professional or peer pressure.

2. *Avoid unnecessary risks*: An unnecessary risk will jeopardize safety without adding valuable gain to the operation.

For example, diving deeper for the sake of it increases the risk of DCS or out-of-air situations without adding any practical value to the dive. In contrast, if a deep dive is needed to reach a specific goal, such as exploring a wreck, then the added risk is part of the operation, and it is reasonable to include it in the overall assessment.

3. *Anticipate risk*: Integrating the ORM process into planning as early as possible provides the best support for making well-informed risk decisions.

For example, the risks associated with a dive should be assessed during the initial phase of the dive planning so that it will be clear what resources are needed and if the overall operation is within the range of the skills/experience of the involved divers.

4. *Take the risk decision to the right level*: Ensure that the appropriate individual makes risk decisions with the knowledge, experience, and position to understand and mitigate the risk.

For example, it could be necessary to refer to the dive leader or the diving safety officer with the experience and authority to decide about the safety of the dive operation.

The ORM follows three basic steps:

1. *Identify the hazard*: The critical point is to identify the root cause of any danger and how this can affect the mission.

2. *Assess the hazard*: For each identified hazard, its associated risk is determined in terms of potential consequences (severity) and likelihood (probability).
3. *Complete risk assessment*: Combine severity and probability levels into a single value. RAM is often used at this stage.

The ORM can be performed at three levels based on the available time.

1. *In-depth*: When time is not a limiting factor, the ORM can benefit from proper research and analysis of all available data.

For example, when designing new equipment or during the planning of diving campaigns, adequate time should be allotted for an extensive assessment of potential hazards and associated mitigation strategies and procedures.

2. *Deliberate*: Time is still not an issue, allowing for brainstorming and using experienced personnel to plan the operations.

For example, during the briefing, the key points of the dive should be reviewed in terms of risk assessment or using a "what if?" approach to identify and fix weaknesses in the procedures.

3. *Time-critical*: Time is limited, such as during an operation, and the operators must quickly address changes. In this case, the ORM is based on four steps:

I. *Assess the situation*: Good situational awareness is essential to apply appropriate resources quickly and effectively.

II. *Balance resources*: Allows for informed and effective risk decisions.

III. *Communicate*: A key factor – loss of communication is often associated with the degradation of the mission.

IV. *Debrief*: Clear feedback and debriefing are essential to learn from the gained experience, use it for future risk management, and improve the following operations.

This is the typical approach if something unexpected happens during the dive requiring rapid changes in procedures and goals. To facilitate a time-critical decision, the development of alternative plans should be integrated into the overall dive planning.

Some errors are common and should be avoided during an ORM procedure.

1. *Over-optimism and misrepresentation*: Personal bias that prevents identification of the actual level of risk.

This is often the case in novice divers who are too keen to achieve the planned goal and may need help in correctly assessing the level of involved risk.

2. *Alarmism*: Planning for a "worst-case scenario" independent from its actual likelihood.

For example, considering a catastrophic failure of the life-support system despite its low probability may require adding an unjustified level of redundancy that can be extremely costly and impractical to manage.

3. *Indiscrimination*: All the information is considered equally relevant for the risk assessment procedure, leading to an overload of data and potential erroneous risk evaluation.

A good diver should be able to identify the information relevant to the risk assessment of the dive, avoiding being distracted by other irrelevant data.

4. *Enumeration*: Difficulty in quantifying human behavior with a numerical value.

Sometimes obtaining numerical values can be challenging or even impossible. In this case, the risk assessment can be qualitative. It will still be helpful, providing a general and informed view of the potential risks involved.

5. *Inaccuracy*: Bad data acquisition.

The data used for the risk assessment should be carefully verified regarding accuracy and usefulness.

An important concept when assessing risk is the "regression to the median." In terms of accidents, it is expected that an improvement of the situation follows a series of particularly adverse events, and vice versa, a period of remarkable safety is interrupted by an accident. This is a natural and unavoidable statistical trend and should be considered when planning and assessing the validity of risk-reduction strategies (6).

For example, during the training of divers, it is very likely that after a series of very positive results, some drop in performance will happen. This should be addressed as a "natural" outcome and clearly explained to the students to avoid losing confidence that could impair the remainder of the training.

On the other hand, a successful dive should not be considered indicative of the actual level of safety if this dive has not been planned following appropriate procedures and standards. This is particularly relevant if the successful outcome follows a deviation from the standards. In this case, the operators could be led to believe that violating the standards will not affect the safety of the dive. This situation is called "normalization of the deviance" (8) and it is a dangerous behavior prompting the operators to disregard good practice. For example, divers could be tempted to dive well outside their knowledge and experience solely because they did it once or multiple times with no adverse consequences. Persisting in such deviance will instead, sooner or later, cause an incident. The importance of knowledge, training, and experience cannot be underestimated when performing a correct risk assessment.

Lessons learned

- "Safe" is not the same as "risk-free."
- Risk is a combination of a hazard's probability and its impact's severity.
- An accident is an event causing damage.
- An incident is an event increasing the likelihood of an accident to happen.

- Even if the risk is objective, its acceptance is subjective.
- The use of a risk assessment matrix helps identify risks and their impact.
- Mishaps in diving activities are very likely to cause injury to the divers.
- A risk assessment is a logical procedure based on a series of steps that aim to identify risks affecting the operation and appropriate mitigation strategies.

References

1. **Craig, P.** *The killing zone: How and why pilots die.* New York: McGraw-Hill, 2001.

2. **Gernhardt, M.** *Exploring and the risk-reward equation.* Monterey, CA : NASA, 2004.

3. **Reason, J.** *Human error.* Cambridge : Cambridge University Press, 2006.

4. **US Navy.** *US Navy diving manual.* Revision VI. Washington, DC : US Navy, 2008.

5. **Blumemberg, M.** *Human factors in diving.* Berkeley, CA : University of California, Marine Technology and Management Group, 1996.

6. **Adams, J.** *Risk.* Abingdon : Routledge, 1995.

7. **HSA.** *Guidelines on risk assessment and safety statements.* Dublin, Ireland : HSA, 2006.

8. **Lock, G.** *Under pressure.* London : Vision Maker Press, 2019.

9. **Greenet, J.** *OPNAV instruction 3500.39C.* Washington, DC: US Navy Operations, 2010.

10. **ECU.** *Information on writing a risk assessment and management plan.* Perth, Australia : Edith Cowan University, 2016.

11. *A risk based approach to safety. Paper 8, marine risk assessment: A better way to manage your business.* **Lamb, I. and Rudgley, G.** London : The Institute of Marine Engineers, 1997.

12. **Liberatore, T.** *Risk analysis and management of diving operations: Assessing human factors.* Berkeley, CA : University of California, 1998.

2. HUMAN AND ORGANIZATIONAL FACTORS

Chapter highlights

Human behavior results from a defined set of characteristics that control our reactions to challenges and problems.

The quality of the interaction between human characteristics and the ambient strongly impacts the outcomes of any operation.

Human action inevitably leads to errors some of the time. Understanding the mechanisms leading to errors is essential to reduce the frequency and gravity of mistakes.

Human factors are often the root cause of major accidents resulting from a chain of related events. Acting on any of these events could interrupt the sequence allowing the system to recover.

Violating rules and standards is the leading cause of diving accidents; environmental stressors can aggravate the impact of human errors.

Looking for feedback helps in validating the correctness of the current decision-making strategy.

A well-organized team will reduce the likelihood of human organizational factors failing; team leaders should facilitate sharing common goals and mental models within the team.

Simple systems and organizations are less prone to failure than overly complex ones but do not have the same degree of redundancy should a failure happen. It is essential to mediate between simplicity and complexity to find the most reliable system.

Introduction

Human and organizational factors (HOFs) can be described as human characteristics that, interacting with ambient and other organizational factors, strongly impact the reliability of any system – mostly when complex environments and procedures are involved. Human factors include attitude, team interactions, communication, and errors (1), (2).

The need to operate in complex and unforgiving technical environments outpaces both the biological and cultural evolution of mankind, making errors and even catastrophic failures more likely (3). It is virtually impossible to avoid errors when interacting with complex systems (2).

As divers, we operate in a dynamic and challenging environment interacting with various life-support systems. Therefore, HOFs play an essential role in our safety. Many of the actions involved in diving require specific training and skills that are not part of our everyday experience, making errors more probable.

HOF failure is generally more deadly when it involves a combination of failures rather than just one isolated problem (3). HOF failure is the leading root cause of diving accidents, mainly when rules and standards are violated; environmental factors such as weather conditions, visibility, currents, and cold waters are contributing factors that may worsen the outcomes of human errors (4).

Diving is a complex procedure involving several interconnected actions and steps; failure in just one of such actions is unlikely to lead to a fatal outcome. However, if errors affect multiple stages, the consequences can be severe or deadly.

Human factors cause about 70% of accidents in complex systems. In an analysis of 93 major aviation accidents, the identified significant causes were all linked to some level of HOF failure (3):

1. Deviation from standard operative procedures   33%
2. Inadequate cross-checking   26%
3. Design fault   13%
4. Maintenance fault   12%
5. Captain ignoring crew input   10%
6. Improper response during abnormal conditions   9%

From these percentages, it is clear that most HOF failures are related to erroneous operative procedures (33%) and omitted checks (26%). To reduce these sources of error, standard operative procedures should be clearly defined during the training phase, and divers should have a habit of following such guidelines as a matter of routine. Checklists should also be enforced, primarily for more complex operations. Chapter 8 of this book will deal with checklists in more detail.

Most of these HOF failures in aviation have a potential parallel in diving:

1. Any diver should follow standards and procedures during any dive; it is not uncommon that divers routinely violate one or more standards, leading to the so-called "normalization of the deviance"; in the long run, this behavior will cause an accident.

2. Pre-dive checks should be mandatory to ensure the correct operativity of the diving system.

3. Even if rare, design errors in diving gear have been involved in diving incidents.

4. Most of the scuba equipment failures are due to poor maintenance.

5. During the dive, reciprocal awareness and communication should be ensured.

6. Sometimes, divers need more time to be ready or trained to respond to changed and unusual conditions.

Human behavior

Human performance is controlled by three main types of behavior: skill-based, rule-based, and knowledge-based (5):

1. *Skill-based behavior*: Related to sensory-motor performance in familiar environments and does not require conscious control. In more complex settings, conscious intention is necessary to modulate the general skill.

Swimming is an example of skill-based behavior that, once learned, is applied without much conscious control of its specific mechanics.

2. *Rule-based behavior*: Controlled by a set of learned rules, its boundary with skill-based behavior needs to be clarified, depending on the individual's level of attention and training. Overlearned rules can generate a skill-based attitude making the response to the problem almost instinctive.

The shifting to an alternate source of breathing gas in case of failure of the primary one, even if rule-based, is performed almost in automaticity by skilled and well-trained divers.

3. *Knowledge-based behavior*: Performance is controlled at a higher conceptual level, requiring a logical analysis of the situation and developing a mental model of the environment. Typical of individuals confronted by unfamiliar and novel situations.

A diver may use these types of behavior to solve an unexpected issue, such as being tangled. In this case, a sequential series of actions must be performed: first, assess the source of tangling (analysis of the situation), then find a logical procedure for removing the problem (develop a mental model), and finally, act.

When confronted with a problem, an individual generally relies on rule-based solutions before attempting a knowledge-based action. Experts, with their extensive knowledge of various situations, can think more abstractly, creating a general model of the problem to be addressed based on similar former experiences (1).

Knowledge-based errors are the most common because, primarily in complex situations, the operators may lack the correct knowledge (2).

Divers with experience in different diving scenarios are more likely to be able to solve unexpected problems using their knowledge gained in former similar, even if not identical, situations. This is one of the main reasons why building experience through diving in various conditions and environments is essential.

Errors in human factors

Errors inevitably affect human performance, but how do we define "error"? We may consider an error an action which did not go as planned or an action which did go as planned but was the wrong action to perform (1).

For example, a diver may fail to complete a gas switch at the correct depth (action did not go as planned) or may complete the gas switch, but the gas used was the wrong one for the depth (improper action to perform).

There are three main elements contributing to the generation of an error (1):

1. *Nature of the task and its environmental circumstances*: Difficult tasks to be performed in challenging environments are more prone to errors.

A leisure dive in calm, warm, clear waters is far easier to be flawlessly performed than a working dive with complex tasks in cold water with bad visibility and current.

2. *Mechanisms governing the performance*: Errors can affect complex procedures more than simpler operations.

Managing a multi-gas dive with consequential switches and complex decompression schedules is more prone to errors than a simple air dive with no decompression.

3. *Nature of the individual performing the task*: Experience, knowledge, and mental attitude determine the capacity of an operator to act.

Novice divers are more likely to make errors than experienced divers, mostly when confronted with unusual and new situations.

Slips and mistakes

It is important to understand what errors we make to define consistent and reliable strategies for their control and mitigation.

Errors can be broadly divided into two main categories: slips/lapses and mistakes (6), (7), (1):

- *Slips/lapses*: These errors typically happen when an unfamiliar activity is performed in a familiar context, breaking a consolidated routine, or when some distraction affects the job in execution. Slips concern mainly skill-based actions where the task is carried out without conscious monitoring. The absence of the expected outcome acts as early feedback for slips, allowing for a prompt reaction of the operator to fix the problem. Slips caused by distraction may affect actions performed with a higher level of conscious control and are more challenging to be promptly detected because they will signal their presence only when affecting the outcomes of the operation.

A diver used to dive with a drysuit and thus "instinctively" controlling the buoyancy using the suit's valves will likely still look for such valves during the first dive performed using a wetsuit. The diver will quickly realize the error (the absence of valves on the suit is the feedback) and use the BCD for buoyancy control.

A diver going through the pre-dive checklist could be distracted, forgetting one or more critical steps, such as fully opening the cylinder valve. This slip can pass undetected until the dive is started and could have serious consequences.

- *Mistakes*: Lack of knowledge or an inappropriate interpretation of the situation causes a logical but erroneous action to follow. Mistakes can be further subdivided into:

  o Rule-based mistakes: In these errors, a rule is incorrectly applied. Information overload and complex and dynamic operative environments can contribute to rule-based mistakes, causing a natural tendency in the operator to follow a general rule which has been so far successfully applied but that is not adequate for the new specific situation. Sometimes the application of a bad rule has not caused accidents in the past, and the user may develop a false sense of self-confidence, leading to further application of the same wrong rule until, inevitably, a failure occurs.

On several occasions, open-water divers have been allowed to enter cave-diving environments without consequences, leading them to think this is an acceptable procedure. This procedure is not proper, as demonstrated by the many cave-diving fatalities caused by untrained divers entering caves.

  o Knowledge-based mistakes: The operator fails to properly understand the situation because of lack of experience, absence or misinterpretation of information, or task overloading. The individual may be fixated on one aspect only of the problem without finding appropriate solutions.

A diver using a new dive computer may fail to understand the information provided, leading to decompression violations.

In both rule- and knowledge-based errors, there is a tendency to ignore any feedback outside the operator's expectations, making detecting the error and its recovery more difficult (1).

Divers can be prone to such "denial" behavior, failing to realize that an error has been made and that the situation is not going as planned. Examples of such errors are represented by cave divers being disoriented and going further inside the cave instead of toward the exit. The feedback provided by the environment is ignored, as the divers are convinced of the correctness of their direction.

Active and latent errors

Human factors are the root cause of many significant accidents in complex systems and environments in the form of active and latent errors (8), (3).

- *Active errors*: They have immediate effects and are most likely caused by the operator.

An example of an active error is a diver failing to switch to the correct gas during a multi-gas dive, thus breathing a mixture that is inappropriate for the depth/phase of the dive.

- *Latent errors*: They can lay dormant for a long time and are usually generated well before the moment in which they become apparent. These errors are difficult to detect and can be the root cause of severe accidents. Latent errors often originate at management level and can go unnoticed for a long time until a series of circumstances make them evident. The use of complex technology and automatic controls can also make errors harder to detect and fix. It is essential to develop a system that allows for the prompt detection of anomalies that could be the sign of a latent error.

For example, the presence of contaminants in the breathing gas due to an error of the filling station operator will affect the diver during the dive only well after the filling procedure is completed. Faulty designs of scuba gear can be the root cause of accidents that happen only when the local circumstances "activate" the latent error introduced in the system by the wrong design.

Chain of events

Generally, an accident is not the result of a single error. Still, more likely the outcome of a series of events with multiple inter-linked root causes (Fig. 2.1). Often, the operator's error is the culmination of a series of errors made by others. Removing even one of these causes may avoid the accident or strongly reduce its severity (3), (9).

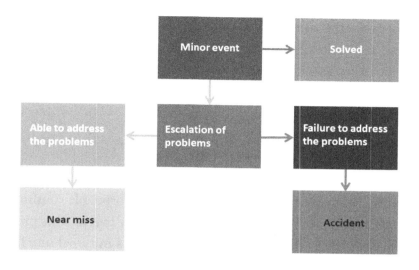

Fig. 2.1. Flowchart of the potential chain of events leading to an accident or a near miss.

The chain of events leading to an accident is usually composed of a well-defined set of circumstances (10), (11):

- *Predisposing circumstances*: The components for a potential accident.
- *Initiating circumstances*: The triggers of the accident, starting the chain of events.
- *Sustaining circumstances*: Further actions/situations that increase the damaging effect.
- *Mitigating circumstances*: Conditions that mitigate the impact of the accident.

For example, a diver forgets to close the weight belt buckle properly (predisposing circumstance); during the dive, the belt becomes loose and falls (initiating circumstance). The diver cannot control their buoyancy, and a fast ascent follows (accident). If the diver can slow down the ascent and no decompression is required, the outcomes can be mild (mitigating circumstances); if, on the other hand, the diver panics, holds their breath, or has a decompression penalty, then the outcomes can be fatal (sustaining circumstances).

Pareto principle

Accident dynamics fit the so-called "Pareto principle" outlined by the 19th-century Italian economist Vilfredo Pareto. This principle states that most events are generated by a minimal number of causes – a "vital few"; therefore, identifying and eliminating these causes strongly reduces the possibility of errors (12), (13).

This principle is fundamental when diving-related mishaps are considered because, as we will see, the vast majority of diving accidents have minimal root causes on which we should focus our attention to control and mitigate errors.

Poor judgment chain

Making a decision is often complicated and stressful, with a tendency to delay it. Even more stressful is having to change a judgment should new information show it was wrong. An FAA report in 1977 showed that over four years, errors in pilot judgment accounted for 50% of aviation fatalities (3).

When an individual is confronted by too much information, is under time pressure, and is task-overloaded, a decision based on wrong judgment may follow, jeopardizing safety. Poor judgment may result from one or more of the following events (7):

- *Distortion of reality*: The actual situation is misperceived.
- *False information*: The wrong information is used to make future judgments which are therefore flawed.
- *No alternatives*: The problem-solving capacity is impaired by a narrowing of focus on very few potential solutions.

To avoid or break a chain of poor judgment, it is necessary to be open to the possibility of error and always look for feedback.

The first step in any good decision is to weigh the inputs from several sources, including memories of similar events, to assess the viable alternatives. The issues with this are that the available information is often limited or incomplete, and personal bias can affect how information is interpreted (3).

For example, a diver under high physical and psychological stress may "over-breathe" the regulator with a feeling of not receiving enough air. As a result, they may start an emergency ascent. It is doubtful that a regulator could fail to provide adequate gas flow; the correct decision would have been to reduce physical activity, calm down and regain control of breathing. Switching to an alternate air source is another good solution if the regulator has a problem. In this example, the poor judgment leading to an emergency ascent was based on a distorted view of reality (that the regulator was not working) and failure to find an alternative (not using a bailout gas source).

System-operator issues

We should consider the interactions between system hardware (our diving gear) and operator actions (how we manipulate such diving gear) when assessing potential failures. In general, human errors in system-operator interactions can be divided into five typologies (14):

1. Operator fails to perform the function.
2. Operator performs function incorrectly.
3. Operator performs function inadvertently.
4. Operator performs the wrong function.
5. Operator actions exacerbate the results of a system failure.

Diving examples of these typologies are:

Type 1: The diver does not inflate the BCD and sinks below the maximum planned depth.

Type 2: The diver fails to control the level of BCD inflation, thus upsetting their buoyancy.

Type 3: The diver inadvertently switches the gas on the dive computer at the wrong depth/time of the dive.

Type 4: The diver pushes the wrong button on the BCD inflator.

Type 5: The diver cannot isolate a free-flowing regulator, thus causing total loss of breathable gas.

HOFs include the interaction with a variety of systems of different complexity. Complex systems are generally more error-prone than simpler systems but may also have more redundancy. Therefore a more straightforward system could be more exposed to being damaged by operator errors (1).

The goal is to mediate between complexity and simplicity to have a system optimized for the task with adequate redundancy but also linear and simple to operate, thus reducing the likelihood of human errors but able to mitigate, through its built-in redundancy, the impact of such errors.

For example, a diver bringing another source of breathing gas, such as a pony tank or a double cylinder with manifold, is intrinsically safer than a diver relying on one system only; on the other hand, the use of multi-gases in complex deep dives exposes the diver to a higher risk of system failure and errors in managing the different gases.

Teamwork and team management

A collection of high-qualified individuals does not necessarily constitute an effective team. Familiarity and good communication are key factors that must be developed to achieve proficiency within a team (3), (2).

Divers that dive together for the first time, as is often the case in charter boats, should be aware that, even if they are very experienced and qualified as individuals, they are all novices when considered as a team. They should therefore be more attentive to each other and not push the safety envelope, considering the unavoidable limits in familiarity and reciprocal trust.

Teamwork and team management are a cornerstone of safety and productivity when operating in challenging environments. A well-organized and managed team can strongly reduce the likelihood of human errors (7), (15). In any team, the less experienced member will set the bar for the whole team's capacity (2).

A diving team should have a good dive leader with enough experience and knowledge to identify areas of strength and weakness within the team, planning the tasks according to the adequate capacity and potential of the group.

In addition, the attitude shown by each team member will make the difference between a good and a dysfunctional team. In general, three central attitudes can be identified (7):

1. *Passive*: The individual allows their ideas and rights to be restricted by others, with anxiety building up to dangerous levels.
2. *Aggressive*: The individual is willing to dominate, being mostly hostile to others' ideas. Communication and relationships are compromised.
3. *Assertive*: The individual recognizes boundaries and others' ideas; there is a constructive approach to problem-solving.

Assertiveness is a positive attitude that should be strongly supported within the team to facilitate a constructive exchange of ideas focused on finding reliable solutions. Lack of assertiveness by subordinates in a team can cause serious accidents, as was the case in the Tenerife aircraft disaster in 1977 when a KLM 747 collided with a Pan American 747 while taking off without proper clearance. The KLM captain was also the KLM chief instructor and had a very strong ego. The hierarchy structure inhibited the other cabin crew members, who did not speak up even if they knew – or at least strongly suspected – that proper take-off clearance had not been given (3).

As divers, we strongly rely on teamwork during our activity; the smallest team is composed of two diving buddies, but much larger teams may be needed for more complex operations requiring attentive leadership and management. A large team may include multiple smaller units, such as the diving team, the topside support team, and the boat crew. Each team will have its structure and team leader; it is essential to ensure clear communication between all the individuals involved during the operations. Moreover, common goals and strategies should be shared between teams.

A team composed of individuals with different skills and knowledge will have a broader capacity to operate in different conditions, as it will be possible to find within the team the needed expertise. On the other hand, if the team's members have similar abilities, the operational horizon of the team will be reduced; however, its redundancy will be greater because if one member fails, others may step in, given that they share some capabilities (Fig. 2.2).

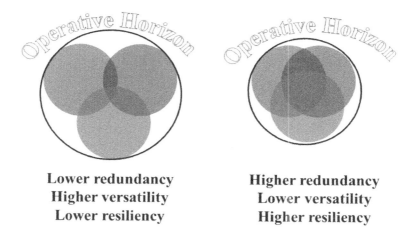

Lower redundancy
Higher versatility
Lower resiliency

Higher redundancy
Lower versatility
Higher resiliency

Fig. 2.2. Different team operative capacities based on members' overlapping skills.

A series of attributes (Fig. 2.3) are needed for the development of a good team able to perform proficient work (15):

• *Leadership*: A leader should be able to direct, monitor, coordinate, and provide constructive feedback on the team's performance. A leader will support teamwork, promoting members' understanding of interdependence and the benefits of working together.

The lead diver should share their mental model with the other divers and support each member's action, providing guidance when necessary.

- *Flexibility and adaptability*: An adaptable team can recognize changes in the operative environment and act accordingly. When a team is involved in constant routine, its members may fail to detect unexpected changes leading to potential errors. It is essential to perform a continuous reassessment of the evolving situation. This is particularly important when the team must operate in stressful conditions.

   In a diving team, alternative plans should be discussed before the dive so that a "what if" response at the team level is promptly available in case of changes in the operational circumstances.

- *Communication*: It is essential to flow information and feedback within the team constantly. Environmental stressors, task and information overloading, team members' bias, and linguistic and cultural barriers may cause a failure in communication.

   Communication among the divers and between the diving team and topside personnel is a cornerstone for the divers' safety and the operation's success. A detailed briefing should precede any dive and involve all the individuals contributing to the operation.

- *Mutual trust*: It must be a shared perception that each team member will act in the interest of the other members engaged in a joint endeavor. Trust in each other will help members accept a certain degree of personal risk and support the positive interpretation of ambiguous events, avoiding suspicion and reciprocal blaming.

Having reciprocal trust underwater is essential, but it requires time to be built. For this reason, the divers should be given enough time to get to know each other before being involved in complex operations.

- *Shared mental models*: Team members must have a common understanding of the tasks to be performed and the operative environment to anticipate each other's needs. Under stress, these models will improve the efficiency of teamwork even when communication is impaired.

The dive plan should be clearly defined and shared between the divers, ensuring that each team member knows their role.

- *Mutual performance monitoring and backup behavior*: In an effective team, each member proactively monitors the others and is ready to support the team's performance, assisting teammates.

Dive buddies should actively monitor each other, ready to assist in need. In more complex operations, using a support diver to monitor the team's safety should be considered.

Fig. 2.3. Key elements for building a good team.

Teams become more effective when the members are used to working together. The most effective team develops when technical skills and teamwork skills are aligned (2). Good interpersonal relationships must be developed before the team can effectively focus on operative tasks. In the beginning, leadership and communication are needed; mutual performance monitoring and backup behaviors develop at a later stage within the team (15). In newly formed teams, the absence of familiarity impacts the quality and effectiveness of communication. It takes time to get used to each other and even longer to anticipate each other's reactions (3).

When underwater, the quality of communication is limited by environmental constraints, making it impossible to share long and complex information; therefore, the divers should have a good level of familiarity with each other to understand their reciprocal needs easily and quickly.

An important part of teamwork is clear communication between members (Fig. 2.4). If the information provided by someone is not clear, we should ask for clarification. An unclear or misunderstood message can result in fatal mistakes during an emergency. Near misses should also be shared to improve future performance without fear of judgment or the false belief that this was just an isolated event not worth mentioning. In an operative situation, mainly in complex and challenging environments, communication should rely on standardized procedures and messages as much as possible to minimize the risk of confusion and misunderstanding (3).

To ensure proper communication, the feedback should always be clear and specific, with the receiver of the message able to repeat in their own words what they understood of the message (2).

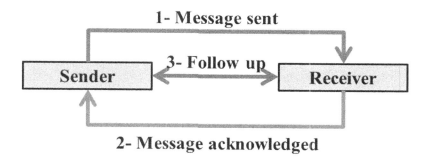

Fig. 2.4. Correct procedure for good communication.

Leadership feedback is important after the task so that the team can receive input on its performance and improve over time. Negative feedback should be provided constructively, avoiding personal blaming and aggressive statements (7).

A dive instructor assessing the poor performance of a group of students should always begin with some positive comments before moving on to analyze what went wrong, providing suggestions for future improvements.

When under very stressful conditions, teams tend to follow standard approaches, with members driven toward a consensus, often ignoring vital information and deferring to individuals who are considered of "higher status" but are not necessarily the most knowledgeable on the specific issue (16).

This can be seen, for example, when a group of divers confronted with an unexpected situation just blindly follows the one whom they consider being "the leader" – such as the most senior or with the highest diving certifications – even if they do not have valuable experience on this specific issue. This can lead to catastrophic outcomes, such as the accident where a group of open-water divers entered a cave following the dive guide. None, including the guide, had any specific cave training, and when visibility was reduced due to silting-up, the group became lost and trapped in the cave – multiple fatalities occurred.

Attitude in divers

Physiological conditions, diving attitude, the complexity of the diving operations, experience and capacity of the divers contribute to defining the level of risk exposure (17). The difference between a safe and a risky dive is almost always due to the behavior of the divers involved, and such behavior depends mainly on the experience and personality of the divers (18).

One of the most dangerous attitudes is that of the "macho," which leads divers to disregard safety in the obsessive pursuit of showing off (3).

A diver with this attitude is a serious risk to themselves and the whole team and will cause an accident sooner or later.

Unsurprisingly research indicates a clear connection between risky behavior and accidents. It has been observed that divers who consider themselves well-experienced and capable have a tendency toward higher risk-taking, likely based on a rational analysis of their adequate capacity vs. the challenges of the dive. Unfortunately, a similar approach is also common in low self-esteem divers who, often lacking proper experience and good capacity, may put themselves and others in danger (19).

As a dive leader, you should be aware of the actual level of expertise of the divers under your supervision. Besides certifications, the logbook should be analyzed to verify the number of dives, the kind of environments they dived in, and the frequency of their dives. While two divers may have the same number of dives in a year, a diver who dives throughout the year will generally be better experienced than a diver who dives mainly or solely during short periods such as holidays.

The core personality of every individual determines human behavior, but it is the interaction with external stimuli that activates the attitudinal response; a risk-averse or risk-acceptance behavior can be due to the way risk is perceived rather than a logical analysis of the possible outcomes. When reliable information is lacking, high-motivated individuals can perceive the probability of success as higher than low-motivated individuals; moreover, it is a human tendency to consider a very low probability as "zero," even if over more extended periods and higher frequencies, it will occur (20).

For divers, this tendency could generate unsafe attitudes, such as disregarding routine checks on gear which is considered to have a very low probability of failing. Even extremely low probability hazards can cause appreciable risk if long exposures are considered.

Thrill vs. relax

For most recreational divers, diving is more a search for comfort and relaxation than a quest for the thrill; a feeling of safety and a relaxed state of mind is associated with diving when the diving buddy is trusted, skilled, and experienced (21). A general interest in new experiences and adventure has also been noted in groups of divers (22).

An analysis of 300 recreational divers from beginner to expert showed that risk and daring motivated the lowest number in diving; fun, observing the sea life, and exploring the underwater world were more relevant. Beginners were more rule-focused on the technical skills of diving. At the same time, expert divers had a more relaxed attitude focusing on socializing, sharing experience and knowledge, and using new technical gear (23).

Similar results were derived from another analysis of the leading diving motivations of 243 divers, with male divers more attracted by the use of technical equipment and female divers more interested in building self-confidence (24).

Another study on the personality of 60 young (16 to 35 years) entry-level scuba divers highlighted four diverse groups of attitudes related to risky behaviors (25):

1. *Adventurers*: The desire to be at the center of attention may push these divers to risky behaviors, endangering their diving partners.
2. *Macho divers*: They have very low self-esteem and self-confidence, using passive-aggressive behavior as a psychological defense mechanism. Are unreliable and could become dangerous.
3. *Dreamers*: Insecure and overwhelmed by the diving environment, these individuals will rely strongly on instructors

and partners. Divers showing this attitude cannot be trusted in case of emergency.

4. *Rationalists*: Rule-bounded individuals who will not take any unnecessary risk as divers; they aim to master scuba diving skills. These are reliable and safe divers who can be trusted in any situation.

Diving activities should be planned to allow divers to enjoy the underwater world, with a controlled approach to risk that can be mitigated by mastering essential skills, building up experience, and growing knowledge. Insecure and aggressive psychological profiles characterize divers as more inclined to risky behaviors that may endanger themselves and their dive buddies.

Lessons learned

- The mastering of skills and rule- and knowledge-based behaviors control human performance.
- Slips/lapses happen when an unfamiliar activity breaks a consolidated routine or when distraction occurs.
- Mistakes are due to a lack of knowledge or an inappropriate interpretation of the situation.
- An error is the result of a chain of related events.
- Few causes are usually at the common roots of errors.
- The difference between a safe and a risky dive is almost always due to the divers' behavior.
- A diver's personality is integral to the attitude toward risky or safe behavior.
- Good teamwork and management strongly improve performance and safety.

References

1. **Reason, J.** *Human error.* Cambridge: Cambridge University Press, 2006.

2. **Lock, G.** *Under pressure.* 2019.

3. **Beaty, D.** *The naked pilot: The human factor in aircraft accidents.* s.l. : Airlife, 1995.

4. **LOR.** *Personal and social dimensions of risky diving behavior.* Melbourne: The University of Melbourne, 2006.

5. **Rasmussen, J.** Skills, rules, and knowledge: Signals, signs and symbols and other distinctions in human performance models. *IEEE Transaction on Systems, Man, and Cybernetics.* 1983, Vol. 13, 2, pp. 257–266.

6. **Embrey, D.** *Understanding human behavior and error.* Wigan: Human Reliability Associates, 2005.

7. **USGS.** *Team coordination training student guide.* Washington, DC: United States Coast Guard, 1998.

8. **Gordon, R.** The contribution of human factors to accidents in the offshore oil industry. *Reliability Engineering and System Safety.* 1998, Vol. 61, pp. 95–108.

9. *Annual fatality dates and associated risk factors for recreational scuba diving.* **De Noble, P., Marroni, A. and Vann, R.** s.l. : DAN, 2010.

10. **Lowrance, W.W.** *Of acceptable risk.* 1976.

11. **Blumenberg, M.A.** *Human factors in diving.* Berkeley, CA: Marine Technology and Management Group; University of California, 1996.

12. **De Noble, P., Caruso, J., de Dear, G., Vann, R. and Pieper, C.** Common causes of open-circuit recreational diving fatalities. *UHM.* 2008, Vol. 35, 6, pp. 393–406.

13. **Reed, J.** The Pareto, Zipf and other power laws. *Economics Letters.* 2001, Vol. 74, 1, pp. 15–19.

14. **Ericson, C. II.** *Fault tree analysis primer.* Charleston, CN: CreateSpace Inc, 2011.

15. **Salas, E., Sims, D. and Burke, S.** Is there a "big five" in teamwork? *Small Group Research.* 2005, Vol. 36, 5, pp. 555–599.

16. **Weisenger H. and Pawlin-Fry, J.P.** *Performing under pressure.* 2015.

17. **Bennett, M.** Risk perception and sport: The doctor as policeman? *SPUMS Journal.* 2004, Vol. 34, 2, pp. 75–80.

18. **Musa, G., Seng, W.T., Thirumoorthi, T. and Abessi, M.** The influence of scuba divers' personality, experience, and demographic profile on their underwater behavior. *Tourism in Marine Environment.* 2010, Vol. 7, 1, pp. 1–14.

19. **Miller, O. and Taubman, G.** Scuba diving risk-taking: A terror management theory perspective. *Journal of Sport and Excercise Psychology.* 2004, Vol. 26, 2, pp. 269–282.

20. **Lopes, L.** Between hope and fear: The psychology of risk. *Advances in experimental social psychology.* 1987, Vol. 202, pp. 255–295.

21. **Dimmock, K.** Finding comfort in adventure: Experiences of recreational scuba divers. *Leisure Studies.* 2009, Vol. 28, 3, pp. 279–295.

22. **Taylor D., O'Toole K., Auble T., Ryan C. and Sherman D.** Sensation seeking personality traits of recreational scuba divers. *SPUMS Journal.* 2001, Vol. 31, 1, pp. 25–28.

23. **Lusbu, C. and Cottreil, S.P.** Understanding motivations and expectations of scuba divers. *Tourism in Marine Environment.* 2008, Vol. 5, 1, pp. 1–14.

24. *An exploration of motivations among scuba divers in North Central Florida.* **Meyer, L., Thapa, B. and Pennington-Gray, L.** 2002. Proceedings of the 2002 Northeastern Recreation Research Symposium.

25. **Coetzeen, N.** Personality profiles of recreational scuba divers. *AJPHERD.* 2010, Vol. 16, 4, pp. 568–579.

3. LEADERSHIP

Chapter highlights

For any team to be effective requires some degree of leadership; this can be formally structured, such as in a diving course where the instructor is the leader, and the students follow their instructions, or more loosely defined, such as in a team of equally expert divers where decisions are shared.

Leaders usually show some common character traits and what is called "emotional intelligence," which is the capacity to understand the feelings and emotions of the team's members and being able to manage these in a constructive way to achieve the planned goals.

Good leadership requires a series of behaviors and attitudes to support and enhance the proficiency and general welfare of the team.

The primary role of a leader is to coordinate the different team's members with their varied expertise, creating a synergistic combination of skills and abilities that is more than the sum of its parts.

Leadership may fail due to both external and internal factors. Two leading causes of failure are leader complacency and the inability to foster a climate of free exchange of information and trust within the team.

Introduction

Teamwork is at the core of diving operations; the size of a diving team can vary from the smallest, composed of just two divers diving together, to teams consisting of multiple divers, tenders, supervisors, and additional crew involved in complex and large-scale procedures.

Whatever its size, any team needs good leadership to be truly effective; the leader's primary role should be linking together the team members' diverse expertise, creating a synergistic structure. The leadership should include shared mental models, common goals, and personal bonds (Fig. 3.1). Moreover, in times of uncertainty, the leader will be the reference figure for the team's members, who will rely on their expertise and decision-making abilities.

Leadership involves persuading others to put a common goal that is important for the group above their desires; this should be achieved by persuasion rather than domination, building cohesive and goal-oriented teams. Performance is often proportional to the efficacy of the leadership (1).

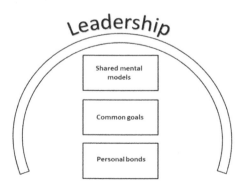

Fig. 3.1. Good leadership should consider critical elements of teamwork, including shared mental models, common goals, and personal relationships.

A good dive leader should persuade the other divers of the importance of their roles for the overall team's performance, even if such functions can appear trivial or not satisfying for the divers. This is a common situation in cave diving exploration: usually, one diver will do "the push" – that is, exploring the deepest/innermost part of the cave – meanwhile, other divers will act in support roles, with tasks such as placing stage tanks in specified places along the cave.

The leader is a crucial figure in the team, defining the team's goals and the paths to achieve them and developing strategies aiming to increase team's efficiency and performance (2). The ultimate goal of a leader is to achieve results; the key is identifying the most effective leadership behavior to reach them (3).

A "direct" leader will influence others through actions and communication strategies; an "indirect" leader is someone whose work and example are inspiring for others even if they are not in direct contact with the leader (4).

A good diving instructor or an exceptional lead diver are examples of direct leadership in scuba diving; an inspiring figure such as Jacques Ives Cousteau is the prototype of an indirect leader, having influenced with his work an immeasurable number of divers.

A leader needs to model teamwork, merging the members' personal goals with the team mission and motivating the team through planning, good coordination, and effective feedback; this is particularly needed when the team operates in complex and dynamic environments (2). The leader's support is often perceived as a reward, increasing the team's motivation (5).

In diving operations, good leadership is the cornerstone of not only proficiency in achieving the team's goals but also the safety, and sometimes the very survival, of the divers. The dive leader should be an inspiring, trusted figure whose opinion is valued and respected by all the other divers.

Leaders' traits

Leaders often show certain common character traits that are instrumental to motivating and managing a successful team and, together with consistent actions, contribute to achieving successful results (4), (6), (7), (8):

- *Emotional intelligence*: Individuals with high levels of emotional intelligence – that is the ability to understand the feelings and emotions of others (as well as their own) and to use such knowledge to regulate emotional reactions within a social context – in leadership positions can motivate the team and stimulate the team's members to work toward the common goal with increased performance and effectiveness. Positive emotions are contagious, elevating team morale and inspiring members to perform more enthusiastically. On the other hand, a leader showing negative emotions such as anger and fear will strongly affect the team, reducing self-confidence and trust in the leader. Overall having a leader with high emotional intelligence surrounded by an emotionally intelligent team will improve decision-making and the team's performance.

The dive leader should be able to gauge the feelings of the other divers, including some degree of frustration that may develop after hours or days of fatigue, motivating them and showing appreciation for their job and, in particular, convincing them that their activity is critical to the success of the operation.

- *Empathy*: Leaders need to be connected with their followers and be able to track the changes in their emotional status.

Being empathic with the team's members is a crucial factor – especially in difficult situations. A leader's high level of empathy is generally more critical than high intelligence.

Diving instructors and team leaders should always be able to connect emotionally with the other divers to foster team unity and trust. No matter how skilled and experienced a diver is, their leadership will inevitably be weak if this is not supported by the ability to create strong emotional bonds.

- *Achievement*: Good leaders strongly desire to achieve goals in a demanding environment requiring technical expertise.

This is often the case with expert divers involved in deep dives, cave exploration, and other complex and challenging diving activities.

- *Ambition*: Personal ambition is essential in the desire for advancement.

Divers involved in leadership training, such as instructor courses, are often motivated by their desire to advance to positions of higher esteem in the diving community.

- *Energy*: Physical, mental, and emotional stamina are required for leadership demands.

Diving is a demanding activity, and high levels of stamina are needed to perform at the highest standards required by the leadership role.

- *Tenacity*: The ability to work hard for long-term goals. Despite having solid plans, reliable equipment, and high-level skills, failure is always possible; sooner or later, we will face a negative outcome. A leader must be able to manage this and continue pushing for the ultimate goal. The situation should always be assessed for what it truly is and not for what the leader wants it to be.

Divers involved in training and courses are familiar with long hours spent reading diving manuals and spending time in the pool and underwater to achieve the desired objective. In complex diving operations, various elements can influence the results. The leader has to be ready to overcome setbacks and delays that can affect any of the team's members.

- *Initiative*: Being proactive instead of just waiting for things to happen.

Underwater this is an essential trait because the diver should always be very aware of the situation and able to forecast the likely evolution of the dive and act accordingly. The dive leader should also be able to take the initiative to optimize the team's performance, often adopting innovative and unconventional strategies.

- *Motivation*: Desire to assume responsibility and influence others for the organization's benefit.

Diving instructors should have a solid motivation to provide valuable learning experiences.

- *Cognitive ability and knowledge*: Above-average intelligence is often associated with good leadership; leaders must also deeply understand the system they are managing. Mastering specific skills is a critical factor in problem-solving under uncertainty and stress. As is the case for the development of technical expertise, good leaders will need ten or more years to develop effective leadership practice. In complex environments, leadership is strictly linked with teamwork and group cohesion, and the leader must establish practical system thinking. These traits will also grow the leader's authority within the team. In general, formal education is less relevant than experience for effective leadership.

Divers in leadership positions, such as instructors, dive supervisors, and dive officers, should be very knowledgeable in their activity and demonstrate a reasonable degree of mental acumen and flexibility to manage the situations likely to be encountered in the dynamic diving environment. Being knowledgeable will also increase the level of confidence that team members have in the leader. Finally, building on former practical experience gained in various diving scenarios, the leader can manage most issues in novel situations.

- *Ingenuity*: In complex systems, multiple elements can fail. Therefore, a high degree of ingenuity is needed by the leader, who should be able to use lateral thinking while maintaining focus even under pressure and stress. Expertise in one field can be transferred into another to spark new ideas and find innovative solutions.

It is common during diving operations that events do not unfold as planned. Changes in environmental conditions, equipment malfunction, and unforeseen circumstances can challenge the leader, who should be able to quickly reassess the situation and find viable alternative solutions to achieve the planned goals, maintaining high levels of safety.

- *Good communication*: Information needs to be communicated to the rest of the team to be effective. Good leaders must therefore be good communicators, involving the team and conveying their vision with inspiring words. The message should follow an accurate, structured narrative to help the team remember the information.

A dive leader should be able to communicate with the team concisely and efficiently. For example, it is important to deliver effective briefings that clearly communicate the diving operations' aims and how to achieve the goals. The leader should be able to develop a standardized structure in the briefing format, assuring consistency; feedback from the team's members should also be requested as proof that the briefing was understood.

- *Humor*: Reducing stress and tension using levity is critical in leadership. Being a leader requires making decisions that will inevitably displease someone sooner or later, and humor helps disable anger. Humor brings confidence to the team, and laughing together increases empathy and cohesion.

Diving is often fun, and this helps maintain the team in good spirits. On the other hand, it is not uncommon to experience stressful conditions linked to the diving environment, such as climate extremes, equipment failure, and fatigue. If the dive leader can maintain a climate of levity, any problem will likely be faced with a more positive attitude.

- *Strategic imagination*: This is the ability to visualize performance in the near and far future based on former experience. A leader should be able to imagine the future situation, the steps needed to achieve the planned goals, the required physical and mental resources, and the team's best members to be involved in the operations.

Every time we have to plan our dive, we should be able to visualize it through a mental rehearsal of logically consecutive steps. Building on our experience as divers, we can identify areas requiring more effort and attention in the planning and execution phase.

- *Self-confidence and emotional stability*: Self-confidence is needed for good decision-making and effective actions in complex situations. A calm and self-confident leader will boost confidence in the team. Emotional stability helps in acting coolly when under stress.

In risky diving environments, self-confidence –based on experience and knowledge – and emotional equilibrium are the basis for good performance and safe behaviors.

- *Honesty and integrity*: Being truthful and showing consistency between words and actions are critical for developing a good relationship between the leader and the rest of the team.

This is extremely important for diving leaders, who should always show consistency between the rules and standards they promote and their actions, mostly when team safety is at stake. It is totally unacceptable to skip basic safety procedures, such as pre-dive buddy checks, on the grounds that experience makes such checks redundant. The dive leader should always act as a role model.

- *Expert knowledge*: When leaders operate within a specific domain, surrounded by other individuals sharing some specific knowledge, they must be recognized as experts in that domain to be trusted and achieve results (4).

In the diving community, good leaders need to be well-experienced and have detailed knowledge of key diving-related issues spanning from dive physiology to techniques and tools. To achieve this level, the leader should be willing to continue their training and always be on top of emerging technologies and methodologies.

- *Charisma*: Charismatic leaders display these three skills/traits (1):

1. Have a vision that others see as compelling.
2. Form teams that share such vision.
3. Develop personal relations within the team to support the vision.

For example, a diving expedition leader should be charismatic because they will need to convince others (including sponsors) of the importance of the mission (point 1), find divers who will participate in the mission, and identify their best role within the team (point 2), and develop strong personal bonds with the divers so that even under stressful conditions the team will remain united and able to perform (point 3).

One final point is that there is a relationship between the effectiveness of leadership and some of the so-called "big-five" personality traits (1):

- *Surgency*: Allows for good communication and the ability to build alliances.
- *Conscientiousness*: Generate a feeling of trust and good organizational skills.
- *Agreeableness*: Good morale building.
- *Emotional stability*: Solving conflicts and being stable under stressful conditions.

To be truly effective, a leader needs to be in emotional contact with their team, who should freely accept their leadership based on shared common values. The leader also needs to create a feeling of belonging to the group (4).

A good diving leader will be able to develop an efficient team of divers tied by shared mental models, common goals, and strong personal bonds. Under stress and in difficult situations, this kind of team will be able to stay united, working together toward a positive outcome.

Leadership styles

A study of 3,871 executives has identified six different leadership styles; the most influential leaders can use them in different combinations based on the situation's needs (3). These behaviors should be the base for actions related to the specific situation to achieve good leadership (2).

1. *Coercive style*: An aggressive top-down style that should be used only in extreme situations, such as during emergencies when a series of actions must be done swiftly and without discussion. If abused, this style will destroy the confidence and morale of the team.

This is the style that a diving team leader may need to use during an emergency, directing the divers with clear, concise, and effective orders. This is mainly needed should an emergency arise during training sessions with novice divers who still must gain the skills or the experience required to assess the situation autonomously.

2. *Authoritative style*: The leader motivates the team showing that the required actions are needed for a larger organizational vision. Standards, feedback, and rewards are defined around this vision, and team members can act creatively and take calculated risks to achieve the planned goals. This is one of the most effective leadership styles, but it loses efficacy if the leader has less experience/knowledge of the team, as when working with a group of experts. In this case, the democratic style (see below) is preferred.

Diving instructors can approach this style when developing advanced skills; the divers will accept the leader's guidance based on their more comprehensive experience and knowledge but will also be motivated to find ways to achieve the planned goals.

3. *Democratic style*: Team members are actively involved in the decisional path, sharing a realistic situation vision. This style works well with teams composed of able and competent members who can provide sound and consistent advice.

The leader of a team of very experienced divers should adopt this style, involving the divers as peers in most of the decisional actions. A typical case is when planning new diving operations with an experienced team whose members have worked together for a long time, gaining adequate knowledge and experience that can be shared, increasing the overall proficiency.

4. *Affiliative style*: Individuals and their needs are valued more than tasks and goals. Loyalty within the team is developed, building strong emotional bonds; positive feedback provides a feeling of recognition and rewards. This style is best used when building a new team, increasing morale, and improving communication among the team's members and with the leader. The limits are that, given that this style primarily focuses on praise, poor performance could go unnoticed, and, in complex situations, the needed guidance from the leader could be impaired. A sound system is to alternate this style with the authoritative style.

A diving supervisor working with new divers may use this style to build good team relations and consolidate personal bonds and communication before pushing the team into more complex situations. Diving instructors can also benefit from this style, focusing on the good results more than on the students' failures; this will improve morale and self-confidence, paving the way to a better performance that will follow once the divers master the new skills.

5. *Pace-setting style*: Another aggressive style where very high standards are set; failing to meet such goals leads to being expelled from the group. It may work within teams of highly experienced and skilled professionals driven by strong self-motivation, facilitating meeting tight deadlines and achieving ambitious results.

This style can be used within high-level training courses such as instructor training or with highly experienced diving teams involved in demanding operations where time-constraints are prevalent. The leader should be aware that such a style will create significant pressure on the team, leading to stressful situations that can only be sustained for a short time.

6. *Coaching style*: The leader helps followers identify their strengths and weaknesses, establish long-term goals, and provide instruction and feedback. To work well this style requires the team/students to have a genuine will to learn and the leader to be able to provide high-quality information. Short-term failures are tolerated and are considered teaching opportunities for growth in terms of knowledge, skills, and experience.

A typical diving situation where this style works is during instructional diving courses. The diving instructor is aware that the students will commit errors, but these mistakes are used to improve skills by providing adequate feedback and guiding the students toward the final goal.

Of these six styles, the authoritative is generally the most effective, followed by affiliative, democratic, and coaching. Coercive and pace-setting styles are primarily negative, as they will impact the team's morale and confidence.

A good leader can move through the different styles, finding the most appropriate one for the situation at hand (9).

Leading a team

The core job of a leader is to identify a clear target and a general strategy to achieve the goal and to share this vision with the rest of the team (2), (7).

The diving leader is in charge of developing the dive plan and sharing it with the other team members during appropriate briefing sessions. Depending on the complexity of the goals, the brief can be a short session immediately preceding the dive where the main points of the dive plan are highlighted or may require multiple meetings well before the planned dive.

The leader's behavior will be considered acceptable and welcomed by the team if the other members feel that it provides valuable guidance to reach the planned goals and that the goals are also linked to the members' ambitions. In clear-cut situations the direction should be limited to the essentials because too many details will be considered redundant and useless (5). This applies primarily to diving teams composed of skilled and experienced divers who should share common goals for the mission, requiring minimal guidance to succeed.

When leading a team, the leader has to consider what is called "organizational climate," which comprises six key factors (3):

1. *Flexibility*: How much the team's members are free to act outside strict boundaries and without direct management.

In a diving team this could mean that the divers are informed of the objectives and scope of the dive but are free to work around the dive plan if new needs arise. To be effective and safe, such a degree of flexibility should only be given to well-experienced and skilled divers.

2. *Responsibility*: Team members are accountable for their actions.

When diving, each diver is accountable and responsible for their safety and the safety of their dive buddy.

3. *Standards*: Define the level of acceptable performance.

This is typical of a diving course where the dive instructor sets the student performance level based on the relevant Agency standards.

4. *Rewards*: Linked to performance.

The diving leader can show appreciation for the team by praising the members and involving them in more exciting and challenging dives.

5. *Clarity*: The mission and values should be clearly stated.

The diving leader should be able to identify the scope of the diving operations and share the information with the rest of the team.

6. *Commitment*: The team members should commit to a common goal.

In a diving situation, this could be mastering new skills, exploring underwater features, or successfully concluding a training session. The leader must involve the team as a group so that each diver feels committed to the general goal.

A leader able to positively impact the organizational climate will contribute about one-third of the overall results (3).

The initial actions of the leader should be more structured and then progressively shift toward fostering team self-management once the team's members have gained enough experience (2).

Typically, a dive instructor will start with a series of skills to be learned in a relatively fixed timeline. Once experience has been built and basic skills mastered, the teaching approach will move toward a more flexible style, with the students being progressively more responsible for their learning schedule.

When under pressure, teams are susceptible to emotional distress. It is up to the leader to mitigate the stress impact, providing a clear vision supported by effective strategies and rules. The leader becomes the primary source of information for the team under uncertainty and temporal urgency (2). Leaders of dive teams involved in complex operations are often exposed to scenarios where stress is high, and it is up to them to reduce the negative impact on team members. Under pressure, tempers can flare, and the leader should be able to address emotional issues, providing coaching and support quickly. They should also know well about the situation to provide meaningful information and reduce uncertainty.

Leaders can follow specific strategies that can be tailored to different operative situations and different team compositions (5):

- *Directive leadership*: The leader establishes standards and provides clear guidelines. This strategy works well in ambiguous situations where a clear path to achieve the planned goals is unavailable, and the team's members have limited knowledge of the system.

Diving leaders may use this approach when managing teams where members conduct dives in unfamiliar environments or perform complex operations. The divers need more extensive and specific experience with the tasks at hand, and therefore need closer guidance.

- *Supportive leadership*: The leader treats team's members as equals, showing a genuine concern for their wellbeing. This strategy works better when the tasks to be accomplished by the team are frustrating and stressful.

This may be a good option in a diving situation when routine and repetitive operations, such as cylinder filling or equipment cleaning, must be performed. Ideally, the diving leader should participate in the activities or at least praise and support the team's efforts.

- *Shared leadership*: The team's members are actively involved in the decisional process, setting their own goals; consequently, motivation and effort will increase. This strategy works well when team members have a good level of knowledge that can be useful for common problem-solving.

This strategy can be used when the diving team comprises equally high-skilled divers who share common mental models of the tasks to be performed. In this case, the chosen leader will act as a facilitator and coordinator of the ideas proposed within the team.

- *Achievement-oriented*: The leader sets challenging goals, showing confidence that the team will achieve such high standards, thus boosting morale and self-confidence. This strategy works well when non-repetitive complex tasks have to be performed.

An instructor trainer can use this approach during an Instructor Development Course (IDC) to stimulate the candidates to perform at their best capacity.

In complex environments, the leader can adopt two approaches that will reduce uncertainty, thus improving the team's resilience and proficiency (2):

1. *Reduction in authority*: A diminished formal hierarchy stimulates lower-ranking individuals within the organization to be more active in suggesting alternatives.
2. *Role diversity*: When forming a team, the leader should identify members with a broader variety of skills and expertise that can be used to develop more accurate models of the complex working environment.

When working within complex and unpredictable environments, traditional hierarchical management needs to be changed into a more flexible approach, with the leader becoming more of a coordinator than a ruler (6).

The diving environment is a typical example of a complex and changing situation where anyone on the team should be able to contribute their ideas to identify viable solutions and alternatives. This approach will work only if the team's members have adequate knowledge and experience; it is up to the leader to ensure an appropriate choice of members.

Operative teams act at the "sharp-end" of the organization and are directly exposed to the hazards involved in the activity. Good leadership is critical for proficiency and the team's survival. A focus on efficiency should be subordinate to the emphasis on safety, and errors and mistakes should be addressed by the leader, who should also provide consistent rules and guidance to be followed during highly demanding situations (10).

For example, firefighting teams usually have four members working together during shifts. The leader plays a pivotal role, acting as a guide and motivator, but to be respected, the leader must have proven themself in action. Once the leader's value has been shown, team members will likely emulate their behavior – especially in emergencies – thus improving the likelihood of successful outcomes and survival (11).

In diving teams operating at the "sharp-end," the dive leader should be aware of the potential risks associated with the diving environment and planned operations, being able to provide consistent and valuable guidance in emergencies. The dive leader must have proven experience in similar environments to be trusted and followed.

Several larger organizations share leadership between individuals in formal and informal management positions. Often each leader's actions influence the others, and a sequential mode, moving through a series of feedbacks, should be followed to produce efficient results (12).

In complex diving operations, primarily in professional settings, the team can become very large, including divers, tenders, surface support personnel, and boat crew. In this case leadership must be shared between the dive leader, dive supervisor, boat captain, etc. It is important that the actions of the co-leaders are well coordinated and that each area of leadership is identified to avoid conflicts and uncertainty. If an emergency arises, the sequence of needed actions should be clearly stated and shared with all the management staff so that appropriate procedures can be applied swiftly and efficiently.

Leadership failure

As with any other human enterprise, an attempt to lead a team may fail. The failure can be due to a variety of internal and external factors to the team.

Faults in team composition, such as character incompatibility or a lack of needed skills, adverse environmental factors that overwhelm the team's coping ability, and limited resources, may cause failure even with good leadership (2).

The leader should be able to identify the likely needs of the operation and select appropriate team members, considering both personal skills and compatibility. This is important during diving operations where stressful conditions are likely to occur. If the operative environment changes so the team cannot manage the situation, the leader should terminate the activity before dangerous conditions develop. Finally, adequate technical resources, such as functional and robust diving gear and procedures, should be available.

Data show that 60% to 75% of the employees in any given organization find the most stressful part of their job is the presence of direct supervisors who fail to act as efficient leaders, becoming obsessed with micromanaging their subordinates, draining confidence and motivation. These leaders also show over self-evaluation and often are chosen by top management on the false belief that displaying certain personality traits – that are erroneously believed to highlight a leadership attitude – is sufficient to ensure actual good leadership (1).

Another problem with leadership is that once a leader is well-established, they can develop an attitude of over-confidence and complacency, becoming less attentive to the decision-making process and failing to evaluate the risk correctly. Once the leader has lost the team's trust, the situation will further deteriorate because it is likely that the team's members will avoid public confrontation and instead withhold critical information (13).

A big problem for a leader is the development of conformity within the team. This is a human habit generated by the tendency to obey authority, go with the flow, and desire to please others. Under the pressure of conformity, subordinates can agree to perform duties they are not ready for, leading to probable accidents. Conformity is also linked to "group-thinking," a tendency away from assertiveness toward passive acceptance of the ideas and behaviors of the rest of the team (14).

Bad leadership in diving operations can be highly damaging, not only leading to a drop in proficiency, but also likely jeopardizing the safety of the divers. Complacency and over-confidence are both dangerous attitudes in a diving leader; challenging such behaviors may be tricky, especially if team members feel subordinate to the leader, as in the case of diving students and their instructor.

Team–leader interactions

A series of propositions have been identified from the study of team–leader interactions. These can be used as a general guideline for good leadership (2), (6):

1. The leader should be able to motivate the team by providing guidance and setting clear goals and strategies.

2. The leader's understanding of the situation positively correlates with the efficacy of the shared mental models within the team.
3. The leader will use their charisma and influence to improve team performance.
4. Leaders who support team members' participation in problem-solving will create a team collectively engaged in information processing.
5. Leaders who set high standards and provide appropriate strategies to achieve the planned goals create teams with higher levels of efficacy and stronger cohesion that are less prone to negative emotional reactions under stressful conditions.
6. Leaders who provide consistent feedback create a more effective team.

When applied to a diving team, these strategies will allow for developing a well-focused group (point 1) that shares a common vision of the operative environment (point 2). A trusted leader will also enhance the diving performance of the team through their example and by involving the other divers in the decision-making process (points 3 and 4). Diving standards and procedures should be set, providing adequate instruction and time to achieve the planned levels of performance (point 5). Finally, the debrief at the end of each dive should give constructive feedback (point 6).

Lessons learned

- Any team needs a good leader to be effective and proficient.
- Good leaders share common traits, including positive self-confidence, stamina, and motivation.

- Different leadership strategies should be applied depending on the team and the operative environment of the dive.
- In complex and variable environments, the team leader should always be able to change their style to manage the team's varying needs.
- In a highly technical domain such as diving, the leader must have deep knowledge of the critical elements and have mastered the relevant diving skills.
- A dive leader should also be an excellent communicator, empathizing with the other divers.
- Under stressful situations, the team will become more dependent on the leader, who, therefore, must be able to handle the crisis, remaining calm, focused, and in control.

References

1. **Hogan, R., Curphy, G. and Hogan, J.** *What we know about leadership: Effectiveness and personality.* 1994.

2. **Zaccaro, S., Rittman, A. and Marks, M.** Team leadership. *The Leadership Quarterly.* 2001, Vol. 12, pp. 451–483.

3. **Goleman, D.** Leadership that gets results. *Harvard Business Review.* 2000, pp. 2–17.

4. **Gardner, H.** *Leading minds.* New York : Basic Books, 1995.

5. **House, R. and Mitchell, T.** *Path-goal theory of leadership.* Seattle, WA : University of Washington, Seattle – US Navy technical report, 1975.

6. **Prati, M., Douglas, C., Ferris, G., Ammeter, A. and Buckley, M.** Emotional intelligence, leadership effectiveness, and

team outcomes. *The International Journal of Organizational Analysis.* 2003, Vol. 11, 10, pp. 21–40.

7. **Kirkpatrick, S. and Locke, E.** Leadership: Do traits matter? *Academy of Management Executive.* 1991, Vol. 5, 2, pp. 48–60.

8. **MacInnis, J.** *Deep leadership.* Toronto, Canada : Knopf Canada, 2012.

9. **Lock, G.** *Under pressure.* 2019.

10. **Heldal, F. and Antonsen, S.** *Team leadeship in a high-risk organization: The role of contextual factors.* Thousand Oaks, CA : Samall Group Research - SAGE, 2014.

11. **Rajnandini, P. and Willars, E.** Transformational leadership, self-efficacy, group cohesiveness, commitment, and performance. *Journal of Organizational Change Management.* 2004, Vol. 17, 2, pp. 144–159.

12. **Spillane, J.** Distributed leadership. *The Educational Forum.* 2005, Vol. 69, 2, pp. 143–150.

13. *How to be a good leader.* **Peake, E.** 2018, Wired.

14. **Beaty, D.** *The naked pilot: The human factor in aircraft accidents.* s.l. : Airlife, 1995.

4. SITUATIONAL AWARENESS

Chapter highlights

Situational awareness (SA) is the ability to be conscious of the surrounding environment and events and their evolution. It is a consequential cognitive process that starts with the awareness of the relevant elements, proceeds with the understanding of their significance, and ends with the capacity to forecast the likely evolution of the situation.

Good SA is essential in monitoring complex systems and when operating in adverse environments, such as when using scuba systems.

Shifting from a low SA to the very high SA needed in emergencies is complex, and in individuals who are not well-trained and experienced, it could lead to panic and failure.

Team SA is more challenging to maintain than individual SA because of the need for good communication between the team members and shared common mental models; as most diving operations are performed as a team, this kind of SA is relevant for divers.

Accidents happen when the divergence between SA and the actual status of the system causes incorrect interpretations of reality.

Loss of SA is often associated with diving accidents and incidents. Good training under realistic conditions is the only way to enhance SA, reducing the likelihood of errors.

Introduction

The first ideas on the importance of being aware of the surrounding operative environment were developed during the First World War by the German Ace Oswald Boelke, the "father" of air dogfighting tactics and mentor of Manfred von Richthofen, the famous "Red Baron." Boelke strongly supported gaining advanced awareness of the enemy's status as a critical strategical advantage; he also advised pilots always to be aware of what was happening on the battlefield, avoiding focusing solely on the closest enemy (1).

The term "situational awareness" (SA) was used in the late 1980s to describe the process of attention, perception, and decision-making utilized by aircraft pilots to generate a mental model of the flying environment (1), (2).

More generally, SA can be defined as being conscious of the surrounding environment, and evolving events and being aware of the "big picture" of what is happening. It is crucial in decision-making that needs to be performed quickly, mostly in complex dynamic environments (3), (4).

The diving environment is dynamic – changes can happen at any time – and complex, requiring artificial life-support systems and specific procedures. For divers, it is therefore mandatory to maintain a high level of SA, being able to forecast the likely development of the situation.

While SA is needed for good decision-making, it is insufficient to guarantee an error-free decisional phase because SA does not necessarily allow for understanding why something is happening, which is a critical factor for correct decisions (5). Poor decisions can still occur even with good SA, as indicated by an analysis of about 400 operational incident reports by flight controllers (1).

A diver should couple good SA with good knowledge of the procedures and with a high level of skills and experience to make correct critical decisions (Fig. 4.1).

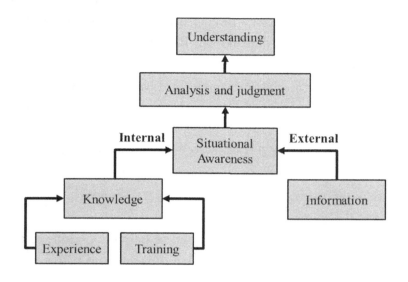

Fig. 4.1. Flowchart of the mental processes leading to good situational awareness and decision-making (modified from Lovering, 2014).

SA is also important in monitoring critical systems, the failure of which could pose a fatal threat to the safety of the operators (6).

A diver should always be aware of the correct functioning of their life-support system (critical system), for example, and be able to quickly react to any anomaly before the issue escalates into an unmanageable system breakdown.

SA is acquired and maintained with a cyclical and adaptive process affected by external (environment) and internal (self) factors (2).

As divers, considering environmental and operational factors, we need to maintain a good level of SA during our dives. Diving mishaps are very often associated with some reduced SA, which allowed minor variances from safe procedures to develop unnoticed; if instead the variance had been discovered in time, then appropriate procedures could have been put in place to avoid the error or, at least, mitigate its consequences (7).

Typology of situational awareness

SA is specific to the situation in which the individual is operating, and a few typologies of the different kinds of awareness that are needed can be identified (8):

- *Environmental*: Awareness of the operating environment.
- *Spatial*: Awareness of the proper position in the reference space.
- *System*: Awareness of the status of all the systems.
- *Communication*: Awareness of the quality of communication.
- *Time horizon*: Awareness of time management.

The sea status, weather, and diving conditions represent the environmental SA during a dive. The knowledge of the team's position in relation to entrance/exit points and monitoring the dive depth is part of the spatial SA. Being in control of the correct functioning of the diving gear represents system awareness. Diver-to-diver communication and diver-to-surface communication are communication SA. Finally, dive time, remaining no-deco time, and deco-stops management correspond to the time horizon SA.

Situational awareness levels

SA is a cognitive process that can be divided into three cumulative levels (3), (8), (9):

- *Level 1*: The identification of the relevant elements in the environment. It can be described as what to look for, when to look for it, and why to look for it. At this level, the operator should be able to critically analyze the surroundings, focusing on the pertinent information and disregarding the rest to avoid distraction.
- *Level 2*: The elements identified in level 1 must be correctly understood and integrated into the current operational goals. Knowledge and former experience generate a mental model of the situation.
- *Level 3*: Building on levels 1 and 2, the operator can project the probable evolution of the situation into the future.

A diver navigating using natural references will focus on the relevant landscape, avoiding being distracted by other elements (level 1). The diver will then correlate the identified landforms with their position underwater (level 2). Finally (level 3), the diver can find their path back to the exit point based on the changes in the landmarks they identified as good navigational references.

A decisional process will follow the SA process. The operator can then use feedback from the resulting performance to reassess the situation and start a new cycle of SA (Fig. 4.2).

During a dive, the SA process should continuously be repeated so that the diver can maintain a good awareness of the surrounding environment and the changes that can affect the evolution of the dive.

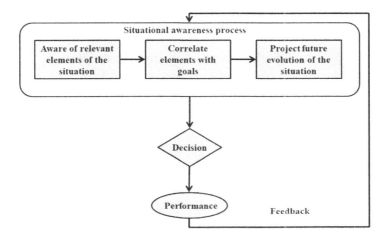

Fig. 4.2. Situational awareness levels (modified from Endsley, 1995).

Situational awareness status

Five statuses of SA have been identified about the operative situation and capacity of the individual (10):

1. *Turned out*: The typical status of an individual relaxed in a safe and familiar environment performing routine tasks.
2. *Relaxed awareness*: Good SA is achieved without overloading the individual's attention capacity. This status can be maintained for a very long time.
3. *Focused awareness*: Typical of a demanding situation where high concentration is needed and will soon deplete the individual's mental and physical energy reserve.
4. *High alert*: Emergency reaction status requires mobilizing

any available resources. This level of SA can be maintained for only a very short time.

5. *Comatose*: The individual is "frozen," becoming unable to cope with the situation; panic will develop.

Shifting from a low-alert to a high-alert status requires time for a successful transition. Being familiar with the operative environment and associated risks improves the quality of SA and the capacity of the individual to react to adverse events.

A diver quietly preparing their diving gear at home is in turned-out status, with no need for any specific SA. During the dive, relaxed awareness should be achieved so that mental reserves are not drained but enough vigilance is maintained. When the diving situation becomes demanding, the divers will shift to focused awareness; this status can be sustained for a limited amount of time, after which tiredness will reduce performance. If the situation evolves into an emergency, the diver must rely on their total capacity and experience to survive. This high alert status is highly taxing. Finally, if the situational demands exceed the individual's capacity, the diver becomes unable to act and will likely be the victim of an accident. When underwater, the time available is limited; therefore, the decisional phase of the overall SA process needs to be performed swiftly and without hesitation. Proper training and former experience will help the diver react quickly and productively to most unforeseen circumstances that can affect a dive.

Team situational awareness

SA in a team is more challenging to maintain than individual SA because it requires not only each member to have good SA but also a good level of communication of this SA within the team. It should include continuous assessment of the evolving situation, with the operators developing shared mental models of the changing system; if a divergence between the mental models of the team members develops, then a breakdown in team SA is likely to follow (11), (12).

A hierarchical structure in a team can help in routine situations with clearly defined procedural steps and roles; for problems requiring a more creative, non-standard solution, a team composed of peers has greater chances of success. Moreover, a strictly hierarchic system may reduce the assertiveness of the subaltern members, resulting in a degradation of team SA. For this reason, role exchange is a standard routine in some teams, such as in flying crews, where the captain and first officer act as pilots in turn (11).

As divers, we almost invariably work as a team, and we should be able to achieve and sustain good team SA. The roles within the team should be identified with a lead diver appointed for the dive. The team should also be allowed flexibility, with the possibility of another diver taking control if new conditions require a shift in leadership. Excellent communication must be maintained throughout the dive so that it will be possible to exchange relevant information and share common mental models of the situation. A critical moment is during the dive briefing; all divers should be required to share their ideas for the mission, ensuring that all (or most of) the possible solutions have been analyzed. During the briefing, the leader should also provide all the critical information shared within the team and correctly understood.

Failure of situational awareness

Failure of SA is often the cause of accidents, especially in challenging working situations such as in the maritime industry and aviation (2), (6). In 221 reports of aviation incidents, loss of SA was the primary cause of 52.8% of the total issues (11). The Australian Transportation Safety Board indicates that failure in SA is involved in 85% of all accidents and incidents reported (8). Accidents may happen when divergence between an individual's SA and the actual status of the system develops (1).

A strategy used by expert decision-makers is to compare the current situation with similar ones they have experienced to classify the events under specific categories in a mental model of the problem and act accordingly. This is particularly valuable when a decision needs to be made based on limited information and under time pressure (13). Maintaining adequate SA becomes progressively more difficult as the complexity of the operational environment increases. Attention capacity and working memory are necessarily limited, and these limits affect the SA capacity of an individual; goals and expectations also influence SA perception. Experience and training support good SA built over time with increased knowledge of the different facets of the operative environment and its temporal evolution. Automaticity also helps overcome the natural limits of human working memory. Still, excessive automaticity can negatively affect SA, with an individual who is too fixed on a routine approach becoming potentially unaware of changes in the situation and environment which require a modification of the usual routine (3), (14).

Expert divers usually have better SA than novices because they can compare the current status with former situations they have been through. It is also essential that these more expert divers share their mental model with the others to avoid misunder-standings and conflictual decisions within the team that will lead to a general failure of the SA.

SA can be affected by errors at each of its levels:

- *Level 1*: Most involved in the failure of novice operators who may be uncertain about relevant data and have difficulties coping with high workloads, attention being shared between too many different goals, and stress (3), (14). Distraction and complacency also affect this level of SA (8). Studies on aviation accidents have confirmed the impact of level 1 failure in fatal mishaps (1).
- *Level 2*: Can be compromised by distraction, lack of experience/knowledge, excessive workload, and failure to connect the data gathered at level 1 with a proper conceptual model (3), (8), (14).
- *Level 3*: Requires a deep understanding of conceptual models to predict the future status of the system. A wrong input in the model, or the use of an incomplete or inappropriate model, will lead to failure in correct forecasting (3), (14). Also, not recognizing that the model needs to be updated or changed because of new inputs is a cause of SA failure (8).

Levels 1 and 2 in SA are particularly relevant in the complex diving environment, and loss of SA was associated with 40% of non-technical failures during diving operations by the US Navy (4). A similar percentage of navigation mishaps was related to loss of SA by the US Coast Guard (15).

Some examples of SA failure at the three different levels in diving are:

- *Level 1*: A diver too focused on the job may fail to check their Submersible Pressure Gauge (SPG).
- *Level 2*: A diver may not understand from the reading of the SPG that they are using more air than usual.
- *Level 3*: The diver cannot foresee a low-air or out-of-air situation developing following increased breathing gas usage.

SA can be reduced in several ways (15), (16):

- Perception based on inaccurate information or faulty processing. Perception is a mental picture of reality and can be affected by the quantity and quality of available knowledge, experience, and expectations.
- Ambiguous information with disagreement between the data.
- Loss of attention on the surrounding environment due to "tunnel vision."
- Failure to follow correct rules and procedures.
- Time pressure.
- Excessive motivation: being motivated is usually good, but the excessive drive to accomplish a given goal may lead to a failure in rational risk assessment.
- Complacency: typical in routine tasks.
- Overload: too many tasks to accomplish in too short a time.
- Fatigue: a fatigued operator will have reduced vigilance and mental capacity.
- Stress: this will affect mostly level 1 SA, narrowing the field of attention and increasing the probability of not being aware of other factors which can seriously affect the safety of the operator.
- Poor communication: this affects SA at a team level.

It is often complicated to detect SA errors; the main clue is usually a mismatch between new information and expectation based on the current SA model.

For example, a diver who thinks they are swimming back toward the shore but is swimming away from it may realize the mistake when they notice that the depth is not becoming shallower as it should be approaching the coastline.

In dynamic environments, workload is another factor that can affect SA in different ways (3):

1. *Low SA and low workload*: In this case, the operator may fail to take adequate action due to vigilance problems, low motivation, or distractions.
2. *Low SA and high workload*: The operator's attention is overwhelmed by too much information, which cannot be correctly analyzed promptly.
3. *High SA and low workload*: An ideal situation where the operator has plenty of capacity and time for analyzing the information.
4. *High SA and high workload*: The operator works hard but within their limits.

The ideal situation of point 3 can be sustained for a long time, which can be achieved by trained operators vectorizing areas of attention/work (14).

For example, during a dive, the different phases of the operation should be identified together with the key parameters to be monitored. In this way, the diver can focus only on a limited number of important issues at any given time, maintaining good SA. If, on the other hand, the diver is overwhelmed by having too many parameters to control simultaneously without a straightforward method, then a drop or even total loss of SA is likely to happen.

Deterioration of SA may lead to several negative consequences (1):

- Failure to detect critical information on the status of the system. This is a level 1 error.
- Failure to understand the meaning of the information. This is a level 2 error.
- Failure to understand tasks and responsibilities. This is an error in team SA.
- Communication failure. This can involve intra-team communication between the team and other groups.

To avoid or at least reduce SA errors, an excellent strategy will include the following key elements, as well as good training (1), (8), (16):

- Plan ahead and identify areas of high workload.
- Delegate/share some duties to reduce the workload of single individuals.
- Be aware of all the available sources of information.
- Cross-check information to eliminate contradictory elements.
- Always consider "the big picture" – avoid fixation on a single problem only.
- Use checklists.
- Buy time to assess the situation better.
- Create visual/audio reminders for interrupted tasks.
- Be able to prioritize attention to different parts of the system depending on its status.
- Enhance multi-tasking capacity.

- Be able to recognize patterns and probable lines of evolution of the system.
- Continuously monitor and evaluate current performance vs. the plan.
- Practice scanning relevant displays in human-machine interfaces.

Some strategies facilitate maintaining a good level of SA in diving situations (4):

- Be aware of the progress of the dive, especially during critical phases such as descending and ascending, and of any abnormal situations (i.e., increase in breathing gas usage).
- Look at the big picture, avoiding focusing only on some aspects of the dive.
- Be proactive during the dive, considering immediate and next steps.
- During the briefing, clearly state all goals and procedures and share your ideas with the other diving team members.
- During the debriefing, review the dive, identify good and bad decisions, and discuss the outcomes with the rest of the team. This process will enhance better SA in future dives.

Some technical aids may support SA; for example, heads-up displays (HUDs) can help facilitate operational tasks by making information more readily accessible. On the other hand, an excessive focus solely on HUD information may be detrimental to environmental SA (17).

Overreliance on automatic features can lead to the loss of effective SA, increasing the risk of accidents. In particular, in the case of malfunctions, the operator should be aware that something is wrong and able to address the issue and override the automatism quickly. Complex systems can make this overriding difficult, leading to accidents. Finally, any automatic system prone to false alarms will undermine the credibility of the warnings, and as a result, a genuine alarm may go unnoticed (18).

It is to be noted that even if good SA increases the probability of good performance, it does not guarantee correct decisions, which must also be based on other skills such as knowledge and experience (3), (4).

SA is the cornerstone on which we as divers build a safety system that includes over-learning key skills, progressive building up of experience, acknowledgment of our limits, and positive mental attitude.

Lessons learned

- SA is based on three levels:
    1. Awareness of the relevant elements of the surrounding environment.
    2. Understanding of the meaning of such elements.
    3. Ability to forecast the evolution of the situation.

- For divers, good SA is essential for controlling the dive.
- Shifting from a situation with low SA to one where higher SA is needed can be difficult and cause actual loss of SA.
- Achieving good SA at the team level is more complex than individual SA.
- Good communication is a crucial feature of team SA.
- Loss of SA is often the root cause of diving accidents.
- To avoid loss of SA experience and training under realistic conditions are mandatory.

- Good dive planning and complete briefings support SA during a dive.

References

1. **Stanton, N., Chambers, G. and Piggott, J.** Situational awareness and safety. *Safety Science.* 2001, Vol. 39, pp. 189–204.

2. **Society, Royal Aeronautical.** *JAA ESSAI Project.*

3. **Endsley, M.** Toward a theory of situation awareness in dynamic systems. *Human Factors.* 1995, Vol. 37, 1, pp. 32–64.

4. **O'Connor, P.** *A navy diving supervisor's guide to the non-technical skills required for safe and productive diving operations.* Panama City, FL : NEDU, 2005.

5. *Odin's ravens: From situational awareness to understanding.* **Lovering, T.** 2014, The Three Swords Magazine, Vol. 27.

6. **Safahami, M. and Tuttle, S.** *Situation awareness and its practical application in maritime domain.* s.l. : SKEMA.

7. *Situational awareness.* **Sadler, R.** s.l. : DAN, 2011, Vol. Alert Diver Winter 2011.

8. **Airbus.** *Human performance: Enhancing situational awareness.* Toulouse, France : Airbus, 2007.

9. **Lock, G.** *Under pressure.* 2019.

10. *A practical guide to situational awareness.* **Stewart, S.** s.l. : Stratfor, March 14, 2012, Security Weekly.

11. **Jentsch, F., Barnett, J., Bowers, C. and Salas, E.** Who is

flying this plane anyway? What mishaps tell us about crew member role assignment and air crew situational awareness. *Human Factors.* 1999, Vol. 41, 1, pp. 1–14.

12. **Dekker, S.** Crew situational awareness in high-tech settings: Tactics for research into an ill defined phenomenon. *Transportation Human Factors.* 2000, Vol. 2, 1, pp. 49–62.

13. *Situational awareness of commanders.* **Juarez-Espinoza, O. and Gonzales, C.** Arlington, VA : s.n., 2004. Proceedings Conference on behavior representation in modeling and simulation .

14. **NOAA.** *Situational awareness and decision making in a warning environment.*

15. **USCG.** *Team coordination training student guide.* Washington, DC : USCG, 1998.

16. **Edwards, D., Douglas, J. and Edkins, G.** Situational awareness. *Flight Safety Australia.* 1998, November, pp. 15–17.

17. **Staal, M.** *Stress, cognition and human performance: A literature review and conceptual framework.* Washington, DC : NASA, 2004.

18. **Beaty, D.** *The naked pilot: The human factor in aircraft accidents.* s.l. : Airlife, 1995.

5. LEARNING AND OVERLEARNING

Chapter highlights

Learning is a process that induces permanent changes in behavior, and it is based on acquiring new knowledge and experience.

Divers continuously learn because they increase their experience and knowledge with each dive. Becoming an expert diver is a long journey that requires focus and motivation.

Mastering a skill involves a series of phases during which the diver moves from simply following a rule to fully understanding the concepts underlying the rule.

Once a skill has been mastered, it should be "overlearned," meaning it is practiced multiple times even after perfectly executed. With this process, the retaining time of the skill is increased, and it will be possible to maintain a high level of quality in the skill even under high-stress circumstances. For this reason, overlearning emergency skills strongly reduces the risk of mishaps.

Every individual learns in their way. Some may be more "visual" learners, some like to listen, and others prefer hands-on practice. An instructor needs to understand the learning style of their students and provide the best and most effective learning experience.

The learned information needs to be stored and retrieved when needed. To achieve this, we have to transfer such information into long-term memory. This process connects new concepts and data with memories already present. In this way, we consolidate the newly acquired knowledge.

Introduction

No one is a "natural born diver"; becoming a proficient and safe diver requires time, dedication, and a progressive building up of experience. Learning is fundamental in acquiring the needed knowledge for becoming a good diver.

This chapter focuses on some basics of learning theory and how these concepts can be used to improve the acquisition of new skills in diving and support mastery of already acquired skills. An experienced and well-skilled diver can better understand and manage any potential risk.

Learning has been defined as "an enduring change in behavior resulting from experience" (1). Through this process, new information is associated with previously learned facts and experiences (Fig. 5.1), generating a new understanding of the situation (2). Facts, concepts, and ideas must be memorized and fused with the already acquired knowledge for learning to occur (3).

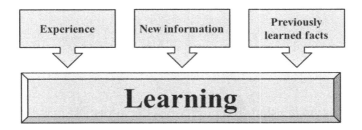

Fig. 5.1. Different components of a learning experience.

From this definition, we can infer some critical information. Once we learn something new, our behavior related to such knowledge is changed, and this change is based on the experience that we build around the newly acquired skill. As divers, we continuously learn, not only when we participate in new courses but also through building up experience every time we dive. Our behavior as divers is therefore changed and hopefully improved once we learn new skills and expand our knowledge in diving.

The "overlearning" concept means that once a given skill has been mastered, further training repetitions will make the response almost instinctive and automatic (4). This is very important in emergencies where a drop in proficiency is inevitable due to the elevated stress levels; overlearning skills will offset most of the stress impact, allowing operators to maintain a good level of efficacy.

How we learn

Learning is not a single-step event but instead follows a series of consecutive levels of cognition that increase in their complexity from the mere basic knowledge of a given fact to a critical judgment of concepts (Fig. 5.2). We can identify five such levels (5):

- *Knowledge*: The information is restated as it was learned.

For example, a novice diver will recall the basic principle of Boyle's law without necessarily understanding its implications.

- *Comprehension*: The purpose of the information is explained.

For example, the diver can now understand that the main point of Boyle's law is that a gas expands when the surrounding environmental pressure drops.

- *Application*: The acquired information is used in practical situations.

For example, the diver understands that they need to exhale when ascending to avoid over-extension of the lungs due to the expansion of the gas following Boyle's law.

- *Synthesis*: Being able to build complex results from different information.

For example, the diver can now correlate the concept of gas expansion and compression with gas density variation and understand why gas consumption at depth is higher than in shallower water.

- *Evaluation*: Judging something against a standard.

For example, the diver can estimate how long the breathing gas will last based on their consumption rate at surface. This operation involves correctly understanding Boyle's law and its application in diving.

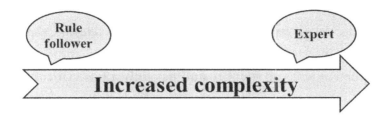

Fig. 5.2. Evolving from novice to expert allows for mastering increasingly complex skills.

The goal for a student is to reach the synthesis and evaluation levels so that the acquired information will be well understood, making memorization easier. To achieve these levels, considerable effort and experience are needed in the initial steps of the learning curve (5).

The acquisition of skills proceeds through a series of phases that can be represented by a five-stage model of consecutive steps (6):

1. *Novice*: The instruction process begins with a series of rules to be applied. These rules must be further explained in their context for the information to make sense.

A diver will likely blindly follow several rules at the beginning of their activity. Once the utility of these rules is better understood, the learning process will be facilitated.

2. *Advanced beginner*: The student learns to recognize meaningful aspects of the situation based on examples and former experience. At this stage, the student is still following instructions.

For example, a diver at this stage understands the need for the "never holding your breath" rule but may still need some prompts from the instructor.

3. *Competence*: At this stage, the student's performance is affected by an overloading of potentially relevant elements that interfere with a clear decision-making process until the student can identify and use only a few critical pieces of information pertinent to the actions to be performed.

For example, divers involved in higher-level training can have an initial feeling of confusion about the large amount of information to be correctly processed; with experience and growth in knowledge, the divers will be able to identify the most relevant elements that need to be taken into account for a proficient and safe dive.

4. *Proficiency*: Proficiency is reached when enough experience is assimilated. Goals are clearly identified, but how to get them is not totally clear yet, and a rule approach is still needed for the more complex situations.

Divers reach this level when they can define all the steps needed for complex diving operations, such as those requiring multiple gases and articulated decompression profiles. At this level, the divers cannot yet define the dive plan autonomously and rely on inputs from more experienced divers or the diving supervisor.

5. *Expertise*: The expert recognizes the situation and immediately knows how to reach the goals. The response to a given situation is intuitive, based on a large body of experience. The ability to make more refined discriminations distinguishes the expert from the proficient performer.

Expert divers can quickly respond to changes, identifying the correct and safest procedures. Their situational awareness is very high, enabling them to manage any challenge posed by the diving environment. Experts can correctly assess the risk and decide if such risks can be managed or if the operation needs to be postponed or canceled.

In the 1980s, Howard Gardner developed the concept that "intelligence" is not a unique entity but instead is the result of different intellectual attitudes and that individuals can have different strengths and weaknesses in their academic structure. For this reason, different individuals learn in different ways (5). The three proposed learner archetypes were:

1. *Visual*: Needs to have visual information.

This kind of diver will more likely better understand skills presented through visual systems such as videos and pictures.

2. *Auditory*: Emphasizes what is heard and spoken.

This diver will respond better to spoken descriptions of the skills to be learned.

3. *Kinesthetic*: Uses the body's movements to learn skills.

This diver will easily learn new skills by practicing them, ideally in a safe and controlled diving environment first, such as in confined water.

Most diving training agencies' current approach to learning considers all these elements, providing programs that include videos, in-person classes, readings, and practical in-water sessions. It is up to the instructor to understand the optimal "blend" of such elements for each student based on the typology of "intelligence" of the student (Fig. 5.3).

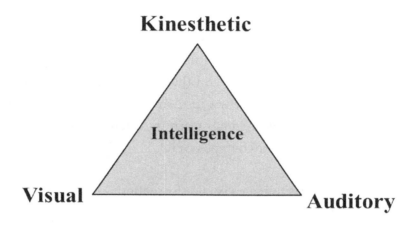

Fig. 5.3. Intelligence is a blend of different capabilities.

Experience plays a central role in the learning process. Knowledge is created by linking new concepts to previously learned ones. Concrete experiences are the basis for observations and reflections, which are assimilated into more abstract concepts (7). On the other hand, misconceptions and erroneous information previously acquired can negatively interfere with learning new ideas (2).

It is up to the instructor to consider all the different attitudes of the students and develop a program that will benefit them. For an instructor, it is essential to understand that the former experience of the learner will affect the current learning outcomes, and they should arrange the information delivery tapping into such previous experiences (1). The instructor must have a deep knowledge of the teaching area to identify the best way of presenting the information (2).

When providing diving training, the instructor should have a good idea of the student's background in diving experience and knowledge of the topics. This should not be intended as a "test" but as a way to identify the needs of the students and, therefore, the most effective way of teaching the needed skills. The instructor may require a pre-evaluation to assess the students' actual level in more advanced training, such as technical diving and rebreather diving.

Memory

Learning will only be helpful if we can store and retrieve the information when needed. For this reason, we have to memorize the newly acquired concepts. There are two types of memory (5):

1. *Working memory*: A short-term form of memory used for new information that is being processed. The information is remembered only as long as it is actively used.

For example, divers may use their working memory when consulting a dive table. It is very unlikely that the diver will be able to recall all the possible combinations on the table once they stop reading them. The different depth and dive time combinations will remain in memory only if continuously analyzed.

2. *Long-term memory*: Permanent memory used to store learned information and skills.

A diver will store in this memory their learned skills and will be able to retrieve them when needed.

Learning is achieved once the information is effectively stored in the long-term memory in an organized and meaningful manner. The learner can then transfer the acquired knowledge to different situations (1).

For example, a diver who learned how to control the BCD using the inflator and deflator valves should be able to transfer this knowledge to similar situations, such as controlling a drysuit or a lift-bag.

To transfer information into the long-term memory, several learning methods can be used, including (5):

1. *Repeated rehearsal*: Practice of skills in several different contexts.

For example, divers can periodically review key safety skills such as gas sharing so that the relative procedure is well memorized.

2. *Building connections*: Using past knowledge to understand new information.

For example, divers involved in Nitrox training may use some of their former knowledge about the laws of gases learned in their introductory scuba course to understand better new concepts related to partial pressure.

Standardization of concepts also facilitates knowledge storage and transfer (1).

More complex information should be divided into basic concepts to make memorization easier. The concepts should then be re-grouped to explain their relationship and the general idea. Analogies can be helpful, but it should be clear that they represent just a simplification of the actual concept. Mnemonics are often used to help store concepts in long-term memory (1), (5).

A typical use of mnemonics in diving is the creation of hints to recall a specific sequence of operations, such as when performing the pre-dive checks.

Examples, experience, and motivation

Most behaviors are learned following appropriate examples more than by trial-and-error. A trial-and-error approach can be inappropriate and too risky in potentially dangerous environments. The students should be provided with a clear explanation of why they should learn a specific topic and get feedback on their performance. More complex skills should be divided into sub-skills to facilitate their acquisition (8).

The best learning level is reached when the students are involved in "doing" rather than just "looking" and when they are required to solve real problems. The learning environment should be stimulating by providing challenges, even within a risk-controlled frame (9). A realistic learning setting will strongly facilitate memorizing the information and skills (1).

Motivation is an integral part of the learning experience, and the student should understand the usefulness of the provided information (5). Motivated students are often emotionally involved in the training, including conscious and unconscious processes (9).

In diving training, examples and feedback are crucial. It would be impracticable and hazardous to proceed by trial-and-error when learning a new diving skill. The instructor should clearly state the importance of the skill and how this will be applied in a real scenario. If complex operations need to be performed, it is wise to learn the sequence step-by-step until each skill has been correctly understood. Motivated divers generally perform better because they have a clearly identified goal. Too much motivation could become problematic because the divers may feel excessive pressure to achieve the planned objective, disregarding the risks. A good balance between motivation and a clear understanding of the needed resources and the risks associated with the operation is always a key factor in diving safety.

Mastery

Repeated practice and reinforcement of the learned concepts continue until a perfect response is obtained without further practice. At this level, the learner has reached mastery of the learned skill (1).

To be fully competent in a given field, it is necessary to possess a strong foundation of factual knowledge, understand facts and ideas within a defined framework, and organize knowledge for easy retrieval (2).

The ultimate goal for a diver is to master the skills needed for a safe and proficient dive.

The stages of mastery can be described using a term borrowed from the martial art of Aikido, the "Shuhari" (10):

- *Shu (protect) – follow the rule*: The rules are followed to the letter, and the procedures are repeated over and over to assimilate them. Following a single well-defined procedure is the most efficient way to learn.

A diver learning a new procedure, such as how to deploy a Submersible Marker Buoy (SMB), will learn the skills following a well-defined technique and repeating it until the skill is perfectly executed.

- *Ha (cut) – break the rule*: The rules are well-known and can be questioned when necessary. The reason behind the rule becomes clear.

A diver well-experienced in a procedure can decide to modify it if the environmental conditions and operational status require so. This can be safely done only if the diver deeply understands the procedure. For example, a diver may change their decompression plan to a more conservative one if they consider the dive more tasking regarding DCS risk.

- *Ri (depart) – be the rule*: The concepts are so well-assimilated that they become instinctive. The student is now the master and can create new rules and methods.

This is a level of mastery that only a few divers reach. They are the ones who will create new standards and procedures. For example, Sheck Exley was the first to develop cave diving standards, rules, and procedures, opening the path for a new diving field.

An important consideration is that under specific circumstances, the diver should be able to deviate from a rule (11). To do this safely and proficiently, they must be an expert able to fully understand the roots of the rule and how it can be modified if needed.

Overlearning

Once a skill is thoroughly mastered, the learning phase is concluded, and the overlearning phase may begin (Fig. 5.4). The percentage of overlearning is defined by the number of times the task is repeated compared with the number of trials needed to achieve the specified level of mastery of the task. For example, if a given task is mastered after ten repetitions, 100% overlearning is completed by a further ten repetitions (4). In overlearning, the performance will level off, not improving more, but additional practice will extend the retention of the skill (12). In general, overlearning is useful when an error-free performance is more important than limiting the time that can be devoted to learning a given task (13). The re-learning of a given skill is also facilitated by good initial learning (14).

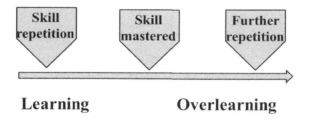

Fig. 5.4. Overlearning happens only after a skill is mastered and requires multiple repetitions.

Divers should use overlearning for skills that are critical elements of diving safety. In particular, any emergency procedure usually not needed during a routine dive should be overlearned so that the correct action becomes almost instinctive and the skills are retained for longer.

Tests indicate that the greater the level of overlearning, the greater the task retention. Generally, 50% overlearning is required for minimal improvement, with 150% for more significant improvements (4), (14).

The overlearned tasks must be practiced in conditions similar to those experienced in the real operative environment (4). Once the skills are fluently executed, responding fast and without hesitation, the overall performance that requires using such skills will improve even in more complex settings (12).

As for any diving training, the skills should be learned and practiced under realistic diving conditions. For example, if the divers often dive in cold water, any skill requiring manipulation should be learned and overlearned, donning the same kind of gloves used in cold water.

Overlearning also prevents disruption to the skill learned when immediately following it up with training on other skills. The effect of overlearning is a hyper-stabilization of the learned task; this status usually lasts for no more than a few hours (15).

This can be useful when divers go through training in similar skills, for example deploying an SMB and using a lift-bag. Overlearning will reduce interference between the skills and improve proficiency.

The automaticity of the skills gained through overlearning allows for performing skills without conscious attention. The individual becomes able to multi-task with minimal effort (12). This is of high importance for situations where the failure of a skill may have seriously damaging consequences (16).

In a diving emergency, the diver has to react to multiple problems quickly, and failing to address even one such problem may result in a catastrophic outcome. Having a high degree of automatism of the skills needed in an emergency, such as closing the correct valve of a free-flowing regulator, can make the difference between life and death.

Both cognitive and physical tasks are improved by overlearning, and both will degrade if no further practice is performed. Overlearning helps retain the skills, and a more extended training period spaced over time helps maintain the skills (18). Studies show that after 19 days, the effects of overlearning halved, and after 31 days, the effects of overlearning disappeared (4). Spacing practice across multiple sessions boosts long-term retention of learned skills (13). This has better results than mass overlearning (17). Critical skills, primarily physical rather than intellectual, that are rarely (or never) used in routine situations tend to degrade if not periodically retrained. Overlearning generally reduces the time needed for retraining in the learned skill (14).

Diving skills will deteriorate if not used. For this reason, the rehearsal of critical skills should be periodically performed. If there is a gap in diving, the diver should progressively refresh their skills before attempting more complex dives. It is a good idea to perform specific skills (for example, gas sharing, deploying the SMB, react to a simulated free-flowing regulator) at the end of each dive to maintain good practice.

Lessons learned

- Learning induces permanent changes of behavior.
- Each individual learns in different ways. It is important to find the "best mix" of learning strategies in order to optimize the acquisition of new skills.
- New knowledge is acquired and memorized building on former knowledge and experience.
- Examples and motivation are key elements for learning.
- Mastery is acquired through multiple phases of learning.

The student will start from the simple "rule follower" stage and move toward complete comprehension of the provided information.

- Overlearning increases the retention interval of any given skill and allows for better execution of such skills even under stress.

References

1. *Behaviorism, cognitivism, constructionism: Comparing critical features from an instructional design perspective.* **Ertmer, P. and Newby, T.** 4, 1993, Performance Improvement Quarterly, Vol. 6, pp. 50–72.

2. **Wilson, S. and Peterson, N.** *Theories of learning and teaching: What do they mean for educators.* s.l. : NEA Research working paper, 2006.

3. **Hammond, L., Austin, K., Orcutt, S. and Ross, J.** *How people learn: Introduction to learning theories.* Stanford, CA : Stanford University School of Education, 2001.

4. **Driskell, J., Wills, R. and Copper, C.** Effect of overlearning on retention. *Journal of Applied Psychology.* 1992, Vol. 77, 5, pp. 615–622.

5. **America, Teacher for.** *Learning theory.* 2011.

6. **Dreyfus, S.** The five-stage model of adult skill acquisition. *Bulletin of Science Technology and Society.* 2004, Vol. 24, 3, pp. 177–181.

7. **Kilb, D., Boyatzis, R. and Mainemelis, C.** *Experimental learning theory: Previous research and new directions.* 1999.

8. **Bandura, A.** *Social learning theories.* s.l. : General Learning Corporation.

9. **On Purpose Association.** *Learning theories.* 2010.

10. **Casali, D.** *Shuhari: A mental model for the phase of mastery.* 2014.

11. **Lock, G.** *Under pressure.* 2019.

12. **Dougherty, K. and Johnston, J.** Overlearning, fluency and automaticity. *The Behavior Analyst.* 1996.

13. **Rohrer, D.** Avoidance of overlearning characterizes the spacing effect. *European Journal of Cognitive Psychology.* 2009, Vol. 21, 7, pp. 1001–1012.

14. **Yeates, P.** *The effect of overlearning and task difficulty on the retention and re-learning of a gross-motor task.* Ottawa, Canada : University of Ottawa MSc thesis, 1973.

15. **Shibata, K., Sasaky, Y., Wonbang, J., Walsh, E., Machizawa, M., Tamaki, M., Chang, L. and Watanabe, T.** Overlearning hyper-stabilizes a skill by rapidly making neurochemical processing inhibitory-dominant. *Nature Neuroscience.* 2013, pp. 470–475.

16. **Rohrer, D. and Pashar, H.** Increasing retention without increasing study time. *Current Directions in Psychological Science.* 2007, Vol. 16, 4, pp. 183–186.

17. **Rohrer, D., Taylor, K., Pashler, H., Cependa, N. and Wixted, J.** The effect of overlearning on long-term retention. *Applied Cognitive Psychology.* 2005, Vol. 19, pp. 361–374.

18. **Kratzing, G.** *Skill retention: A test of the effects of overlearning and skill retention interval on maintenance of infrequently used complex skills.* Regina, Canada : University of Regina, Ph.D. thesis, 2016.

6. STRESS AND PERFORMANCE

Chapter highlights

Stress is part of our daily experience, affecting us every time physical and mental challenges confront us.

If we manage to deal with the stress, the outcomes can be positive because we can focus on the most critical aspects of the problem, reducing distraction. On the other hand, failure to cope with stressful situations may lead to the onset of panic that triggers uncontrolled, frantic, and ineffective reactions.

Time pressure and workload are two of the main stressors affecting the capacity of the individual to stay in control of the situation.

The more complex the action to be performed, the more it will be affected by stress. Knowledge, experience, and overlearning can offset part of the stress, allowing for better performance.

Divers are exposed to potentially high-stress levels deriving from being in an unfamiliar environment and having to perform multiple tasks in a limited timeframe. Moreover, several physical stressors are present in the diving environment, including cold, poor visibility, and fatigue.

Panic is one of the leading causes of diving fatalities, and panicked divers represent a danger to their safety and to everyone on the diving team.

Training in realistic conditions helps boost confidence, thus reducing the likelihood of panic under stress.

Introduction

Hans Selye defined stress in 1936 as "the nonspecific response of the body to any demand for change" (1). It can be induced by emotion, frustration, distress, and personal situations (2).

Stress is part of our daily life; whenever a challenge confronts us, we react physically and mentally, ready to respond to the situation (3).

A degree of stress, often defined as "eustress" or "good stress," is positive because it triggers a logical cognitive process of evaluation of the actual status of the situation to find appropriate solutions; the individual's available resources balance the demand, creating a positive feeling of "being in control." On the other hand, if the individual experiences a gap between their ability and the situation's needs, this will generate negative feelings of stress and anxiety (4), (5).

A total absence of stress is also harmful because the lack of stimuli may lead to boredom, reduced situational awareness, and complacency, with an increased risk of careless errors and a drop in performance (2), (6).

The reaction of an individual to a stressful situation is controlled by several factors (7):

- Trait-anxiety and trait-arousal levels typical of the individual.
- Individual's assessment of the actual level of stress.
- Individual's capacity to control the stress level.
- Previous exposure to the stimulus.

In divers, the trait-anxiety and trait-arousal factors are part of the individual psychological profile. Appropriate training may improve the stress response, providing a previous experience that will help control stress levels when similar conditions are encountered during operative dives.

Tolerance to stress varies between individuals, and for the same individual can vary on different days even if the situation is the same. Anxious individuals can become victims of feeling unable to cope with the circumstances, whatever those may be and becoming incapable of performing any logical actions. Knowledge, experience, and training play a central role in the operator's capacity to manage stressful situations, especially when immediate action is required (8), (9), (10).

A well-skilled and experienced operator, even when under stress, should be able to (2):

- Take care of an emergency while maintaining good situational awareness of the other parts of the system.

For example, a diver faced with a low-air situation should still be able to control the other parameters of the dive, including depth, dive time, and navigation.

- Quickly estimate the probable outcomes of the different possible actions.

For example, a dive instructor may need to swiftly decide if the problem their student is experiencing can be safely addressed underwater or if the dive must be terminated.

- Rapidly reorient priorities as the situation deteriorates or improves.

The diving environment is fast-changing, and divers should be able to adapt quickly to such changes to control their dive.

A way to better tolerate stressful situations is to overlearn basic skills and emergency procedures. Overlearning is defined as continuous training after performance improvement has been maximized, enhancing the resiliency of the learned skill (11). The overlearning concept is analyzed in more detail in Chapter 5.

A well-trained and knowledgeable diver will be able to manage the stress, being more confident and relaxed during the dive, focusing on the key elements of the plan without fear of not being able to cope with the workload. In an emergency, their reaction will be quicker and more effective.

Impact of stress

Most research shows that stress negatively affects decision-making, leading to poor rational analysis, narrowing of attention, reduced working-memory capacity, and longer reaction time. Moreover, a tendency toward avoidance develops with the individual becoming unable to recognize the existence of a problem (2), (12), (13), (14).

Well-learned skills are more resilient to the impact of stress because they are embedded in the brain's long-term memory, leading to automaticity and reduced usage of cognitive resources. Under very high stress, this strategy may fail, with even expert individuals reverting to a step-by-step approach in decision-making, often regressing to former behaviors which are not necessarily the best for the current situation. Increased stress may also cause "tunnel vision," with a diver focusing only on one main task or stimulus, reducing situational awareness (2), (4).

All divers must overlearn critical safety skills to make their cognitive load manageable even under high-stress levels. New skills require more time to be mastered, so their application to the current situation can become automated, avoiding regression to former and potentially inadequate skill sets.

Under stress, divers often cannot develop realistic expectations, with wishful thinking emerging. Individuals may see what they expect to be there rather than what is there (2).

This behavior can be hazardous when diving because it can delay appropriate reactions to a changing situation, wasting precious time that, when underwater, is always a limited resource.

Physical stressors, such as thermal extremes and noise, reduce working-memory performance, with more complex tasks most affected. This degradation is usually progressive and linked to an increase in stressors. Motor skills are also affected; for example, manual dexterity is impaired when the skin temperature of the hands drops below 11°C (53°F). However, motivation and peer support can mitigate the impact of thermal stressors (4).

It is not unusual for divers in cold water to become so uncomfortable that their only thought is to terminate the dive and exit the water as soon as possible. The cold acts as a "distractor," reducing the capacity to focus on the tasks, making mistakes and slips more likely.

Dodson-Yerkes curve and performance under stress

A classical relation between stress level and performance is illustrated by the Dodson-Yerkes curve (Fig. 6.1), which is an inverted U, Gaussian-type curve (bell-shaped) where the level of performance (y-axis) is shown in relation to stress levels (x-axis). Performance increases until an optimal status is reached, the curve's apex, and then performance drops for any further increase in stress, reducing the ability to react (7), (15).

Dodson-Yerkes curve

Fig. 6.1. Dodson-Yerkes curve. The best performance is achieved when an optimum stress level is reached.

In tasks requiring processing multiple pieces of information, low levels of stimulation are associated with attention paid to non-relevant cues, leading to a drop in performance. Boredom may also cause inappropriate actions that are initiated to reduce such boredom. When arousal increases, there is a better focus on more relevant information until a threshold is reached. Further stress causes attention tunneling with loss of relevant cues, thus reducing the performance (2), (3).

It is important to highlight that this relation between arousal and attention is questionable in its simplicity due to the complex nature of human responses to stress. Different stressors can affect performance in different ways (4).

Simple tasks, such as endurance and basic physical activity, benefit from a higher arousal level than tasks requiring elaborate processing of information and mental effort, which are better performed under low levels of stress; there is also a general preference toward stimuli and tasks that have a medium arousing potential (6), (10).

Stress reinforces dominant responses in familiar and well-known tasks but inhibits the performance of newly acquired and unfamiliar tasks (16). This performance deterioration generally affects secondary tasks; meanwhile, central tasks are still performed well or improved (7).

Under elevated stress levels, attention span is reduced, and the individual can effectively focus only on limited aspects of their situation. These aspects are not automatically those requiring more attention in terms of potentially hazardous consequences (2), (17).

Depending on the situation, this narrowing of attention can enhance some aspects of performance with a greater focus on one task. It can also impair performance when a broader sense of situational awareness is needed (4).

Under stress, expert divers may perform better as they become more focused on the task at hand; inexperienced divers may instead show a significant drop in performance when exposed to unexpected and stressful environments. This makes novice divers much more at risk of mishaps when under tension.

When attention is totally focused on one specific task, it is easy to forget other important clues to act on different issues. One example of such a situation was an aviation accident where a perfectly functioning aircraft crashed because the crew was so focused on a faulty landing gear indicator that they forgot to control the remaining fuel level (2).

Over-focusing on a single issue when diving can be dangerous; for example, a diver under high stress due to swimming against a strong current could be tempted to focus only on fighting the current, forgetting to check their air consumption, which will likely be increased by the effort of swimming, leading to a potential out-of-air scenario.

Time pressure and workload

Workload and time pressure are strictly related and represent one of the most common stressors in decision-making. The level of task load and the associated processing time quantify the time needed for a correct decision. This value, divided by the available time, generates time pressure, which may trigger anxiety with further build-up of stress (4).

Time pressure stress could be an evolved trait, as slower ancestors could more easily fall victim to predators. Running out of time also alters any prior planned schedule, adding to the stress. This may lead to dangerous shortcuts and rushed actions that are against one's best judgment (2).

For example, a diver confronted by multi-tasking activity and under the stress of a limited bottom-time may feel extreme time pressure, substantially decreasing performance and causing poor decision-making. To reduce this stress, more complex operations should be divided into multiple smaller tasks to be performed in a series of consecutive dives. If they have to be done only within one dive, they should be split between different divers sharing the burden of the tasks.

Selective attention

Under stress, "tunnel vision," or selective attention, develops following three main patterns. Only one (attention approach) leads to an increase in performance (4):

1. *Attention approach*: The individual is focused on the main task only, with increased performance.
2. *Capacity resource*: Attention is focused on the most easily accessible task, which is not necessarily related and congruent to be achieved. A drop in performance may develop.
3. *Thought suppression*: Hypersensitivity toward task-irrelevant cues develops under stress at an unconscious level as to-be-suppressed thoughts. This wasting of mental resources impairs performance.

For example, a diver focused on controlling the dive parameters (depth and gas consumption) and with good situational awareness of the overall status will likely perform a proficient dive achieving the planned goals. If the stress rises above a level that can be well-managed by the diver, then their attention span could be narrowed to the easiest task, such as controlling depth, failing to correctly manage the gas reserve, or any of the planned operational tasks. A drop in performance and reduction in safety is likely to follow. Finally, under very high stress, the diver can become concerned by irrelevant issues or even fixated on nonexistent threats (such as potential attack from hazardous marine life), neglecting to control the dive parameters, leading to failure in achieving the planned goals and becoming a victim of a diving accident.

Responses to stress

Strong physiological reactions may develop in extreme situations, including increased heart rate, respiratory rate, muscle tension, and skin conductance (7).

Under very high-stress levels, humans develop a "flight or fight" response, an innate and instinctive reaction in our cognitive structure (18).

This reaction is triggered by the hypothalamus stimulating the sympathetic region of the autonomic nervous system and the adrenal medulla. The physiological response is immediate, with large amounts of glucose and oxygen becoming available for the brain, skeletal muscles, and heart. At the same time, activities considered non-essential for facing a threat are inhibited, such as the digestive, urinary, and reproductive systems (19).

In divers, the mobilization of oxygen leads to an increase in respiratory rate that will deplete the available breathing gas reserve faster, adding further stress and time pressure to an already critical situation. Adequate control of the respiratory drive is important for the divers because it will reduce breathing gas usage and because being in control reduces their overall stress levels.

Underwater a "flight" reaction is often dangerous, leading to frantic actions (20). On the other hand, if the escape reaction develops as a controlled action, it is not necessarily a wrong response, as it can result in removing the individual from danger-ous circumstances. For example, a diver experiencing an out-of-air situation may have a controlled "flight" reaction, performing an emergency ascent safely (10).

Under high stress, the individual tends to regress, perform-ing actions and developing behaviors based on previously learned procedures that are no longer beneficial. The greater the similarity between old and new procedures and stimuli, the greater the chance of confusion. A sense of delusion and denial may also develop, with the situation being perceived as one wishes it to be rather than as it is. For this reason, often emergency procedures are delayed until it is too late, and fatal-ities may result (2).

Overlearning critical skills and procedures protects from mistakes under stress. Divers in an emergency could delay act-ing on the false belief that the situation is not truly dangerous due to denial, believing that "it cannot happen to me." Under high stress, the diver could also regress, reverting to old inap-propriate operational procedures for the emergency. This, for example, could be the case of divers using models of Closed Circuit Rebreathers (CCRs) that differ from previous ones in their operational modes, leading to mistaken emergency pro-cedures.

More experienced individuals can better manage stress. For example, a study of parajumpers highlighted that, for the ones with more experience, the moment of maximum avoidance and stress was the night before the jump. Novices instead had strong avoidance very close to the actual time of the jump (7). Removing the stress away from the real action is one coping strategy. In divers, a loss of dexterity was directly correlated with increased depth and poor diving conditions, both perceived as more dangerous, thus triggering higher stress levels. A decrease of 16% in manual dexterity was measured in divers tested at 30 m (100 ft) in a high-anxiety situation, compared with divers operating at 6 m (20 ft) with negligible stress (7).

"Seyle's General Adaptation Syndrome" is an individual's response to high levels of stress, and it is composed of four consecutive phases (21):

- *Phase 1*: The individual is startled by the onset of an unexpected event and cannot react due to shock and alarm.
- *Phase 2*: The body reacts, releasing hormones (e.g., adrenaline) to increase the level of reaction. The individual initiates actions to respond to the stressful situation.
- *Phase 3*: Physical and mental reserves become depleted.
- *Phase 4*: The individual is exhausted. In this phase, mishaps are likely to occur.

In general, the resistance reaction of phase 2 allows the body to withstand the stressful episode; if this does not happen, then phases 3 and 4 will follow (19).

In a diving situation, the four phases will develop over a very short time, in minutes, and the diver will soon become unable to cope further with the stress, more likely to commit errors and mistakes (22). This is why a timely and effective reaction is of the essence in a diving emergency, to act before mental and physical capacities are exhausted.

From stress to panic

Failure to control stress levels may lead to panic, causing a break-down of the logical and rational mental processes, leading to the incapacity of proper reaction (8).

Panic is characterized by specific physiological changes, such as increased and irregular heart rate, shortness of breath, and chest pain associated with a feeling of losing control. If no corrective action is taken, the symptoms will further escalate, triggering a panic attack within ten minutes or less (20). A panic reaction is a self-fueling situation where a vicious circle is generated, with the individual exposed to increased mental stress becoming unable to react constructively (Fig. 6.2).

Fig. 6.2. Panic is a vicious circle of irrational self-feeding faear.

Three types of panic attacks have been identified (20):

- *Situational bound*: Triggered by a specific event and is usu-ally associated with a phobia of the individual.

For example, claustrophobic divers may panic if exposed to restricted environments like caves.

- *Situational predisposed*: The panic attack may be delayed requiring multiple exposures before it is triggered.

For example, a novice diver may dive under the same conditions several times before a sudden panic attack happens.

- *Spontaneous*: There is no apparent reason/trigger for the panic attack. This is the most dangerous, being unpredictable. It is often associated with some kind of mental pathology.

Individuals with recurrent episodes of this kind of panic should not dive and seek specific medical advice before entering dive training.

Panic is the leading non-technical cause of diving accidents (8). It is extremely dangerous and can easily result in fatal outcomes. Panic triggers inefficient, shallow, and rapid breathing, leading to hypercapnia and hypoxemia. The diver "over-breathes" the regulator and can rush to the surface for more air (23).

An individual in panic is also dangerous to other divers because panic behavior can cause increased aggressiveness when they are approached by a rescuer (20). For this reason, one should be extremely careful in approaching a panicked diver and be well-trained in the appropriate rescue procedures.

Stress and panic in divers

Being underwater is a significant source of stress, as demonstrated by several tests on divers in dry chambers vs. open sea and shallow water vs. deep water. Divers showed a drop in performance and an increased rate of failure in situational awareness when they were exposed to environmental conditions which they felt were potentially dangerous. The stress level increased from dry chamber tests to shallow water tests and finally to deep water tests. More experienced and motivated individuals can learn to inhibit their anxiety when exposed to high-stress levels by displacing it away from the moment of perceived maximum danger to better cope with the situation. Despite this, performance in real conditions is always worse than during training, and this should be considered when planning and training for more complex diving activities (24).

During training, a diver's goal should be to achieve at least above-average levels, and possibly outstanding levels, to create a sort of buffer that will offset the inevitable drop in performance observed when they are exposed to a real scenario. This is particularly critical for emergency drills because the high-stress level triggered by an emergency will cause a strong performance drop.

Several studies show that up to 50% of divers experienced some form of panic or near-panic during one or more dives in their lifetime. Panic was often triggered by hyperventilation and exposure to multiple stressors, which overloaded the mental capacity of the individuals. A typical perilous response was a fast ascent (25), (26), (27).

Fast ascent, comparable to the "flight" response of an individual faced with a dangerous situation, strongly increases the risk of over-expansion lung injuries and the development of DCS. The divers should overlearn that the correct response to a problem is to stop and think and that most of their issues can be solved underwater.

A study on 12,087 recreational divers highlighted that the likelihood of a diver experiencing panic during a dive is almost twice as high for individuals with a personal history of panic and seems unrelated to the level of certification. Training made a difference in how the divers managed the panic. About 80% of the divers who experienced panic obtained further training after the episode, gaining confidence and the ability to handle potential future emergencies (25).

An analysis of the performance of a group of 649 divers of the Spanish Armed and Security Forces showed that better underwater adaptation was achieved by individuals more psychologically stable and with higher intellectual capacity. Divers with more prominent anxiety-prone traits had lower-quality performance (28).

Even if a formal psychological assessment is generally not required, before starting any sport-diving training, the candidates should be well aware of any underlying anxiety, which could be exacerbated by the stress induced by being underwater, particularly in beginner courses. They should disclose this issue to the instructor so that a specific training approach can be followed to minimize stress and the associated risk of panic. A psychological assessment could be required for professional divers, especially for leadership positions such as safety diving officers.

Time pressure, environmental hazards (low visibility and cold), and potential human-related negative interactions, such as ship traffic and errors by inexperienced surface supervisors, were the main concerns and causes of stress in 39 Finnish commercial divers. Their general attitude was very professionally focused, with no acceptance of unnecessary risks. Their way of managing the stress was to be in charge of arranging their work schedule, with particular attention to selecting the surface tender (29).

This highlights the importance of trusting the other components of the wider team and being able to assess the risks, avoiding those considered too high.

Correct stress management techniques are needed to maintain self-control in emergencies and to be able to focus on the solutions to the problem (9). Intellectualization is a cognitive strategy to distance oneself from a stressful situation emotionally, enhancing the feeling of being in control and increasing the ability to cope (4).

In a diving environment, there may not be enough time to apply the usual stress-reduction techniques of relaxation; the diver should therefore be well-trained and able to quickly focus on the practical responses needed to assess the situation (10).

Training can increase performance under stress by developing mental models which can be applied to an emergency using a rule-based approach. Continuous information processing and decision-making under stress should be emphasized during training sessions (8). Mental rehearsal of the potential emergency helps reduce the degree of uncertainty and the associated stress level (20). Phased training involves learning new skills under minimal stress, followed by progressive exposure to more realistic stressors only once the skills are mastered. It is to be noted that training is helpful only for scenarios that have been rehearsed and is therefore very task-specific; it is good to correlate newly acquired skills with already learned ones, where possible, to enhance the automaticity of new procedures (4).

Overlearning emergency skills is needed to ensure an instinctive, fast, and appropriate reaction even under extreme stress, reducing the likelihood of a panic attack (8), (20), (26), (30).

Decision failure under stress can be mitigated by a series of strategies, as follows (12):

- *Pre-assessment*: Analysis of potential risks and benefits associated with the decision.
- *Checklists*: Use a list of criteria to check for potential alternatives.
- *Reminders*: Be aware of the consequences of failure.
- *Reducing information load*: Avoid being overwhelmed by excessive information.
- *Prioritizing*: Rank the tasks following their priority.

Understanding potential causes of stress and being able to manage them before they escalate into panic is an essential survival strategy for divers. Overlearning, continuous training, and experience will help divers to be in control of the situation, allowing for safe underwater operations.

Lessons learned

- Some degree of stress is positive, allowing for a sharper focus on the tasks at hand.
- Total absence of challenge can lead to boredom, complacency, and a drop in performance.
- When an individual feels that there is a gap between their ability and the skills required by the situation, stress develops.
- Stress reduces the efficiency of decision-making, likely leading to poor decisions.
- Workload and time pressure are the most common stressors.
- Environmental stressors, such as cold and poor visibility, can deteriorate performance.
- Under a high-stress level, a "fight or flight" reaction may develop with potentially uncontrolled outcomes.

- If stress is not managed, it may develop into panic.
- Panic is the leading non-technical cause of diving accidents.
- Overlearning essential and emergency skills, continuous rehearsal of emergency procedures, and good planning are critical to reducing stress in diving.

References

1. **Selye, H.** A syndrome produced by diverse nocuous agents. *Nature.* 1936, Vol. 138, 3479.

2. **Beaty, D.** *The naked pilot: The human factor in aircraft accidents.* s.l. : Airlife, 1995.

3. **Kahnerman, D.** *Attention, and effort.* Englewood Cliffs, NJ : Prentice Hall, 1973.

4. **Staal, M.** *Stress, cognition and human performance: A literature review and conceptual framework.* Washington, DC : NASA, 2004.

5. **Lock, G.** *Under pressure.* 2019.

6. **Teigen, K.** Yerkes-Dodson: A law for all seasons. *Theory and Psychology.* 1994, Vol. 4, 4, pp. 525–547.

7. **Idzikowski, C. and Baddeley, A.** Fear and dangerous environments. [book auth.] J. Hockey. *Stress and fatigue in human performance.* 1983.

8. **Blumenberg, M.** *Human factors in diving.* Berkeley, CA : Marine Technology and Management Group, University of California, 1996.

9. **O'Connor, E.** *A navy diving supervisor's guide to the non-technical skills required for safe and productive diving operations.* Panama City, FL : NEDU, 2005.

10. **Bachrach, A.J. and Egstrom, G.H.** *Stress and performance in diving.* San Pedro, CA : Best Publishing, 1987.

11. **Shibata, K., Sasaky, Y., Wonbang, J., Walsh, E., Machizawa, M., Tamaki, M., Chang, L. and Watanabe, T.** Overlearning hyper-stabilizes a skill by rapidly making neurochemical processing inhibitory-dominant. *Nature Neuroscience.* 2013, pp. 470–475.

12. **Gok, K. and Atsan, N.** Decison-making under stress and its implications for managerial decision-making: A review of literature. *International Journal of Business and Social Research.* 2016, Vol. 6, 3, pp. 38–47.

13. **Raghunathan, R. and Pham, T.** All negative moods are not equal: Motivational influences of anxiety and sadness on decision making. *Organizational Behavior and Human Decision Processes.* 1999, Vol. 79, 1, pp. 56–77.

14. **Weisenger, H. and Pawlin-Fry, J.P.** *Performing under pressure.* 2015.

15. **Bougherara, D., Grolleau, G. and Mzoughi, N.** Is more information always better? An analysis applied to information-based policies for environmental protection. *International Journal of Sustainable Development.* 2011, Vol. 10, 3, pp. 197–213.

16. **Zajonk, R.** Social facilitation. *Science.* 1965, Vol. 149, pp. 269–274.

17. **Endsley, M.** Toward a theory of situation awareness in dynamic systems. *Human Factors.* 1995, Vol. 37, 1, pp. 32–64.

18. **Cannon, W.** *Wisdom of the body.* New York : Norton & Company, 1932.

19. **Tortora, G., Reynolds, S. and Grabowski, G.J.** *Principles of anatomy and physiology.* New York : Harper Collins, 1996.

20. **Yarbrough, J.** Understanding diver panic. *Alert Diver SEAP.* pp. 16–21.

21. **Seyle, H.** The general adaptation syndrome and the diseases of adaptation. *The Journal of Clinical Endocrinology and Metabolism.* 1946, Vol. 6, 2, pp. 117–230.

22. **Lewis, S.** *Staying alive: Risk management techniques for advanced scuba diving.* Toronto, Canada : Techdiver Publishing & Training, 2014.

23. **Nevo, B. and Breitstein, S.** *Psychological and behavioral aspects of diving.* North Palm Beach, CA : Best Publishing Company, 1999.

24. **Baddeley, A.D.** Selective attention and performance in dangerous environments. *Journal of Human Performance in Extreme Environments.* 2000, Vol. 5, 1, pp. 86–91.

25. **Colvard, D. and Colvard, L.** A study of panic in recreational scuba divers. *The Undersea Journal.* 2003, First Quarter, pp. 40–44.

26. **Colvard, D.** Fathoms of fear. *Alert Diver Asia – Pacific.* 2006.

27. **Campbell.** Psychological issues in diving: Anxiety, phobias in diving. [Online]

28. **Plaza et al.** Prediction of human adaptation and performance in underwater environments. *Psycothema.* 2014, Vol. 26, 3, pp. 336–342.

29. **Honkasalo, A.** Finnish divers' view of occupational risks and risk taking. *Applied Ergonomics.* 1992, Vol. 23, 2, pp. 202–206.

30. **Gilliam, B.** *Deep diving.* Locust Valley, NY : Aqua Quest Publications, 1999.

7. ENVIRONMENTAL AND PHYSIOLOGICAL HAZARDS

General introduction

Divers are exposed to various hazards due to the inherent hostility of the environment and the impact that diving has on the physiological response.

Environmental hazards include:

- Cold water, which will affect the divers, topside personnel, and gear exposed to low temperatures.
- Low visibility leading to potential disorientation and enhancing the risk of trapping/tangling.
- Polluted waters posing severe health risks for the exposed personnel.
- Differential pressure that is created when water flows from higher to lower hydraulic heads leading to an increased risk of entrapment.
- Depth, affecting breathing gas usage, narcosis, oxygen toxicity, and decompression risk.
- Physiological hazards include:
- Hypoxia and hypoxemia causing loss of consciousness and increasing the risk of drowning.
- Fatigue, reducing the mental and physical performance of divers, increasing the risk of incidents and mishaps.

The following sections will assess the risks associated with such hazards to identify mitigation procedures for safe and effective diving operations.

7.1. COLD

Chapter highlights

Water has a very high thermal conductivity and can quickly remove massive amounts of heat from a diver's body even when the ambient temperature is relatively elevated. Exposure to this dense medium triggers a variety of physical and behavioral responses aimed at reducing heat loss.

The body will enhance heat production by shivering and reducing peripheral blood circulation to maintain a stable core temperature. Despite these protective measures, hypothermia will develop if the exposure time is long enough, leading to a drop in performance and, in extreme cases, life-threatening conditions.

Cold water will impact divers' capacity to perform manual operations due to the loss of dexterity caused by reduced blood circulation in the extremities. It will impair higher mental functions following a modest drop in core temperature.

Cold exposure also negatively affects diving gear, with the potential for failure of regulators due to freezing, a drop in battery performance involving electronics such as dive computers and rebreather systems, and plastics becoming brittle.

Diving in cold water, therefore, requires careful planning focused on mitigating the specific risks associated with heat loss.

Introduction

Cold is a powerful environmental stressor that triggers physiological and behavioral reactions that aim to reduce heat loss. If any of these reactions fail, the body's core temperature can be reduced, leading to hypothermia – a severe medical condition.

A hypothermic diver is strongly impaired and is more likely to be involved in diving incidents or accidents. The impairment is both physiological (reduced peripheral blood circulation leading to loss of dexterity) and mental (affecting short-term memory and brain activity). Decompression stress is also increased.

Topside personnel are likewise exposed to the impact of cold weather, and appropriate sheltering and insulation should be considered.

Cold water also negatively affects diving gear, with the potential for failure of critical elements such as the regulators, which may freeze, leading to free flow. Several materials can become brittle in frigid temperatures, with an enhanced risk of breakage.

Thermoregulatory mechanisms

The human body is adapted to function within a very narrow range of core temperature around 37°C (98.5°F); a variation of 4°C (7°F) above or below this value will impair both the physical and mental capacity of divers. Usually, core temperature is maintained within 1°C (2°F) of its average value, with maximum core temperature reached in mid-afternoon–evening and the lowest during the midnight–early-morning period (1).

A series of thermoregulatory mechanisms have evolved to maintain this core temperature independent from the temperature of the external environment. These mechanisms are most effective on land, becoming less efficient in water (2).

A constant core temperature is due to a correct heat balance based on the following equation (3), (4):

$$M = W + E \pm C \pm K \pm R \pm S$$

M = Total metabolic rate
W = Measurable external work
E = Evaporation
C = Convection
K = Conduction
R = Radiation
S = Heat storage

Both sides of this equation are equal in a state of thermal balance, and the body temperature is stable. If the body gains heat, it must also dissipate it through enhanced peripheral blood flow, sweating, and heat radiation. If the body loses heat, peripheral vasoconstriction and shivering develop to reduce heat loss and improve metabolic heat production. A diver's average metabolic heat rate is around 415 Kcal/hour (4). From this value, it is easy to see how diving causes a fair amount of energy expenditure even to maintain adequate metabolic heat production. Appropriate caloric intake should be considered when diving in cold climates, as thermogenesis cannot adequately occur without calorie consumption.

For a diver immersed and in thermal equilibrium, the heat storage (S) is considered 0, the radiation component is also negligible, and conduction and convection are included in a single term considering the overall coefficient of heat transfer by conduction and convection at the swimsuit/water interface. This heat transfer is also inverse to the thickness of the swimsuit material (4).

Body temperature is maintained within the comfortable range by the coordinated actions of several systems (5):

- *CNS and autonomic nervous system*: Vasoconstriction and shivering.
- *Endocrine system*: Release of specific hormones.
- *CNS alone*: Voluntary muscle action.

The body's reaction to a cold stimulus is mainly controlled by the central nervous system (CNS). Thermal receptors are located in different body areas, both in the skin and the core, and send signals to the hypothalamus within the brain to trigger behavioral and physiological responses. These responses include increased heart rate, tensing of the muscles, increased metabolism, and peripheral vasoconstriction. The autonomic nervous system also mediates this latter. The result of vasoconstriction is forming of a "cold shield" in the outer 2 cm of the body, with its thermal conductivity becoming equivalent to that of cork (3). The hypothalamus uses the sensory information from peripheral and central receptors to control sweating mechanisms, vasomotor changes in the blood vessels, and muscle motor neurons, which affect the body's temperature (1).

To maintain a constant core temperature, deliberate muscle activity can increase heat production 15-fold compared to a body at rest. However, this increase in metabolic demand results in an enhanced peripheral blood circulation of up to 52%, resulting in additional heat loss, thus reducing the effectiveness of heat generation (6).

Shivering is an involuntary tensing of the muscles that will increase heat production up to five-fold, also causing an increase of two or three times the oxygen consumption (7), (8). Shivering can be triggered in response to cold stimulation of the skin receptors, despite the actual status of the core temperature (9). It begins from the neck muscles, progressively involving the pectoral and abdominal muscles, and finally, the extremities. Shivering can be halted by a slight increase in skin temperature, causing a false sensation of normothermia, even if the heat loss is still happening, leading to potential hypothermia (10). A skin temperature of 32.7–34.4°C (91–94°F) corresponds to a feeling of thermal comfort (4).

In a diving environment, thermoregulation is affected by several non-thermal factors (2):

- *Inert gas narcosis*: The narcotic effect of breathing nitrogen at high partial pressure inhibits the stimulus from the cold receptor, reducing shivering and related heat production by up to 40%.
- *Hypoglycemia*: Low glucose level caused by prolonged exertion, such as when performing long underwater activities; reduces intensity and duration of shivering, leading to potential hypothermia.
- *Dehydration*: The reduced blood flow in peripheral circulation during cold exposure, if coupled with a general reduction in blood plasma due to dehydration, such as that caused by increased diuresis during a dive, may increase the risk of cold injuries to the tissues.

Hypothermia

Hypothermia is defined as a decrease in core temperature below its average value, that is, for a fit adult, around 37°C (98.5°F). There are two main forms of hypothermia (6):

1. *Primary hypothermia*: The individual's thermoregulatory response is normal but overwhelmed by the external cold environment.
2. *Secondary hypothermia*: Thermoregulation is impaired by some physiological conditions including fatigue and a drop in glucose availability.

Primary hypothermia may affect divers when diving in cold water for extended periods or if the adopted thermal protection is inadequate.

Strenuous dives may cause over-exploitation of divers' energy reserves, leading to secondary hypothermia.

Hypothermia is implicated as a factor in 20% of diving fatalities. Even if it is not the direct cause of death, it worsens the ability to manage other critical situations that arise (7).

For example, a hypothermic diver can become so incapacitated that they cannot manage the BCD, thus losing control of the buoyancy leading to a potentially fatal fast ascent.

Based on the causes and rate of development of hypothermia, further classification is possible (3):

- *Acute hypothermia*: Caused by a sudden drop in temperature due to exposure to cold environments. The individual may rewarm quickly once removed from the cold conditions.

- *Chronic hypothermia*: The heat-production resources of the body are depleted. Even when removed from the cold environment, the individual cannot self-rewarm, requiring external heat sources.

A diver exposed to cold water without adequate thermal protection may initially be a victim of acute hypothermia; chronic hypothermia may develop if the exposure is prolonged. The dive should be terminated if the diver feels they are becoming too cold; continuing to dive in the cold increases the risk of developing severe hypothermia.

Depending on the degree of core cooling, hypothermia is classified as (3), (11):

- *Mild*: Core temperature between 32.2°C and 35°C (90–95°F). At this level, peripheral vasoconstriction develops, followed by shivering, fast breathing, and increased heart rate. Impairment of mental functions is often associated with this hypothermic state. The skin may be reddish because of the trapped oxygenated blood that cannot release its oxygen, being too cold.
- *Moderate*: Core temperature between 28°C and 32.2°C (82–90°F). Shivering no longer occurs, heart rate decreases, cardiac arrhythmias may develop, and respiratory functions are suppressed. The body becomes progressively unable to cope with the cold and cannot rewarm independently.
- *Severe*: Core temperature below 28°C (82°F). At this stage, pulmonary edema is likely, altered mental status and coma occur, and ventricular arrhythmia develops, leading to cardiac arrest and death.

Divers in cold water are more likely only to be exposed to mild hypothermia (12). This is because the discomfort associated with generalized cooling of the body will prompt the divers to terminate the dive before more profound hypothermia can develop (13). If the divers cannot leave the water, such as when long decompression stops are required, then the level of hypothermia may increase.

Using a drysuit with adequate thermal undergarments, an adequately insulated diver is unlikely to become seriously hypothermic within the timeframe of a scuba dive. But a more subtle danger may develop, mainly when multiple cold-water dives are performed, in the form of "silent hypothermia." This is a slow loss in core temperature, which causes a feeling of cold, fatigue, and general uneasiness, and that may require long rewarming time and rest to be resolved (12), (13), (14).

A phase of cold stress precedes hypothermia. During this phase, the individual becomes progressively more uncomfortable due to the loss of body heat (10):

- *Mild cold stress*: Core temperature is normal with normal total body heat. The individual may be uncomfortable in a cold environment, but this is not affecting proficiency.
- *Moderate cold stress*: Core temperature is still average, but total body heat is reduced. The individual feels colder and experiences very cold extremities, often with pain; proficiency is diminished.
- *Severe cold stress*: At the boundary with the beginning of hypothermia, total body heat is severely reduced, and the core temperature is below average but above 35°C (95°F). The individual is very uncomfortable, and proficiency is severely reduced.

In mild hypothermic individuals, shivering can be very intense to a level that impairs voluntary movements. Short-term memory is reduced, and the quality of judgment deteriorates (10), (12).

The effects of hypothermia can be very debilitating for a diver, who could become unable to swim, climb a ladder to exit the water, and, due to overall reduced mental capacity, also be unable to address any emergency adequately.

It is necessary to wait at least 24 hours and have proper food, hydration, rest, and rewarming to be restored after a dive that caused even the mildest hypothermia (5).

Heat loss

The head is exposed to heat loss due to reduced insulation and lack of vasoconstriction. Heat loss is linear with time (Fig. 7.1.1), and heat is lost from the human body at different rates depending on how much fat insulation is available and how much vasoconstriction is achievable. At $0°C$ ($32°F$) ambient temperature and at rest, up to 35% of the body's heat production is lost via the head. This value drops to about 19% when working at half the maximum individual's capacity. Small bodies have a larger surface-to-volume ratio leading to more heat loss through the skin; for the same reason, the extremities are more exposed to heat loss (8), (9).

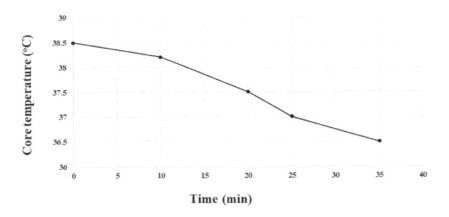

Fig. 7.1.1. Core temperature drop over time for full-body immersion in water at 10°C (modified from Wattmers and Savage, 2001).

Besides the head, the most heat lost is from the chest, particularly during the first 30–40 minutes of immersion (15). In a test dive in water at 8°C (46.4°F), the skin temperature of the torso dropped by about 12–13°C (22–23°F) in the first ten minutes, with a minimal decline thereafter (16). Another path of heat loss is the production of urine which is warmed at core temperature; diuresis, induced by cold and immersion, enhances such loss in addition to causing dehydration in the divers (10).

An essential factor enhancing heat loss is the convection process, also referred to as "wind chill." It is possible to correlate the actual air temperature with the wind speed, creating a chart that indicates the potential for cold-induced injuries against exposure time (see Tables 7.1.1a– and b). The "limited danger zone" allows for five hours of exposure; in the "increased danger zone," exposed flesh will freeze within one minute; in the "great danger zone," exposed parts may freeze within 30 seconds (1).

Wind speed (MPH)	Air temperature°F													
	35	30	25	20	15	10	5	0	-5	-10	-15	-20	-25	-30
0	35	30	25	20	15	10	5	0	-5	-10	-15	-20	-25	-30
5	33	27	21	16	12	7	1	-6	-11	-15	-20	-26	-31	-35
10	21	16	9	2	-2	-9	-15	-22	-27	-31	-38	-43	-47	-50
15	16	11	1	-6	-11	-18	-25	-33	-40	-45	-51	-60	-65	-70
20	12	3	-4	-9	-17	-24	-32	-40	-46	-52	-60	-65	-76	-81
25	7	0	-7	-15	-22	-29	-37	-45	-52	-58	-67	-75	-83	-89
30	5	-2	-11	-18	-26	-33	-41	-49	-56	-63	-70	-78	-87	-94
35	3	-4	-13	-20	-27	-35	-43	-52	-60	-67	-72	-83	-90	-98
40	1	-4	-15	-22	-29	-36	-45	-54	-62	-69	-76	-87	-94	-101

Table 7.1.1a. Wind chill factor for air temperature in°F and wind speed in miles per hour. Limited danger zone is white, increased danger zone is pale gray, and great danger zone is dark gray.

Wind speed (KPH)	Air temperature°C													
	2	-1	-4	-7	-9	-12	-15	-18	-21	-23	-26	-29	-32	-34
0	2	-1	-4	-7	-9	-12	-15	-18	-21	-23	-26	-29	-32	-34
8	1	-3	-6	-9	-11	-14	-17	-21	-24	-26	-29	-32	-35	-37
16	-6	-9	-13	-17	-19	-23	-26	-30	-33	-35	-39	-42	-44	-46
24	-9	-12	-17	-21	-24	-28	-32	-36	-40	-43	-46	-51	-54	-57
32	-11	-16	-20	-23	-27	-31	-36	-40	-43	-47	-51	-54	-60	-63
40	-14	-18	-22	-26	-30	-34	-38	-43	-47	-50	-55	-59	-64	-67
48	-15	-19	-24	-28	-32	-36	-41	-45	-49	-53	-57	-61	-66	-70
56	-16	-20	-25	-29	-33	-37	-42	-47	-51	-55	-58	-64	-68	-72
64	-17	-20	-26	-30	-34	-38	-43	-48	-52	-56	-60	-66	-70	-74

Table 7.1.1b. Wind chill factor for air temperature in°C and wind speed in kilometers per hour. Limited danger zone is white, increased danger zone is pale gray, and great danger zone is dark gray.

The wind chill factor should be carefully addressed because it will strongly increase the risk of hypothermia in topside personnel and for the divers before and after the dive unless shelter is available. When using a boat as a diving platform, the airflow induced by the vessel's movement, mostly at higher speed, can produce an appreciable wind chill factor. Divers, personnel, and material should be protected from the direct impact of the airflow.

The heat conductivity of water is about 23 times that of air, and its specific heat is about 3,500 times higher. Consequently, heat loss when submerged happens 4–5 times faster than in air. For any given temperature, water has a cooling effect of 11°C (20°F) cooler than that of air (3). The combined heat transfer coefficient for convection and conduction in water varies from 38 Kcal/m²h°C in still water to 55 Kcal/m²h°C in stirred water (15).

In water, the heat flux from the skin surface increases four- to six-fold, from 50–70 W/m² in air to 200–400 W/m² in water (2). This enhanced heat loss has a substantial impact on the velocity of the cooling of the core. As an example, a drop of about 0.5°C (0.9°F) in core temperature is observed after about one hour of exposure to air at 0°C (32°F), but only after 20 minutes of immersion in water at 10°C (50°F) (9). For these reasons, the thermoneutral temperature (at which the metabolic heat generation perfectly balances the heat loss at rest) in water is 35°C (95°F) compared with 26°C (78.8°F) in air (5).

Performing muscular work, mostly with leg movements, produces metabolic heat that can help maintain a stable core temperature in water temperatures as low as 18°C (64.4°F). This exercise must be of high intensity to be effective in thermogenesis. Otherwise, the increased convection heat loss due to the movement of the water surrounding the body and the reduced vasoconstriction in the muscles will cause a decrease in core temperature (8), (15). In general, exercising in cold water increases overall heat loss because body movements accelerate the convective circulation of the surrounding water, and shivering increases the peripheral blood flow to the limbs with associated heat transfer from the core to the skin (17).

Even if the primary heat loss in water is due to conduction and convection, evaporation also plays a role in the air passages leading to the lungs when breathing cold, dry air, such as the air from scuba cylinders in cold environments. This evaporation will also contribute to dehydration in the form of "insensible water loss" from the mucosa linings of the airways (9). Respiratory heat loss represents about 8–10% of the metabolic heat production, but this percentage increases at depth due to the denser breathing medium. In practical terms, respiratory cooling is a limiting factor only for very deep dives below 180 meters (13). At 30 ata, breathing gas at 4°C (39.2°F) can cause the loss of 100% of the metabolic heat of a diver (5). These depths are well beyond the usual depth of most scuba dives but are within the range of several deep saturation dives.

The respiratory heat loss is proportional to the difference in temperature and humidity between inspired gas and lungs and will vary depending on the respiratory volume (4).

Cold water immersion

A variety of physiological and behavioral reactions are triggered by immersion in cold water. Some of them happen immediately once in contact with water; others will develop progressively with the cooling of the diver's body:

- *Cold shock*: The fast cooling of the skin following sudden immersion in cold water causes shock that develops within the first two minutes. This sudden cooling, mainly in the torso area, stimulates the peripheral cold receptors leading to a powerful drive to breathe. The blood pressure rises rapidly due to peripheral vasoconstriction, the heart rate increases, and breathing becomes more frequent, leading to hyperventilation. Hyperventilation causes a drop in blood PCO_2, which reduces cerebral blood flow, resulting in dizziness. In some cases, this response can result in sustained cerebral vasoconstriction, causing loss of consciousness. In water colder than 15°C (59°F), breath-holding capacity is reduced to about 15–25 seconds, one-third of the expected time for a fit individual. In water colder than 10°C (50°F), an unprotected swimmer will be incapacitated within 10 to 15 minutes. Increased amounts of subcutaneous fat do not reduce the cold shock because the thermal receptors are located in the periphery and are exposed to the cold water (3), (5), (9), (12), (18), (19).

- *Core temperature drop*: In prolonged exposure to cold water, a degree of hypothermia is inevitable. The core temperature may drop as fast as 2–6°C/hour (3.6–11°F/hour) in waters at 10°C (50°F), 3–9°C/hour (5.4–16.2°F/hour) in waters at 4–6°C (39–43°F), and 6°C/hour (10.8°F/hour) in waters at 0°C (32°F) (19). Human survival is impossible at core temperatures of 25°C (77°F) or less (20). In a static immersion test that lasted six hours, total heat loss was 1082 kJ in water at 10°C (50°F), compared with only 37 kJ in water at 34°C (93°F). The heat flow from the immersed body increased during the first 40 minutes before becoming stable for the remainder of the immersion time (17). In cold water, cold diuresis develops, with urine output increasing up to three times the rate of normal production, reaching 350 ml/hour. This diuresis is caused by peripheral vasoconstriction, which shifts blood volume toward the central circulation. This increase in blood flow to the kidneys is sensed as hypervolemia. Thus diuresis is activated to restore the perceived correct fluid balance. The cold also negatively affects the capacity of the kidneys to reabsorb water, further enhancing diuresis (3), (5), (9), (12). The core temperature may decrease even once the exposure is terminated. A diver in a flooded drysuit in water at −1.9°C (28.6°F) for 43 minutes had their core temperature reduced to 34.8°C (94.6°F); this drop in temperature lasted for some time after the end of the dive (19). Operative capacities can be degraded for up to four hours after a dive in cold water (around 10°C or 50°F) (17). Divers exposed to water temperature in the range of 6–8°C (43–46°F) for about 40 minutes reported a feeling of cold lasting for about two hours after the dive, even after consuming warm food and beverages, taking a hot shower, and resting in a warm room. Very long sleeping hours (ten or more) were reported for the night following a cold dive (16).

- *Breathing gas consumption*: The cold shock associated with sudden immersion in cold water can cause a diver to "over-breathe" the regulator and hyperventilate with obvious adverse consequences. An increase from 25 to 100% in breathing gas usage has been recorded in divers exposed to 5°C (41°F) water compared to 20°C (68°F) water. The metabolic oxygen use in cold water dives ranges from 1.7 to 3.4 liters/minute (5), (21). In a swimming test involving ten proficient swimmers, who were required to swim for ten minutes in water at 5°C (41°F), only three completed the test. The failure was due to a massive 122% increase in respiratory rate making proper stroke coordination impossible (3). The metabolic need for oxygen for a given work level increases when the core temperature drops below average. Individuals who experienced a drop in core temperature of 0.5–1.0°C (0.9–1.8°F) required an increase of up to 50% in oxygen to perform work compared to normothermic individuals (9). During a six-hour immersion in cold water (10°C or 50°F,) the estimated oxygen used was around 250 liters/hour, corresponding to the oxidation of approximately 330 grams of glucose; an increase of the basic MET from 1 to 3 was also observed (17). This increase in the use of oxygen should be carefully addressed by divers, mainly when using rebreathers whose oxygen injection is based on an assumed metabolic oxygen demand (22).

- *Dexterity impact*: The fingers are effective heat-loss structures and are therefore affected early by vasoconstriction during cold exposure (1). This vasoconstriction directly reduces manual dexterity. Observation of individuals exposed to cold air showed that when the skin temperature falls below 12°C (53.6°F), manual dexterity is strongly impaired even if the rest of the body remains warm; cooling the body to 20°C (68°F) degrades manual performance even if the hands are kept warm. In general, cooling the skin affects tactile sensitivity, and the cooling of deeper tissues reduces muscle strength and slows the movements of joints. Below 9°C (48°F), neural conduction is impaired (16). In sub-freezing water, the temperature in the fingertips can drop to 10–12°C (50–53.4°F) in less than 30 minutes, even if the diver is using a drysuit; at this level, acute pain develops. Further cooling to 8–10°C (46.4–50°F) causes numbness and can lead to non-freezing cold injuries with swelling, pain, itching, and potential permanent hypersensitivity to future cold exposure (12). During tests in cold water, the drop in the manipulative capacity of the hands was estimated to be 17% compared to a warm water dive (21). Further tests showed a reduction in manual dexterity by up to 45% following a 20-minute exposure to water at 8°C (46.4°F) (23). Muscles lose power by 3% for each 1°C (1.8°F) of temperature reduction; nerves lose impulse transmission capacity in 15 minutes when cooled to 15°C (59°F) (3). Physical activity becomes impossible when muscles are cooled to 25°C (77°F) (10). After six hours of immersion in water at 10°C (50°F), the skin temperature dropped from 35°C to 25°C (95°F to 77°F), with the more significant drop occurring during the first ten minutes of immersion and a concrete leveling off after about 3 hours; the temperature of the hands in the same conditions dropped to 13°C (55.4°F) (17). The rapid cooling of the superficial skeletal muscles causes a decrease in swimming capacity, and drowning may happen to individuals with insufficient buoyancy to maintain their airways above the water (19).

- *The "hunting reflex"*: The initial vasoconstriction is followed by vasodilatation in cycles of three to five times per hour, increasing the heat loss and improving blood circulation in the hands. This effect is called the "hunting reflex" (9). The "hunting reflex" helps divers regain some dexterity, but this temporary status will last just a few minutes and will be followed by further vasoconstriction and loss of manipulative capacity. Due to this intense vasoconstriction of the hands, the body heat loss through them is minimal; gloves will help protect from localized cold impact but have minimal effects on total heat loss (15).

- *Mental impact*: The impact of cold on the brain can alter motor control, interfere with the circadian rhythms and affect the quality and duration of sleep (6). The effect on mental capacity can be most relevant regarding working-memory impairment and slower reasoning processes. Using arithmetic tests and a list of names to be recalled by divers exposed to cold water showed a 9% slower mental calculation speed and an increase in recall errors by up to 32% (21). The mental impact of hypothermia is more severe when complex tasks have to be performed and when a continuous stream of information needs to be elaborated upon. Once stimulated, cold receptors in the skin cause the arousal of the reticular activating system (part of the brain that controls the wakefulness and sleep-wake transition) that leads to cortical stimulation, interfering with higher-order mental processes. Cold stress affects familiar tasks less, and more skilled individuals are more resilient to performance degradation due to cold. In general, cooling causes an increase in the time required to complete tasks of all kinds (13). Cold has a further effect on the mental capacity of individuals, as it acts as a distraction, making it more challenging to focus on the task at hand (16). Rapid cooling to 34°C (93°F) is also associated with short-term memory loss (13), (24). The sense of the passing of time during the dive is often altered, with divers perceiving that less time has elapsed than has (10). This can seriously impact the safety of a dive because unless a timing device is frequently checked, the divers risk staying underwater longer than planned, leading to increased inert gas loading and decompression stress. More prolonged exposure to cold water also causes further heat loss, affecting performance and creating a feedback loop. During their debriefing, the divers may fail to recall important information and events that happened during the dive because of memory impairment by the cold conditions (21). This is a severe issue for scientific divers who often collect data and information during the dive.

- *Decompression*: Thermal factors can affect decompression stress, increasing the associated risk based on the length and magnitude of the thermal stress (19).

  DCS risk increases in cold-water diving, especially if the diver is cold during the decompression phase because the cold-induced peripheral vasoconstriction will modify the off-gassing capacity of the tissues, making the model used in the decompression calculation unreliable (10), (13), (19). In a hypothermic individual, the interval between heart contractions is prolonged, and blood viscosity is increased, resulting in a marked reduction in coronary blood flow and increased risk of thrombosis and myocardial ischemia (10), (25). This slowing in circulation and increased viscosity can affect the inert gas exchange, allowing larger bubbles and/or blockages to form. Sudden rewarming of divers following a cold dive may induce the local release of inert gas bubbles, decreasing adequate tissue perfusion and thus increasing the risk of DCS (2).

Cold injuries

Exposure to a cold environment may lead to physical injuries due to tissue damage following partial or total freezing of the tissues' fluids.

The risk of such injuries can be calculated as (26):

Risk = (Time of exposure × Intensity of exposure) / (Adaptability to cold × Protection technology)

Several factors can amplify the intensity of cold exposure. For example, evaporation from wet clothing can account for 80% of body heat loss (26). Therefore, at the end of the dive, a diver should remove any damp garment as soon as possible to avoid heat loss by evaporation.

Non-freezing cold injuries (NFCIs) may develop when the temperature of the tissue is below 17°C (63°F) (3), resulting in damage to peripheral tissues (primarily in the extremities) exposed to cold temperatures for a prolonged time. The pronounced vasoconstriction associated with cold exposure may cause local blood flow reduction, leading to tissue hypoxia and ischemia. Dehydration, even if moderate, enhances the likelihood of experiencing an NFCI and reduces tissue perfusion. Fatigue, immobility, and stress can also contribute to NFCI (3), (26). Due to the typical conditions of cold-water diving, divers are more likely exposed to NFCI, mostly in their hands and feet. These are the most distal body parts most affected by vasoconstrictive responses. The ideal rewarming procedure after an NFCI should be slow inside a protected, warm environment (26). Subsequent NFCI can significantly compound damage caused by the initial cold insult. Therefore, warmed extremities should be kept warm, avoiding new cold exposure. In some cases, after suffering an NFCI, the individual may present with increased sensitivity to cold in the damaged tissues that lasts forever (3).

Prevention of hypothermia in divers

Proper dive planning: The most common cause for mild hypothermia in divers is planning a dive that requires prolonged cold-water exposure, mainly during the deco phase when the divers are already experiencing cold stress. When diving in cold climates, proper planning should include appropriate thermal protection, reduction in exposure time, and sufficient time for rewarming between dives. In repetitive dives, the failure of adequate rewarming between the dives leads to continuous loss of heat (12).

Nutrition: In cold environments, performing physically demanding work requires about 4,000–4,500 Kcal/day, and 4 liters/day of liquid should be ingested to offset the loss of body water that can go unnoticed in a cold setting (26), (27). In cold water diving, up to 1,000 Kcal can be lost during a one-hour dive (15). Therefore, appropriate hydration and food intake are needed for sustained thermogenesis in such environments (28). The divers should have a balanced and nutritious diet with ample carbohydrates when diving for multiple days in cold water. After the dive, ingesting warm non-caffeinated fluids also contributes to regaining heat and proper hydration.

Insulation: Divers should be protected from the cold during the dive and the time spent at the surface. Multi-layered clothing made with fibers that can remove body moisture is preferred (26). A full wetsuit (5 mm) exposed to water temperature of 12°C (53.6°F) causes a cooling rate of 0.5°C/hour (0.9°F/hour); an insulated drysuit in the same conditions causes a cooling rate of 0.3°C/hour (0.54°F/hour) (5). The insulative capacity of neoprene is reduced by 45% at 2 ata, and by 52% at 2.5 ata, compared to its value at surface. This is due to the squeezing of the internal air cells by the increased environmental pressure (15). Radiative barriers added to the diving suit have minimal effect, as there is no substantial physical separation between the body and suit. Conduction being the most significant cooling factor, a space should be maintained between the diver's body and the surrounding water to reduce heat transfer away from the body (19). Thick gloves are bulky and increase the surface area of the fingers, thus increasing potential heat loss. Mittens have less exposed surface area and are better at reducing heat loss. When using electrically heated undergarments, attention should be paid to the adequate heat transferred to the body; if this is too modest, then the effect could only mask the actual heat loss with the potential for the development of hypothermia. Using heated gloves may also cause tissue damage by overheating, mainly if the blood circulation is reduced by strong peripheral vasocon-striction (5). Using electric heating at depth increases inert gas intake, and this, significantly if associated with a loss of heating during the decompression phase, may increase DCS risk (19).

The best insulation strategy is using a drysuit with a three-layer structure (19):

- Base layer – a hydrophobic garment helps to move the con-densation away from the body, reducing evaporative heat loss.
- Mid layer – provides insulation, further reducing heat loss. Using a semi-rigid matrix or an aerogel can strongly enhance heat insulation.
- Shell layer – the waterproof barrier that surrounds the diver.

CCRs reduce respiratory evaporative heat loss by retaining humidity in the breathing loop and due to the heat released from the CO_2 absorption's exothermic reaction (19).

Acclimation

A degree of "cold acclimation" has been observed in individu-als routinely exposed to cold environments. In these individuals, an increase in metabolism, reduction and delay in the shivering reaction, and a general decrease in cold discomfort have been observed (1). One of the main effects is the delayed onset of cold vasodilatation in the hands of individuals used to working in the cold, thus allowing for better manual dexterity (23).

The repeated cold stimulus may lead to increased local skin tem-perature and reduced pain associated with episodes of cold exposure.

Cold-shock attenuation is obtained with as few as six three-minute immersions in cold water and lasts up to 14 months (28).

In an experimental study following four cold water (12°C or 53.6°F) head-up immersions of 2.5 minutes each, the breath-holding capacity increased significantly (up to 70 seconds). Respiratory drive and cardiac components of the cold-shock response (that peak during the first 30 seconds of cold-water immersion) were strongly reduced. Psychological conditioning could also play a role in enhancing the breath-holding capacity in cold water. It is important to note that such adaptations for a diver using a breathing apparatus reduce the demand on the system when immersed in cold water, thus reducing the risk of free-flow and/or "over-breathing" the regulator (18).

In general, divers used to cold water show a degree of cold adaptation in terms of delayed shivering with an increase in non-shivering heat production (2), (8).

The degree of such acclimation is variable in different persons depending on physical attributes such as the thickness of the subcutaneous fat, mass/surface ratio of the body, genetic heritage, age, and level of fitness (29), (30).

The fact that acclimation/habituation to cold can effectively improve performance under cold stress is supported by anecdotal stories, needing consistent data analysis. Moreover, individuals showing decreased sensitivity to cold can become hypothermic without being aware of this effect (13). Therefore, the level of effective and proficient work that even an acclimatized diver may sustain for a long time still needs to be determined.

Divers used to operating in warmer climates are less resilient when diving in cold waters. When a team of divers work in cold water, the least acclimated member of the group will dictate the acceptable exposure limits. This is an important point to consider if the team is composed of divers from different experience levels in terms of diving environments.

Post-dive issues

When the diver exits the water, the sudden drop in hydrostatic pressure causes a return of fluids from the central core towards the periphery and the legs under the pull of gravity. If this effect is further enhanced by fast rewarming, such as hot showers or entering overheated locker rooms, or if the diver is dehydrated, a hypovolemic condition may develop, causing decreased cerebral flow and sudden loss of consciousness. A sudden rewarming can also trigger the formation of inert gas bubbles in the tissues, mainly the skin, enhancing the risk of DCS (2), (5), (13). It is, therefore, essential to rewarm progressively and slowly after a dive in cold water.

When the diver exits the water in a very cold environment (with air temperature below freezing), the wet gear may quickly freeze, making its removal difficult or impossible. For this reason, tenders should act promptly, helping to remove the gear before it freezes. If this is not possible, the diver should have access to a heated shelter to allow the ice formed on the gear to melt. Shelters should be available for both divers and topside personnel and their equipment.

Team management in cold environments

Fatigue and the challenging environment require very high stamina and motivation; self-confidence and knowledge of proper limits are key factors for success in cold cli. Performing any job takes longer in the cold because cold affects the body and critical capacity, often inducing lethargy. Team leaders should be aware of the strain posed by the cold on team members, maintain good communication, and avoid very tight and rigid schedules that will have little chance of working (31).

Rewarming breaks should be planned between operations to allow proper rest, food intake, and changing clothes if needed (32).

The divers in the water and topside team members will likely be exposed to the cold environment. The most vulnerable members are the standby divers and, in tethered diving, the tenders who may need to spend time sitting or standing still in the cold. Under no circumstances should a standby diver be allowed to don wet gear. Evaporation from the diving suit will enhance heat loss, and if the environment temperature is below the freezing point, ice may form within the regulators. The team leader should enforce appropriate rotation of the divers, use of shelters, and adequate rewarming intervals.

Cold impact on diving gear

The main impact of a cold environment on the diving gear is the increased risk of regulators malfunctioning due to freezing. This risk is substantial when diving in waters below 4.5°C, and divers should be well aware of it (33).

Moisture condenses and may freeze on cold parts inside the regulator affecting its functioning; the probability of freezing depends on (34):

- Ambient temperature.
- Rate of gas flow.
- Relative pressure drop (first stage).

- Moisture content of the breathing gas.
- Shape of the air passages inside the regulator.

The typical scenario of a regulator freezing is the formation of ice inside the second stage, leading to malfunction of the demand valve and subsequent free flow. Another problem is the formation of what is defined as "free ice," where ice builds up in the second stage but does not cause free-flow; particles of this ice can be carried by the airflow inside the airways of the diver, causing severe respiratory problems, similar to those caused by inhaling foreign objects.

Ice formation is possible even in warmer waters (10°C or 50°F) due to the cooling of the gas following the drop in pressure from the high pressure inside the cylinder to the intermediate pressure inside the first stage. The associated Joule-Thomson effect can generate gas at –25°C (–13°F) when using a full (200 bar or 3,000 psi) cylinder at 20 meters (60 ft) of depth when high gas flow is required (62.5 l/min). Using lower cylinder pressure may strongly reduce the cooling effect; for example, if the cylinder is at 100 bar (1,500 psi), the air temperature at the exit of the first stage is –13°C (8.6°F). During the transit inside the low-pressure hose, the airflow from the first to the second stage is partially rewarmed by the heat absorbed from the surrounding water, raising its temperature by about 5–10°C (9–18°F). The specific design of the regulator, with a large surface area and mass, can help absorb heat from the surrounding water, thus reducing the likelihood of freezing. If the water temperature is below 3.5°C (38.3°F), there is not enough heat to allow this rewarming process. A sealed first stage reduces the risk of ice formation on the diaphragm or piston that can upset the intermediate pressure regulation leading to free flow (33).

Because gas cools down when expanding, high-flow situations should be avoided, such as inflating the drysuit and BCD at a high rate and using the purge valve on the second stage (34). Some divers retrofit the original BCD inflator system with a "high-flow" inflator to reduce the time needed to fill the BCD. In cold water, this could cause excessive cooling of the airflow, increasing the risk of the regulator freezing.

Plastic material may become brittle at low temperatures, and rubber gaskets lose elasticity, thus affecting their sealing capacity (34). Careful handling and good O-ring lubrication help reduce the risk of gear damage.

These materials can be damaged by sudden changes in temperature when rewarmed. For this reason, frozen gear should not be exposed to sharp rewarming, such as pouring hot water on it, and should be handled with extra care. In certain situations, such as during ice diving, the gear should be protected from the cold environment; avoid leaving it in the snow or in the open.

Risk identification and mitigation strategies

We have seen that divers exposed to cold environments undergo considerable physical and mental stress. If this stress is not assessed and dealt with, the situation can degenerate, creating damaging effects with potentially life-threatening consequences in the case of severe hypothermia.

Diving gear is also exposed to potential damage and malfunction in cold climates.

Lessons learned

- Cold is an extreme environmental stressor affecting both physical and mental capacities.
- Proper thermal insulation is mandatory during cold weather operations.
- When planning dives in cold water, the dive time should be limited to avoid excessive heat loss.
- In multiple dives, adequate rest and rewarming between the dives should be granted.
- Some cold adaptation is possible, but its real positive effect is questionable.
- Performance in cold environments is reduced, and extra time will be needed to complete any operation compared with warmer settings.
- Diving gear is also affected by the cold, with an increased risk of malfunctions.

References

1. **Ramsey, J.** Heat and cold. [book auth.] G. Hockey. *Stress and fatigue in human performance.* New York : John Wiley and Sons, 1983.

2. **Mekjavic, J., Tipton, M. and Eiken, O.** Thermal considerations in diving. [book auth.] A. and Negman, T. Brubakk. *Bennet and Elliott's Physiology and Medicine of Diving.* 5th edition.

3. **Golden, F. and Tipton, M.** *Essentials of sea survival.* 2002.

4. **Penzias, W. and Goodman, M.** *Man beneath the sea.* New York : Wiley Interscience, 1973.

5. **Tipton, M., Mekjavic, I. and Golden, F.** Hypothermia. [book auth.] Bong and Davis. *Diving medicine.*

6. **Pozos, R.S. and Danzi, D.** Human physiological responses to cold stress and hypothermia. *Textbook of military medicine.* Vol. Vol. 1: Medical aspects of harsh environments.

7. **Danzi, D. and Lloyd, E.** Treatment of accidental hypothermia. *Textbook of military medicine.* Vol. Vol. 1: Medical aspects of harsh environments.

8. **Bookspan, J.** *Diving physiology in plain English.* Durham, NC : Undersea and Hyperbaric Medical Society, 1995.

9. **Wattmers, L.E. and Svage, M.V.** Cold water immersion. *Textbook of military medicine.* Vol. Vol. 1: Medical aspects of harsh environments.

10. **Lioyd, E.** *Hypothermia and cold stress.* 1986.

11. **Epstein, E. and Kiran, A.** Accidental hypothermia. *BMJ.* 2006, Vol. 332, pp. 706–709.

12. **Sterba, J.** *Field management of accidental hypothermia during diving.* Panama City : NEDU, 1990.

13. **The Diving Medical Advisory Committee.** *Thermal stress in relation to diving.* 1981.

14. *The under ice dive.* **Somers, L.** s.l. : AAUS, 1987. Special session on cold water diving AAUS.

15. **Sagawa, S. and Shiraki, K.** Thermal regulation in dry and wet hyperbaric environments. [book auth.] Y.C. and Shida, K.K. Lin. *Man in the sea.* 1990, Vol. Vol. 1.

16. **Bowen, H.** Diver performance and the effects of cold. *Human Factors.* 1968, Vol. 10, 5.

17. **Riera, F., Hoyt, R., Xu, X., Rellin, B., Regnard, J. and Bourron, L.** Thermal and metabolic responses of military divers during a 6-hour static dive in cold water. *Aviation, Space and Environmental Medicine.* 2014, Vol. 85, 4.

18. **Barwood, M., Datta, A., Thelwell, R. and Tipton, M.** Breath-hold time during cold water immersion: Effects of habituation with psychological training. *Aviation, Space and Environmental Medicine.* 2007, Vol. 78, 11.

19. *Thermal physiology and diver protection.* **Pollock, N.** s.l. : Rebreather Forum 3, 2012.

20. **Wenger, B.** *The regulation of body temperature.*

21. **Davis, F.M., Baddeley, A.D. and Hancock, T.R.** Diver performance: The effect of cold. *Undersea Biomedical Research.* 1975, Vol. 12, 3, pp. 195–214.

22. **Bozanic, J.** *Mastering rebreathers.* 2013.

23. **Hoffman, H.** Human psychological performance in cold environments. *MAHE.*

24. *Thermal problems during cold water diving.* **Mekjavic, I.** Seattle WA : AAUS, 1987. Proceedings of special session on cold water diving. AAUS, University of Washington, Seattle, WA. .

25. **Golden, F., David, G. and Tipton, M.** *Review of rescue and immediate post-immersion problems.* s.l. : HSE, 1997.

26. **Roberts, D. and Hamlet, M.** Prevention of cold injuries. *Textbooks of military medicine.* Vol. Vol. 1: Medical aspects of harsh environments.

27. **Headquarters, Department of the Army.** *Soldier's handbook for individual operations and survival in cold-weather areas.* s.l. : Department of the Army Headquarters, 1986.

28. **Daanen, M.** Finger cold-induced vasodilation: A review. *Journal of Applied Physiology.* 2003, Vol. 89, pp. 411–426.

29. **Brown, M., Bird, G., Delahayt, D., Green, J., Hatcher, J. and Rage, J.** Cold acclimatization. *Canada M.A.J.* 1954, Vol. 70, pp. 258–261.

30. *Human adaptations to heat and cold stress.* **Sawka, M., Castellani, J., Pandolf, K. and Young, A.** Dresden, Germany : s.n., 2001.

31. **Command, Naval Facilities Engineering.** *Cold weather operations manual.* Alexandria, VG : Naval Facilities Engineering Command, 1989.

32. **Young, A., Roberts, D., Scott, D., Cook, J., Mays, M. and Askew, E.** *Sustaining health and performance in the cold.* Washington, DC : US Army Research Institute of Environmental Medicine, 1992.

33. **Ward, M.** *Scuba regulators freezing: Chilling facts and risks associated with cold water diving.* Panama City, FL : Dive Lab Inc., 2014.

34. **NOAA.** Cold water diving. *NOAA Diving Manual.* 5th edition.

7.2. LOW VISIBILITY

Chapter highlights

The loss of visual stimuli, such as when working in very low or zero visibility environments, may strongly affect the operators, leading to "spatial disorientation" (SD).

SD is a central issue when operating in complex tridimensional environments. For example, it is estimated that up to 69% of fatal accidents in aviation were linked to some degree of SD.

Mental models of the surrounding environment based on former experience gained in working under similar conditions can reduce SD.

Diving in zero visibility exposes the divers to increased risk of tangling, becoming lost and dive-buddy separation.

Waters with very low visibility are often polluted by organic and chemical contaminants, thus posing other hazards for the divers.

Communications are more challenging because zero visibility makes visual aids useless and requires tactile or acoustic signals.

Adequate training should be undertaken to develop consistent diving procedures for zero visibility situations.

Introduction

Several factors affect underwater visibility that in extreme situations can drop to zero, creating a high-risk situation for the divers.

Silt can be easily stirred from a soft bottom. Enclosed environments, such as the inside of wrecks and caves, are often filled with very fine sediments that can become waterborne once disturbed not only by the kicking of the fins but also by the rising stream of the exhaust bubbles. The presence of tannic waters can create a "black water" situation. Diving under artificial structures such as piers or the hulls of large ships is usually characterized by reduced light and low-visibility conditions.

Diving in such situations is extremely challenging, exposing the divers to a variety of risks, including entanglement, entrapment, and loss of orientation.

Waters with low visibility may also indicate the presence of pollution due to organic and chemical contamination, posing further hazards for the divers.

Our senses have developed to make us aware of our spatial position; the submerged environment, mostly when visibility is reduced, can trick these senses, leading to potentially severe disorientation.

Learning to plan and manage dives in zero visibility requires time, knowledge, and practice. Specific training can be undertaken for realistic but controlled simulation of zero visibility diving. The diving gear configuration should also be specifically designed for zero visibility operations.

Finally, the psychological element should be considered: assessing the fear some divers can experience when diving in low or zero visibility, leading to intense stress and potential panic, is important.

Spatial disorientation

Spatial disorientation (SD) has been defined in aviation as the pilot's inability to understand the aircraft's position in relation to "up and down" and its relative motion. SD in these situations can result in total loss of control or "controlled flight into terrain" of the aircraft, with very often fatal consequences (1). SD contributes to at least 25–33% of all aircraft mishaps (2) and about 80% of pilots have experienced some kind of SD during their flights; about half of them were not immediately aware of being disoriented (3). SD is increased by wrong mental models of the surrounding environment that facilitate sensory illusions (2).

Underwater our senses are dulled by the environment, making it easier to become disoriented, particularly in limited visibility. To maintain a good understanding of "up and down," a descending line (shot-line) is helpful, allowing for a visual reference. Some diving computers, such as the Dive System iX3M2, show the ascending or descending velocity plus arrows indicating up or down. This can help reduce disorientation, especially when moving through the water column without reference points.

"Brown-out conditions" are caused by the stirring of dust clouds by helicopter rotors. This can cause a false illusion of motion in helicopter pilots, leading to SD. In Afghanistan and Iraq aircraft operations, this issue accounted for about 75% of SD cases (2).

In a diving situation, the presence of dense floating particles, such as silt or plankton drifting with the current, can create a similar "dust effect," with the diver becoming disoriented about the actual direction of movement. This is more evident when floating in mid-water. Swimming close to the bottom (if depth allows) or nearby some structure (such as a rocky outcrop) helps reduce SD.

The senses that typically provide orientation are (1), (4):

- *Visual system*: The eyes sense our position based on what we see; 80–90% of spatial information comes from this system.
- *Vestibular system*: The inner ear balance organ can detect accelerations along the three spatial axes. A threshold of $2°/\sec^2$ is needed for the acceleration to be detected.
- *Somatosensory system*: Composed of the nerves in the skin, muscles, and joints that feel the gravitational pull.

SD is likely to happen if the divers are exposed to water with reduced visibility or swim above a featureless seafloor, such as a flat muddy bottom. The leading cause of SD is loss of visual reference due to zero visibility situations or a lack of reference points over featureless terrain (1), (4). However, being submerged also strongly reduces the effectiveness of the vestibular and somatosensory systems regarding spatial awareness.

Two modes of vision have been defined (5):

1. *Focal visual mode*: Uses the central $30°$ angle of the visual field and is important for identifying fine details in the visual image.
2. *Ambient visual mode*: An unconscious mode that relies on the peripheral visual field to determine orientation concerning the surrounding environment.

In minimal visibility, the ambient visual mode is compromised, with tunneling of vision and loss of spatial awareness.

When diving in zero visibility, divers may need to rely on the readings of their instruments only, such as the bearing of a compass or the depth indications of a dive computer, using the focal visual mode. This requires greater mental processing of the information, and it is a skill to be learned.

Contradictory signals from the vestibular system may induce a series of involuntary eye movements (nystagmus), leading to vertigo that, in turn, can cause strong SD (1), (4).

Illness, medications affecting the CNS, and alcohol can affect the vestibular system (1). Too low mental workload is also a pre-disposing factor for motion sickness that can be exacerbated if visual references are lost (6). It is not uncommon for divers to experience seasickness when diving, mostly in reduced visibility or above terrains with moving features such as seagrass oscillating in the current or the waves.

Over-stimulation of the vestibular system can happen in hyperbaric conditions (alterno-baric vertigo). It is a strong but short-lived sensation of vertigo more often associated with the ascending phase of the dive, with the divers experiencing feelings of spinning and tumbling (7). If this happens the diver should stop ascending, get hold of a stationary object (such as the shot-line) and wait for vertigo to subside.

There are three types of SD (1):

- *Type 1 SD*: Often associated with loss of situational awareness; it is not recognized until too late. A fatal outcome is very likely.
- *Type 2 SD*: The SD is recognized, and corrective measures can be applied.
- *Type 3 SD*: The SD is recognized, but the operator cannot take appropriate action, being overwhelmed by the situation – often aggravated by fatigue and excessive workload.

Divers entering caves without proper knowledge, training, and equipment can be victims of Type 1 SD, becoming lost without being aware until too late. Divers with good situational awareness can instead quickly recognize the cues of SD (Type 2 SD), such as vertigo, and act accordingly. Finally, divers involved in too complex and fatiguing dives, for example, when performing multiple tasks in very low or zero visibility, can realize they are disoriented but cannot act promptly (Type 3 SD).

It has been demonstrated that pilots who experienced some degree of SD become more resilient to further SD episodes. Developing appropriate training for SD is critical to address situations potentially prone to generating SD (1).

Standard training for divers includes using a blinded mask with the diver required to perform various tasks. During this training, a support diver should always be in contact with the trainee diver and be ready and able to interrupt the training and help the diver if need be. Divers used to dive in very low visibility develop a better orientation capability, becoming able to generate consistent mental models of the surrounding environment.

If a "zero visibility" situation develops, the operators should follow the instruments, disregarding their "body signals," which will likely be misleading (1).

Closely observing the depth gauge is required to maintain the planned depth profile for dives in zero visibility. A compass can help retain the correct swimming direction, but a guideline may be needed as a reference in extreme situations. Cave diving techniques can help in diving in low visibility. For example, the reel will allow a continuous link between the diver and the exit point. When using lines, the divers should be careful to correctly manage them to avoid entanglements that can be even more dangerous in poor visibility conditions.

Reduced and zero visibility diving

Poor visibility affects the divers in multiple ways: added stress due to potential loss of orientation, difficulties with remaining in contact with the rest of the diving team, and the potential for tangling hazards to go undetected until too late. Moreover, murky waters are also often polluted (8), (9), (10) (see Chapter 7.3). Subconscious irrational fears can also develop when diving in zero-visibility waters. Tactile senses become predominant, and slow, deliberate movements are needed.

Even an experienced diver can be unsafe in zero visibility if supervision and appropriate safeguards are not in place (11).

When using more complex diving systems, such as rebreathers, the diver must monitor multiple parameters on the handset, which can become very challenging in zero visibility (12). A heads-up display and a "semaphore code system" (where colored LEDs provide basic information on the system's status) help reduce visual workload.

In case of zero visibility, the buddy system should be implemented, using buddy-lines where appropriate, ensuring that contact between the divers is retained throughout the dive (11).

The risk of a zero visibility situation should be clearly stated during the briefing so that the divers are well aware of potential SD (11). Moreover, if divers feel uncomfortable diving in zero visibility, they should declare so during the briefing and refrain from diving.

Some activities, such as photography or visual survey, can be impossible or extremely slow in low visibility. If these activities are the reason for the dive, then the operations should be postponed until better visibility is present.

Technological aids are available to partially offset the negative impact of poor visibility. These technologies include video augmentation devices and sonar that can be fixed on a diver's helmet or full-face. For example, the US Navy has recently approved for use one such system where a see-through head-up display is integrated into the diving helmet, allowing the diver to see augmented reality overlays during the dive (13). Another system has been developed by Blackwater Vison, composed of a hand-held device that generates a flow of clear water to displace the turbid water around the area to be observed. The device also has a video camera with feeds to topside and to the diver (14).

Training for zero visibility

Given the difficulties of diving in very low or zero visibility, the divers should be properly trained before attempting operations in such conditions.

Training should be progressive, allowing time for the divers to learn the specific skills needed to operate safely in zero visibility (8).

Using an obscured mask, the divers should be able to complete 3D puzzles, assemble tools, recognize objects, and operate on the diving gear. An underwater maze can be assembled on the bottom of a swimming pool or other similarly confined waters, and the divers should learn how to move through it wearing an obscured mask (9), (10).

During training, special attention should be given to the well-being of the divers who may experience an elevated degree of stress. A safety diver should always be in the water with the divers in training to ensure that the situation is under control and to quickly act in case of necessity.

A psychological assessment of the divers should rule out any fear that could jeopardize the safety of the diving team during zero visibility operations. Suppose a diver feels uncomfortable diving in reduced visibility even after proper training. In that case, they should not be forced to overcome this feeling because, under the added stress of an actual emergency, their behavior could become unpredictable (15).

Risk identification and mitigation strategies

The specific risks associated with zero visibility are analyzed, and some mitigation strategies are presented in this section.

- *Tangling*: In reduced or zero visibility, the risk of being tangled or trapped is increased. The main issue with a trapped diver is the possibility of running out of breathing gas. To mitigate this risk, a standby diver should be readily available with a rigged scuba unit to be carried to the trapped diver. Conservative planning around breathing gas consumption should be adopted as a further safety measure (16). In surface-supply diving, the risk of running out of breathable gas is strongly reduced. Still, hypothermia may develop if the diver remains submerged for long periods in cold water.
- *Communication*: Visual communication is strongly reduced and impossible in zero visibility. Tactile or audio signals should be used (9). Tethered diving should be considered with an established code for rope-pulling signals (16). Acoustic signals can be used from the surface crew to advise the divers of the approaching the end of the dive time, and a specific "emergency recall" signal should also be established (8).

- *Diving gear*: The "Hogarthian configuration" is preferred, and an alternative air source must be available to each diver in the form of a pony tank, doubles with manifold, or multiple independent cylinders (8). The divers should carry appropriate cutting devices and use a streamlined set of diving gear to reduce the likelihood of tangling; the use of pockets, pouches, and straps instead of dangling equipment is enforced (8), (9). The cutting devices should be placed in body areas that can be easily reached even by a severely tangled diver. The upper torso area and the forearms are good places for placing cutting devices. Also, consider carrying devices able to cut different materials. For example, EMT shears are suitable for cutting through various materials. Razor blades are helpful for fishing monofilaments. Serrated knives can be needed for cutting larger and stronger lines. Some synthetic lines, such as Spectra ropes, can be very strong and cut-resistant; monofilaments are also very strong and can go undetected, especially in reduced visibility, enhancing the risk of tangling, so use extra caution when diving around such lines.
- *Visual aid*: Under extreme "black water" circumstances, a Ziplock-style bag filled with clear water can be used as a "viewer" for instruments, measuring devices, and tables. The bag is placed between the mask visor and the object to be seen (8). More sophisticated methods include using sonar and video-enhancement systems that can be carried underwater by the diver.
- *Standard procedures*: The safety drill should focus on the ability of the divers to reach and operate the valves of the cylinders by touch only. A "lost buddy" procedure should also be pre-arranged between the divers and between the diving team and the surface crew (8).

Risk	Personnel and equipment affected	Mitigation/avoidance strategies
Tangling	Divers	• Multiple cutting devices. • Standby diver ready to be deployed. • Use of streamlined configuration.
Running out of air following entanglement	Divers	• Redundant air sources. • Conservative air management. • Standby diver ready to be deployed.
Spatial disorientation	Divers	• Use of instrument references such as compass and depth gauge. • Training and experience in low-visibility diving.
Potentially polluted waters	Divers and topside crew	• Assess the level of pollution. • Special procedures may be required.
Loss of visual communication	Divers	• Use of acoustic communication. • Rope signals.

Lessons learned

- Diving in zero visibility is stressful.
- Disorientation is likely to happen, particularly when reference points are lost.
- To reduce the risk of tangling, a streamlined set of diving gear should be used, and the divers should carry multiple cutting devices.

- Training and overlearning key skills can strongly enhance the divers' performance.
- If a diver does not feel confident in zero visibility diving, they should not be forced onto such dives for any reason because panic could develop.

References

1. **Newman, D.** *An overview of spatial disorientation as a factor in aviation accidents and incidents.* Camberra, Australia : Australian Transport Safety Bureau, 2007.

2. **Gibb, R., Ercoline, B. and Schar, F.** Spatial disorientation: Decades of pilot fatalities. *Aviation, Space and Environmental Medicine.* 2011, Vol. 82, 7, pp. 1–8.

3. **Lawson.** *Training as a countermeasure for SD mishaps: Have opportunities for improvement been missed?* s.l. : NATO – S & T Organization.

4. **AOPA.** *Spatial disorientation.* 2004. Safety Advisory 17 - 8/4.

5. **South African Civil Aviation Authority.** *Disorientation.*

6. **FAA.** *Spatial disorientation.*

7. **Lundgren, C.** Alternobaric vertigo: A diving hazard. *British Medical Journal.* 1965, Vol. 10, 1136.

8. **Hayes, R. and Howe, D.** *Archaeological diving in low visibility or zero visibility.* s.l. : Institute of Maritime History.

9. **Sibthorp, R.** *Full-face mask and zero visibility training for scientific black-water divers.* s.l. : AAUS, 1995.

10. **Sellers, S.H.** Bridging the experience gap: Technologies for reducing the stress of zero visibility training. [book auth.] W. Jaap. *Maritime archaeology.* Costa Mesa, CA : Springer, 1993, pp. 313–322.

11. **US Coast Guard.** *Finding of concern 002-19.* Washington, DC : USCG, 2019.

12. **Hires, L.** Cavediving community. [book auth.] R.D., Denoble, P.S., Pollock, N.W. Vann. Orlando, FL : s.n., 2012.

13. **McMurtrie, P.** Diver augmented vision display ready for fleet issue. 2019, Vol. 23, 2.

14. **Blackawater Vision.** Clearview System II. 2018.

15. **Niewiedzial et al.** The problem of experiencing anxiety among divers: Experiment in hyperbaric exposure conditions. *Polish Hyperbaric Research.* 2019, Vol. 1, 66, pp. 47–59.

16. **NOAA.** *NOAA Diving Manual.* 5th edition.

7.3. POLLUTED WATER

Chapter highlights

Even apparently clear and clean waters can instead be polluted by biological or chemical contaminants, which pose a risk to the health of those exposed.

Areas of higher risk are bodies of water with reduced circulation surrounded by anthropized, farmed, and industrialized areas from which raw sewage or chemical spills can move into the water. This is more likely after heavy rainfall due to water runoff.

Bottom sediments can accumulate chemical and biological contaminants and, if stirred, can expose the divers to a high concentration of potentially harmful substances.

The most reliable protection is to be fully encapsulated using a diving helmet mated to a vulcanized rubber drysuit and dry gloves.

If planning to dive in biologically compromised waters, the divers should have updated and appropriate immunizations.

Dive time should be kept to a minimum to reduce exposure, also considering that several chemicals can damage the diving gear and penetrate the fabric of the protective suit in a relatively short time.

Attentive decontamination must follow for both the diver and the used gear. The personnel involved in the decontamination procedure should be protected from exposure to the contaminants.

Introduction

Most of the water bodies in which we can dive have some degree of contamination, with biological pollutants being the most likely to be present (1).

It is generally difficult to assess the presence of pollution in water without using specific analytic techniques. Often apparently clean waters can instead host a variety of pollutants of biological, chemical, or, more rarely, radioactive origin (2), (3), (4). Acute intoxication may develop if the concentration of the toxic compounds is high; lower contamination levels can still cause chronic effects even years after the exposure (2).

Contaminants can accumulate in bodies of water with poor and limited circulation such as lakes and harbors (2). Water circulation paths in estuarine systems can create parcels of highly polluted water that move through the larger body of water with reduced dilution, thus representing a hazard for divers working within the system (4).

Divers are exposed to severe health risks when diving in polluted waters, and a specific risk assessment is required based on the level and typology of pollution and exposure (5). Microbial and chemical contaminants can affect the human body through skin contact, ingestion, inhalation, impingement, and absorption through the mucosa membranes (2), (6). Regarding water ingestion, while diving, a 50 ml/hour figure is used in calculations; this estimation is based on the same value observed in swimmers (7). This is likely higher than the actual amount, given that the divers' airways are more protected by the use of regulators than for swimmers.

Sediments can concentrate both chemical and biological contaminants and allow for microbial proliferation; if disturbed by divers or diving activities, such as sampling or construction operations, the sediments can release the pollutants (1), (2), (4). Divers can also ingest some sediments during the dive or even post-dive, mostly if food is consumed during the surface interval and hands are contaminated (7).

Biological pollution

The level and typology of biological contamination vary across several parameters, including location, climate, population density, and industrialization level (1). Sewage and agricultural run-off are the primary sources of biological contamination, especially after heavy rainfall that can overflow the treatment plants (2), (4). The main sources and impact of biological contaminants are indicated in Table 7.3.1.

Most water parasites with high human health risks are found in warm freshwater. Colder waters, and seawater in general, host parasites that are less dangerous. Algal blooms are especially harmful because the released toxins can cause strong dermal, respiratory, and even neurological damage (2).

Divers can easily be contaminated when diving in polluted waters; a study of divers working in polluted waters showed alteration of the skin microflora composition that tends to reflect the kinds of bacteria present in the water even after relatively short (< 30 minutes) exposures (8).

External otitis is a common problem for divers, and it is often associated with an increase in gram-negative bacteria in the external ear canal during dives. An increase of up to 46.7% in the microbial flora in the external ears was observed when using a hood that likely caused an outflow of bacteria from deeper skin layers and sweat of sebaceous glands. The preventive use of ear-drops at 2% concentration of acetic acid reduces bacteria growth and colonization (9). This procedure should be adopted as a standard prophylactic method even when diving in apparently clean waters (4).

To limit the risk associated with exposure to biological contaminants, divers should have a series of immunizations, including (4), (6):

- Tetanus
- Diphtheria
- Typhoid fever
- Hepatitis
- Cholera
- Polio

Fecal contamination

Fecal contamination is caused by human and animal raw sewage waters. It causes mostly enteric illness and, more rarely, can cause acute febrile and respiratory maladies. The final outcomes can be fatal in some circumstances, such as heavy exposure to Leptospira spp. and Vibrio cholera. Divers are exposed to such contamination by swallowing water, inhaling droplets through the regulator, and absorbing microorganisms through the nose, ears, or open wounds. Organisms associated with fecal contamination are (1), (3):

- Bacteria:
  - o *Escherichia coli*

- o *Vibrio vulnificus* and *Vibrio cholerae*
- o *Campylobacter spp.*
- o *Leptospira spp.*
- Viruses:
  - o *Polioviruses*
  - o *Hepatitis A*
- Protozoa:
  - o *Cryptosporidium parvum*
  - o *Giardia lamblia*
- Worm:
  - o *Ascaris helminths*

Fecal coliforms *Escherichia coli* and *Enterococci spp.* can be used as indicators for the quality of freshwater. In marine water, only *Enterococci spp.* are used as indicators. Acceptable counts are (1):

- *Escherichia coli*   126–200 cells in a 100 ml sample
- *Enterococci spp.*   35–40 cells in a 100 ml sample

Aeromonas

Another source of potentially serious infections is the bacteria of the genus *Aeromona*. These are Gram-negative bacteria showing resistance to multiple antibiotics and can colonize humans, producing cytotoxic and enterotoxic substances; these bacteria are mostly present in warm waters (> 20˚C) (8). *Aeromona hydrophilia* is the most frequently isolated species associated with infections and can act as a secondary opportunistic pathogen but also as a primary pathogen in humans (10). *Aeromona spp.* are prevalent in many harbor waters and often associated with other pathogens, including *Vibrio parahaemolyticus*, *Escherichia coli*, *Klebsiella spp.*, and *Salmonella spp.* (4). (8). *Aeromona spp.* were found in the external ears of more than 90% of divers diving in contaminated waters; these pathogens also showed an inverse correlation with the levels of oxygen concentration in water (8).

Amoebae

Amoebae present a severe hazard to humans exposed to contaminated freshwaters. Primary amoebic encephalitis (PAR) is caused by the amoeba *Naegleria fowleri* that enters the body through the nostrils and follows the olfactory nerve infecting the brain. *Entamoeba histolitica* causes intestinal disease and is due to human fecal contamination of freshwater. The genus *Acanthamoeba* includes eight different species that can cause brain and spinal cord inflammation if colonizing the CNS and keratitis if entering the eyes; the infective route is through the nostrils, ingestion, inhalation, and open wounds. The risk of amoebae contamination in seawater is reduced because amoebae will not survive for long in the marine environment (3), (4).

Pfiesteria piscicida

Pfiesteria piscicida is a toxic dinoflagellate that can cause open sores and brain damage with symptoms similar to dementia. During the cold winter months, it is dormant, becoming active in warming waters and when high levels of other pollutants, such as animal waste, are present (11).

Algae and cyanobacteria

In marine waters, health risks are associated with skin exposure, ingestion, or inhalation of cyanobacteria that can cause acute dermatitis and skin burns. In freshwater, microcystins (hepatotoxins produced by cyanobacteria) are the most common toxins that can cause severe liver damage and are absorbed mainly through inhalation. Cytotoxins cause liver and kidney failure. Divers should not enter waters containing blue-green algal blooms (1).

Contaminant	Source	Presence	Impact
Fecal	Raw sewage	Freshwater and seawater	Serious to fatal
Aeromonas	Water organisms	Freshwater and seawater	Gastrointestinal
Amoeba	Water organism and human fecal contamination	Freshwater	Serious to fatal
Pfiesteria piscicida	Water organism	Freshwater and seawater	Serious brain damage
Cyanobacteria	Water organism	Freshwater and seawater	Serious liver damage

Table 7.3.1. Most common biological contaminants in water.

Chemical pollution

A degree of chemical contamination is likely present in almost any body of water except very pristine environments. The primary chemical sources are industrial spills, agricultural runoff, sewage, and ships (2), (3). In general, the level of chemical contamination in open water is not high enough to cause serious health risks for the divers. Still, exceptions are present with areas of local high contamination (1). Sediments can host pockets of heavy metal contamination (6). It is essential to know the composition of the chemicals and their interaction; their impact on the diving gear should also be quantified (12). The presence of chemicals can also alter the bacteria population, favoring an abnormal development of some species against others. Chemicals may also cause a reaction in the body, stimulating allergy or cutaneous rashes (4). Floating chemicals, such as gasoline, represent a severe hazard to the divers who have to swim through them to exit the water. At the other side of the spectrum, sinking chemicals can create pockets of very high concentration on the bottom (3).

Hydrocarbons

A carcinogenic polyaromatic hydrocarbon known as creosote is used as a wood preserver. It may leach from treated wood such as pilings and dock supports. Its concentration is usually higher in new structures. Exposure to water contaminated by this chemical exposes the divers to absorption through the skin or ingestion (2). A variety of other hydrocarbons are so dangerous for human health that when present diving should be totally avoided (1). Rubber-based diving gear can deteriorate and fail quickly if exposed to even modest concentrations of hydrocarbons; halogenated organics are extremely dangerous because they can penetrate suit material and skin. In this case, no exposure should be allowed (13). One issue can be accidental contact of the diving suit with traces of hydrocarbons that could be present on the deck of the diving platform.

Other organic contaminants

Tributyltin (TBT) is the main component of various biocides, including marine anti-fouling paints. Its residuals are likely present on the bottom of harbors (1). In September 2008, a ban on TBT was enforced by the International Convention on the Control of Harmful Anti-fouling Systems on Ships (14). Since then, the levels of TBT are likely to have dropped, but potential residual accumulation in harbor waters is still possible.

PCBs and DDT are highly toxic and can accumulate in sediments where they remain stable for a very long time. Even though their use has been banned since 1977 in North America, their presence is still being identified on the bottom of different bodies of water (2).

Other contaminants, such as atrazine and glyphosate, are unlikely to reach concentrations in water high enough to be a risk for divers. In some areas, such as close to agricultural runoff sites, there may be zones of higher concentration (1).

Heavy metals

These metals are dangerous when in ionic status dissolved in seawater, combined with organic compounds, or absorbed into sediments (2). Mercury and lead are insoluble and will accumulate within sediments (1).

Of particular concern is tetraethyl lead, which used to be an additive in fuel. This chemical can penetrate several materials, including those used for diving gear. In 1977 a recovery operation involving deep dives (98 meters) and using surface-supply to the wreck of the "Cavtat" about 3.5 miles offshore from Capo d'Otranto (Italy) aimed to retrieve a large number of drums holding tetraethyl lead. Some divers developed lead contamination symptoms; it was discovered that some tetraethyl lead had penetrated the umbilical.

Equipment

When diving in polluted water, the type of equipment that is needed will be assessed regarding the contaminants present, their concentration, and the job to be performed (2). The topside personnel should also use adequate protective gear (15).

Standard scuba gear does not offer any appreciable degree of protection; in particular, wetsuits are totally inappropriate because neoprene can absorb contaminants, and the water trapped between the skin and suit creates a microenvironment that enhances the risk of dermal exposure to contaminants (1), (7), (13).

A full-face mask coupled with the use of a drysuit and dry gloves may offer some degree of protection from microbial hazards, preventing nose and mouth exposure – mainly if it can operate in positive pressure (in this way, any rupture in the seal between mask and face will cause the regulator to temporarily free-flow preventing water ingression). It is to be noted that this mask will not protect the ears, and it is prone to potential leaks (2), (4), (15), (16). A full-face mask will also protect the diver's airway in case of loss of consciousness (17), enhancing the chances of survival and rescue.

The best protection is offered by a diving helmet mated to a vulcanized rubber drysuit with dry gloves often sealed at the wrist with extra duct tape to prevent detachment of the latex/

silicone seal and covered by external protective gloves (2), (16). This encapsulation is mandatory if the exposure can result in severe illness or death (15). A disposable over-suit can be used to reduce the gear's exposure to contaminants (2). If a helmet and surface-supplied gas are used, it is important to be sure that no chemical can penetrate and deteriorate the umbilical (15). One of the main points of weakness is the second stage and the helmet exhaust valve; water may leak through them, spreading contamination. For this reason, a double exhaust system, or similar technological solution, should be used even if this will increase the breathing resistance (2), (16), (15).

With their continuous flow of water, hot-water suits protect from the ingress of polluted water from the environment but need an ample supply of clean water. Any failure in the circulation system may result in contamination (16).

A variation of this suit is called the "suit-over suit." It comprises a tight 3 mm neoprene inner suit covered by a large heavy-duty vulcanized rubber suit. Clean water is then pumped at a rate of about 4 liters/minute between the suits, and it is dumped through two one-way valves at the ankle and shoulder of the external suit. The positive pressure generated by the water flow prevents the ingress of contaminants (18).

Decontamination

A critical phase of polluted water operations is the final decontamination procedure, which should be aimed at both the gear and the diver. During decontamination, it is essential to avoid spreading contaminants from the gear to the environment and the surrounding personnel (2). If the fluids produced during the decontamination procedure can be contained and disposed of, then the killing/inactivation of biological contaminants and neutralization of chemical agents onsite may not be needed, thus simplifying the procedure (19). Prompt decontamination of the gear should follow each biological exposure to avoid proliferation of pathogens (4).

The general sequence for decontamination is (13), (16), (19), (20):

- Freshwater pressure washing of the diver still suited. The water should be sprayed at low pressure (< 70 psi) to avoid damage to the materials and forcing the contaminants into the seals. The water spray should be from top to bottom at about 1.5–2.0 ft (45 – 60 cm) of distance to avoid excessive backsplash.
- Removal of the outer disposable suit (if used).
- Scrub the diver still suited with a soap solution.
- Rinse the soap with clean freshwater spray.
- Undress the diver with particular attention to avoid ingress of residual contaminants.
- The diver will take at least two five-minute showers with soap and clean water.
- Further cleaning of the used gear; the valves must be checked for damage and disassembled for final cleaning. Particular attention should include seals, zippers, and boot soles.
- Soaking of ancillary equipment and umbilical in a cleaning solution.
- Final clean freshwater rinse of all gear that should be left to air dry in a clean area.

The gear should be treated with adequate products aimed to remove and inactivate the contaminants. Povidone-iodine is suitable for the removal of microorganisms without damaging the gear. Exposure to a 10% solution of this compound (that is commercially known as Betadine) for ten minutes will kill most pathogens (4), (19). Sodium hypochlorite (bleach) at 10% concentration can be used as a biological cleaner for ten minutes of contact time. Isopropyl alcohol can be used for wiping down the areas under the seals of a full-face mask. Some materials can be damaged by exposure to bleach or alcohol (19).

If the gear comes into contact with chemicals that cannot be safely removed and inactivated, it must be discarded even after one single exposure (15).

Monitoring the diver's health, including blood and urine testing, is important within four hours of the dive (5). If any malady develops, the medical personnel should be promptly and clearly informed of the potential exposure of the diver to contaminants (6).

Planning for dives in contaminated waters

The diving and support teams should be appropriately and continuously trained in hazmat procedures and on the correct use of the protective gear (20).

It is often difficult to assess all the possible contaminants that can be present in water; especially those diffused into the water column. Biohazards can be less visible and more difficult to assess than other pollutants (11). In general, only a qualitative assessment is possible supported by some quantitative analysis on specific pollutants allowing for a generic classification of the waters (2):

- Category 1: Highest level of chemical and biological contamination.
- Category 2: Moderate contamination with level of pollutants above normal.
- Category 3: Baseline contamination with no acute effects on divers.
- Category 4: No pollutants are present.

Some other guidelines can be derived from accepted levels of contaminants in recreational waters (1).

When planning for diving in polluted waters specific diving scenarios could present a higher risk of contamination. For example, runoff channels and drainage pipes can feed contaminants to the abutting waters with a strong local increase in pollution (1), (2).

A standard plan for diving in contaminated waters should include (12):

- Identification and, if possible, quantification of the hazards (chemical, biological).
- Evaluation of the potential effects on the diver and the diving gear.
- Limits for toxicity and lethal doses.
- Exposure time limits.
- Decontamination procedures.
- Protection of topside personnel (with decreasing levels of protection from A to D depending on the contamination risk):
  - A: Fully encapsulated with SCBA (self-contained breathing apparatus).
  - B: Hooded chemical splash suit with SCBA.
  - C: Hooded suit with purificator respirator.
  - D: Splash suit without respirator.

The need for total encapsulation exposes the divers and the support personnel to an overheating risk. Appropriate shelter and limited exposure time should be planned in advance (15).

Before entering the water, all divers' suits should be checked for leaks, ideally immersing the diver in a large tank of clean water. If this is unavailable, then a soap-spray leak-check should be performed (15). It is the tender's duty to double check the integrity of the seals before allowing the diver to enter the water (20).

Dives in contaminated waters should not need decompression, and bottom time should be as short as possible for the job to be performed. The "rule of thirds" should be applied to the available breathing gas for extra safety. Divers with any kind of open wound should not be allowed to dive. A contaminated diver who needs hyperbaric treatment must be totally decontaminated before being allowed to enter the chamber. Pollutants in a confined space can be extremely dangerous (2), (5), (20).

In surface-supplied diving, if an onsite compressor is used, it should be placed far from any polluted zone, assuring that no contaminants can enter the feeding inlet (2).

It is also very important to ensure good communication between the divers and the topside team; a tether with hardwired communicators is the best solution (15). A downline should be used to guide the divers to the working zone without delay (20).

A series of zones have to be identified to provide efficient and safe decontamination procedures (Fig. 7.3.1) (19), (20):

- *Exclusion zone*: The "hot zone" where the use of appropriate PPE (personal protective equipment) is mandatory. Decontamination is compulsory for anyone exiting the zone.
- *Contamination reduction zone*: The area where primary

decontamination of the diver is achieved. PPE must be used by topside personnel.

- *Support zone*: A clean and safe area where topside personnel and divers can rest, and non-frontline operations are conducted. This is also the area where the control box and compressor for surface-supplied diving are placed.
- *Emergency decontamination area*: Used for emergency procedures on injured divers.

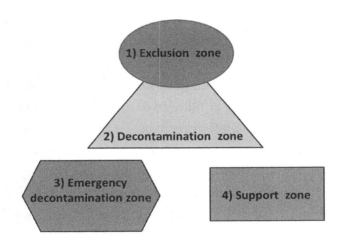

Fig. 7.3.1. Diagram of the different areas in a polluted-water diving operation.

Risk identification and mitigation strategy

Diving in biologically and chemically polluted waters exposes the divers to a variety of health risks that need to be mitigated through the use of appropriate prophylactic measures, including inoculations and, in particular, adequate isolation from the surrounding environment. Some of these risks are also shared by the support topside crew, who can be exposed to the same contaminants both during diving operations and in the post-dive cleaning phase. The diving gear can also be damaged by various chemicals, and it needs to be properly and thoroughly cleaned and sterilized soon after the dive. Overall, diving in polluted waters is one of the riskiest diving operations and requires very careful planning, the use of specific diving gear, and proper procedures and training.

Risk	Affected elements	Mitigation/avoidance strategies
Biological contamination	Divers and surface crew	• Prophylactic inoculations. • Encapsulation.
Biological contamination	Diving gear	• Washing off pollutants soon after the dive. • Proper sterilization.
Chemical contamination	Divers and surface crew	• Encapsulation. • Limited exposure time.
Chemical contamination	Diving gear	• Limited exposure time. • Use of chemical-resistant material. • Inactivation and washing off chemicals at the end of the dive.
Long-term health effects	Divers and surface crew	• Medical monitoring. • Minimize exposure to known contaminants.
Spreading of contaminants	Environment	• Recovery and proper disposal of washed off fluids. • Proper disposal of condemned contaminated gear.

Lessons learned

- If unsure, always consider water to be polluted.
- Full encapsulation is the only real protection for diving in polluted waters.
- Accurate planning is needed before operating in contaminated waters.
- Decontamination procedures must be followed, and the resulting fluids must be appropriately disposed of.
- Despite any protection used, diving in contaminated water exposes the operators to high health risks.
- Topside personnel should also be protected from potential contamination using appropriate PPE and procedures.

References

1. **Que Merais, B.** *Diving in contaminated water: Health risk matrix.* Toronto, Canada : Defence Research and Development Canada, 2006.

2. **Navy, US.** *Guidance for diving in contaminated waters.* s.l. : Sea Systems Command.

3. **Barsky, S.** *Diving in contaminated water: The dangers.* 1991.

4. **Colwell, R., Hatem, M. and Ahearn, H.** *Microbial hazards of diving in polluted waters.* 1982.

5. **International, Phoenix.** *Diving in contaminated waters: Past, present and future.* s.l. : NAVSEA SUPSALV, 2006.

6. **Online, Diving Medicine.** *Diving in polluted waters.* 2002.

7. **Sheldrake, S., Davoli, D., Poulsen, M., Duncan, P. and Pedersen, R.** *Diving exposure scenario for the Portland Harbor risk assessment.* Washington, DC : EPA, 2009.

8. **Seidler, R., Allen, D., Lockman, R., Colwell, R., Joseph, W. and Daily, O.** Isolation, enumeration and characterization of Aeromonas from polluted waters encountered in diving operations. *Applied and Environmental Microbiology.* 1980, Vol. 39, 5.

9. **Brook, I., Coolbaugh, J. and Williscroft, R.** Effect of diving and diving hoods on the bacterial flora of the external ear canal and skin. *Journal of Clinical Microbiology.* 1982, Vol. 15, 5.

10. **Joseph, S., Daily, O., Hunt, W., Seidler, R., Allen, D. and Colwell, R.** Aeromonas primary wound infection of a diver in polluted waters. *Journal of Clinical Microbiology.* 1979, Vol. 10, 1.

11. **Barsky, S.** *Every dive may be a polluted water dive.* 2000.

12. **Reclamation, US Department of the Interior – Bureau of.** Contaminated water diving. [book auth.] US Department of Interior – Bureau of Reclamation. *Diving safe practices manual.* 2006.

13. **Amson, J.** Protection of divers in waters that are contaminated with chemicals or pathogens. *Undersea Biomedical Research.* 1991, Vol. 18, 3.

14. **International Maritime Organization.** *International Convention on the Control of Harmful Anti-fouling Systems on Ships.* London : International Maritime Organization, 2001.

15. **Barsky, S.** *Diving in contaminated waters: Equipment.* 1991.

16. **Steigleman, W.** *Survey of current best practices for diving in contaminated water.* s.l. : NEDU, 2002.

17. **Harris, R.** Rebreathers: Overcoming obstacles in exploration. [book auth.] R.D., Denoble, P.S. and Pollock, N.W. Vann. Orlando, FL : s.n., 2012.

18. **Tejara, S.** Safe diving in polluted waters. *EPA Journal.* March, 1985.

19. *Environmental response team: SOP for contaminated water diving operations.* **Humphrey, A., Grossman, S. and McBurney, J.** s.l. : AAUS, 2010.

20. **Barsky, S.** *Diving in contaminated waters: Techniques.* 1991.

7.4. DIFFERENTIAL PRESSURE

Chapter highlights

Differential pressure (DP) is caused by a pressure imbalance between two adjacent bodies of water. In these conditions, water speed can suddenly increase, and a diver can be dragged toward the DP source, becoming trapped and seriously injured.

DP is mainly due to the presence of artificial structures such as dams, water inlets, pumps, and propellers.

Even modest depths and small openings may generate DP that is dangerous for divers. Moreover, the area affected by DP is hard to detect from a safe distance.

To mitigate the risk associated with DP, the boundaries of a "danger zone" are identified where water velocity exceeds 0.5 m/s (1 kt), considered the maximum current that a diver can negotiate. Divers must avoid entering this zone using restraints and physical barriers.

If a diver is caught by a DP, the chances of rescue are minimal, as other divers attempting rescue will be exposed to a high risk of being trapped or injured themselves.

Risk avoidance is the best strategy when DP is present; the use of ROV should be preferred to deploy divers.

Scuba is not permitted when operating in an area where active DP is present. In this case, surface–supply is mandatory.

Introduction

Differential pressure (DP) is caused by an imbalance in pressure in the water between upstream and downstream areas that are connected by some opening (Fig. 7.4.1). The flow caused by a given DP may drag a diver toward the opening generating a force that will pin the diver or even suck him within the opening. A "danger zone" is defined as the area surrounding the DP source where the speed of the induced water flow is above 0.5 m/s (1 kt), which is considered the maximum velocity of a current negotiable by a diver (1).

DP is present primarily on or near water-control structures where a pressure difference exists (2). It is a latent hazard with no risk when no water is flowing, but once DP is initiated, the resulting force can draw divers holding them indefinitely. DP is insidious, being almost undetectable at a safe distance but becoming quickly overwhelming when the safe distance is breached (3).

Specific plans and procedures must be followed when diving in active DP areas; scuba is not permitted; instead surface-supply with voice communication is required (4).

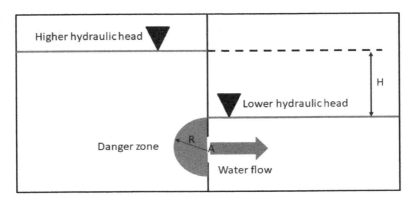

Fig. 7.4.1. Differential pressure zone created by a water flow between areas at a different level.

DP risk zones

DP is created mainly by artificial structures that generate zones where water is adjacent to voids or where water with higher hydraulic head/higher pressure is adjacent to water at lower hydraulic head/pressure. Some of the most common situations where DP may exist are the following (1):

- *Locks*: Allow navigation in waterways with a difference in water level. The areas where DP may develop are the seals of the lock, the gates, and the water discharge channels.
- *Coffer dams*: Used to isolate a section of a water body and drain it. The main areas for DP are the bottom of the coffer dam and the junctions in staked coffer dams.
- *Hydraulic dams* are used to create water reservoirs for hydroelectric production and storage. DP can be generated by damage in the dam's face, leaks at the base, and water outlets.
- *Pumping stations*: Designed to move large amounts of water. Areas of potential DP are the water intakes, trash rakes, submerged pumps, and water-supply channels.
- *Storage tanks/reservoirs*: Used for water storage, the water level within can drop very quickly based on the supply demands. DP can be present near the flanges and between the access hole and the water surface.
- *Vessels*: Several areas of DP are present around the vessel's hull, including water intakes, sea chests, propellers, thrusters, and breaches in the structure.
- *Pipelines*: Deployed in a dry state and must be progressively flooded. DP is a risk during the flooding procedure when cutting an old pipeline (that could be void) and when

removing the flange protection in newly deployed pipelines.

- *Inflatable shutters*: Plugs used to block valves, hoses, and pipelines temporarily. A shutter failure can trigger a sudden DP; redundant shutters should be used.
- *Airlifts and pumps*: Use DP for removing silt and debris from the bottom of bodies of water. The suction can be very strong, with potential injury to the hands and limbs of the diver handling the system.

Diving near any water intake is hazardous, exposing the diver to DP risk. In these areas, scuba is not to be used (2), (4), (5).

When working near headgates in a dam, the downstream flow should be reduced to a minimum to limit DP (5).

DP incidents and accidents

DP incidents are almost always due to a failure of risk-control measures (3). DP accidents are the leading cause of occupational diving fatalities, with 127 events from 1975 to 2014 and no sign of any decrease throughout the years (1), (2).

In one analysis of DP-related accidents, 74 divers were involved in 66 incidents, with 54 fatalities, 6 injuries, and 14 near misses. Dams were the structures with the most (26%) DP accidents. Inland commercial diving activity was the most affected (59%) by DP incidents. The various origins of the DP were the following (3):

- 41% due to changes in water levels.
- 29% due to the presence of water intakes.
- 22% due to the presence of air-filled voids.
- 5% due to the action of propellers and thrusters.

The most common injury mechanism (49%) involved in DP accidents was "primary event trauma, "an adverse event causing immediate loss of life with limited or no opportunities for rescuers to help the diver. At a depth of more than 10 meters, this was the predominant cause of fatalities. Entrapment and drowning accounted for 22% of the fatalities (3).

DP risk involves mostly professional divers, who represented 89% of the analyzed accidents and incidents (3).

DP accidents are often deadly, with the diver becoming unable to perform any self-rescue and with very limited possibility of intervention from topside personnel and rescue divers, who could instead become further fatalities.

Quantification of DP

The water flow through an opening can be calculated as follows (1), (2):

$$Q = A \times V = A \times \sqrt{(2gH)} = C \times A \times \sqrt{H}$$

Q = Flow rate

A = Area of the opening

V = Water velocity

g = Gravitational acceleration (constant equal to 9.81 m/s^2)

H = Depth of water above the opening or difference between two adjacent levels

C = 4.43 (values in meters) or 8.02 (values in feet)

The speed of the flow is therefore (1):
$$V = Q/A = C \times \sqrt{H}$$

The boundaries of the DP area are defined by a hemisphere centered on the opening (Fig. 7.4.1). The velocity of the water at these boundaries is calculated by dividing the flow rate by the hemispherical flow area (2):

$$V = Q/2\pi R^2$$

$$2\pi R^2 \times V = Q$$

$$R^2 = Q/2\pi V \rightarrow R = \sqrt{(Q/2\pi V)}$$

Considering the velocity as 0.5 m/s (that is the maximum speed of the water that a diver can work in safely), the radius (in meters) of the danger zone is:

$$R = \sqrt{(Q/\pi)}$$

If the suction opening is near the junction of two bulkheads at a right angle, then the area is half of a hemisphere (πR^2), therefore considering V as 0.5 m/s:

$$0.5 = Q/ \pi R^2$$

$$R^2 = Q / 0.5\,\pi = Q / \pi/2 = 2Q/\pi \rightarrow R= \sqrt{(2Q/\pi)} = 1.4 \sqrt{(Q/\pi)}$$

If the suction is at the corner of three bulkheads, then the surface is a quarter of a hemisphere, and the radius is:

$$R = 2 \sqrt{(Q/\pi)}$$

The presence of structures around the source of suction alters the ideal configuration of the flow, and the distance at which the danger zone is active is increased by a factor (f_c) that depends on the geometry of the structures. This increases the risk of a diver being dragged toward the opening that is the source of the flow (1).

- Two walls at right angles $f_c = 1.4$
- Three walls at right angles $f_c = 2$
- Three walls at right angles and one inclined inwards $fc = 4$

Considering an ideal configuration (hemispheric danger zone), the safe distance to be outside of the danger zone depending on the flow rate is (1):

Flow (m³/s)	Distance (m)	Flow (gal/s)	Distance (ft)
0.1	0.17	26	0.55
0.5	0.40	130	1.31
0.8	0.50	210	1.64
1.0	0.56	264	1.83

From these values it is evident that even large flows (of the order of 1,000 liters per second, or 265 gallons per second) generate a danger zone of modest dimension with a radius of around

0.5 meters (1.6 ft). This makes it very difficult for a diver to be aware of the presence of DP until they are very close to its source, further increasing the risk of being trapped by the flow. The speed profile of the water in a DP danger zone causes a quick acceleration once the danger zone is entered (Fig. 7.4.2), generating very strong pulling forces that will make an escape from the area extremely difficult, if not impossible.

The force generated by the DP depends on the depth of the water and the pressure change per unit increase of depth (that is, the density of the water multiplied by the depth). This means that saltwater (denser) creates stronger forces than freshwater (2):

$$F = DP \times A = D \times Pc \times A = D^2 \times \rho \times A$$

F = Force generated by the DP

DP = Differential pressure (D $\times$ Pc)

A = Area of the opening

D = Water depth

Pc = Pressure change per unit increase of depth ($\rho \times D$)

ρ = Water density

Given that the suction force is linked to the square of the water depth, even a modest water depth ($\approx$ 0.5 meters – 1.6 ft) can generate a strong DP, resulting in dangerous conditions (1). For example, at a depth of 0.5 meters (1.6 ft), the force generated over a pipe intake of 30 cm (12 inches) in diameter is over 18 kg

(40 lb). Fatalities due to DP have occurred in water as shallow as 3 meters (10 ft) (3).

If pumps are present, their suction head will add to the force exerted by the water depth above the intake. Positive displacement pumps may create a suction head of ≈ 10 meters (25–29 ft) (2).

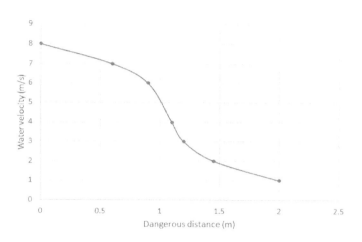

Fig. 7.4.2. Increased water velocity with reduced distance from the ΔP source.

Detection of DP

The upstream and downstream areas of a potential DP zone should be visually checked for the presence of whirlpools, vortexes, and eddies that are indicators of fast-moving waters (1), (3). Other signs of DP are water leakages downstream of a retaining structure such as a dam, lock-gate, or bulkhead (2).

Another way to detect DP from the surface is to use a rope (diameter around 10 mm – 0.4 inches) weighted with a small shackle and slowly lowered in front of the suspected danger zone. If a flow is present, then the rope will vibrate/oscillate. This procedure works only in still water where no currents, other than the ones created by the DP, are present. For more significant DP, the shackle can be replaced by a bag (20 liters -5 gal) filled with sand. This method can also be used by a diver with a 3 mm (0.12 inches) diameter rope dangling in front and below him for about 3–5 meters (9 – 16 ft) (1).

Dye released near an area where DP might be present could be used to detect the water flow and its direction.

Underwater cameras and ROV can also be used to visually detect a DP zone by the movement induced on a strip/ribbon placed in the camera's visual field. Similarly, in good visibility, a diver can use a pole with a rag/mop at the end to detect the water flow (1). Areas affected by DP are often characterized by low or zero visibility, making the underwater visual identification of the danger zone very difficult or impossible (3).

Acoustic Doppler Current Profilers can be used to track the water movement around a structure before deploying the divers (1).

When underwater, the diver may be aware of the presence of DP by the associated noises produced by fast-flowing water (1), (3). However, due to the difficulty in locating the source of sounds underwater, the position of DP hazards is rarely correctly pinpointed by divers (3).

The velocity profile of the flow generated by DP makes it almost impossible for a diver to detect the presence of the hazard at its boundaries. The diver can be easily trapped without notice (3).

The safest detection method is to identify the DP from the surface or use remotely operated systems before the divers enter the water. Relying on the diver to locate the source of the flow exposes the diver to a high risk of being trapped.

Risk identification and mitigation strategies

DP risk is present when operating in any of the following situations (3):

- Water level between adjoining areas varies (locks, dams).
- There is a boundary between water and a void space (pipelines, hulls).
- Water intakes are active (pumps, sea-chests, drainage channels).
- Propulsors, impellers, and thrusters are operative.

The hazard is considered active when a flow is known or suspected to be occurring; a latent DP hazard is present where conditions have the potential for generating a water flow (3).

Scuba is not permitted in areas where a DP hazard is present and cannot be eliminated before the divers enter the water. Surface-supply with helmet and voice communication must be used. The diver must also wear a harness to facilitate lifting from the water (1), (2).

The ideal goal is to eliminate the DP risk; this can be achieved in different ways (1):

- *Balancing the pressure*: Equalize water levels before the divers enter the area.
- *Lock-out*: The elements able to generate DP are physically locked.
- *Clogging*: The opening causing the DP is sealed.

The equipment able to generate any kind of DP, such as pumps, propellers, valves, and gates, must be secured and locked before the divers enter the water. The key must be unique and held by the diving supervisor until the divers exit the water and the job is concluded (5).

If DP cannot be eliminated, other strategies can be used to reduce the risk. Engineering controls are the next best step. For example, the divers can be separated from the DP source by operating within a specifically deployed chamber or by using deflectors that deviate the water flow away from the operational area (1), (3).

Finally, procedural risk control methods, information, and training are other, if less effective, ways of controlling the risk (3).

Divers operating near a DP source can be protected from entering the danger zone by limiting the length of the umbilical and tether. This length is easily calculated by applying the Pythagorean theorem (1), (2):

$$C = \sqrt{(A^2 + B^2)}$$

C = maximum length of umbilical/tether to deploy

A = water depth (plus any height above the water surface)

B = distance from the danger zone

The actual length of the tether/umbilical will be 3–5 meters (1–2 ft) shorter than the maximum calculated length to add an extra safety buffer (2).

The force required to free a diver trapped by a DP depends on (2):

- DP intensity across the diver.
- Area affected.

- Water flow rate.
- Frictional force between the diver and the opening generating the suction.

In several situations, this force is very elevated, and even if it could be applied to a diver using appropriate mechanical systems, this will likely overcome the resistance of the diver's body, causing severe injury or even resulting in a fatal outcome.

Lines should be in place to be used by the diver as a guide to move without entering the danger zone. A 5-meter buffer is the minimum boundary when in open water for a safety zone around the DP hazard (1), (2). Diving within 15 meters (50 ft) of an active flow ≥ 190 liters/minute (≥ 50 gallons/minute) is not authorized (3).

If the diver is caught by the DP, he should try to position laterally to reduce the pressure area. If the helmet is trapped, the diver should open the free-flow to counter the likely blockage of the second stage due to the DP-induced depression that can also induce a squeeze via the exhalation valve of the helmet (1).

It is almost impossible for a diver to free himself once caught by a DP suction. Rescue divers are also exposed to a very high risk of becoming further fatalities, and there are no indications of effective reciprocal rescue in dive buddies. The only effective measure is to equalize the pressure differential (3).

Topside personnel should try to stop the sources of DP before lifting a trapped diver; as a last resort, if the dimensions of the opening allow, the diver could be sent through it to reach the safer downstream area. This maneuver is extremely risky and should be considered only if all other action fails (1).

Time pressure leads to unsafe practices, especially when DP hazards are involved (3).

Risk	Affected elements	Mitigation/avoidance strategies
Trapping	Diver Umbilical	• Restrain the diver's movement by controlling the length of the umbilical/tether. • Handle the umbilical with minimal slack and away from the danger zone.
Primary trauma	Diver	• Avoid operating close to a DP source.
Drowning	Diver	• Use surface-supply with redundant gas reserve if the diver is trapped underwater for a long time.
Air starvation	Second stage regulator	• Open the free-flow in the helmet if trapped by DP.
Hypothermia	Diver	• Use appropriate insulation, considering the diver may be trapped in cold water for a long time.

Lessons learned

- DP hazards are extremely dangerous and insidious.
- If trapped by DP, self-rescue is virtually impossible.
- DP accidents are often fatal.
- Rescue divers are exposed to very high risk and will likely become further victims.
- Risk avoidance is the best approach. DP should be neutralized before the divers enter the water.
- Engineering controls are effective only if correctly applied by expert personnel.

- When DP is present or suspected to be present, alternative working methods should be considered, such as the use of ROVs.
- In an area of active DP, the use of scuba is forbidden. Surface-supply must be used with appropriate voice communication.

References

1. **Hermans, E.** *Delta P in diving: Risks and prevention.* 2018.

2. **CADC.** *Guidelines for diving operations on dams and other worksites where delta-P hazards may exist.* s.l. : CADC, 2011.

3. **Fisher, A., Gilbert, B. and Anthony, T.** *Differential pressure hazards in diving.* s.l. : HSE, 2009.

4. **USACE.** *USACE Diving Operations: Section 30.* s.l. : USACE, 2014.

5. **Joiner, J.** *Commercial diving training manual.* 5th edition. s.l. : Best-Publishing, 2007.

7.5. DEPTH

Chapter highlights

Deep diving exposes divers to higher stress levels with a higher risk of adverse outcomes in case of errors or mishaps.

Gases that are normally inert at sea-level pressure, such as nitrogen, instead have narcotic effects when breathed at depth.

Oxygen can become toxic when breathed at depth. Its partial pressure in the breathing mix must remain below a certain level to avoid oxygen toxicity. This is achieved by respecting the chosen gas's maximum operative depth (MOD).

Inert gas intake increases (dive time being equal) with deeper diving, leading to a more significant decompression penalty. A good risk management strategy should negotiate between the maximum allowable depth and maximum decompression time that the divers are willing and able to perform.

Divers involved in extreme deep dives can be affected by other neurological issues, such as high-pressure neurological syndrome (HPNS) and some long-lasting brain alterations.

Exposure to hyperbaric environments, primarily if associated with fast decompression and decompression injuries, can cause permanent damage to the long bones and the development of dysbaric osteonecrosis (DON).

> High pressure stresses the diving gear, increasing the risk of flooding and implosion. Respecting the MOD of the gear and good maintenance help reduce the risk of damage.

Introduction

The deeper we dive, the more challenging and potentially stressful the conditions we encounter; our body and our gear are exposed to progressively higher pressure, which has consequences on the dive's physics and physiology.

Following Boyle's law, the breathing mix becomes denser proportionally with the increased ambient pressure; therefore, we consume more gas when diving deeper. The respiratory effort is also increased.

The main physiological effects of depth are caused by the increase in the partial pressure of the gases we breathe. Gases that are physiologically inert at sea level, such as nitrogen, are not so once at depth, affecting the central nervous system's response (CNS); even life-sustaining oxygen can become toxic if its partial pressure increases above a certain threshold.

The progressive inert gas saturation of our body due to the dissolution of non-metabolic gases within the tissues leads to the decompression stops to avoid the formation of bubbles big enough to cause damage upon resurfacing.

Diving gear is also exposed to higher hydrostatic pressure at depth, with an enhanced risk of leaks or implosion in some components, such as video housing and battery compartments.

Narcosis

Since the 1800s, symptoms similar to alcoholic intoxication have been observed in individuals breathing air at high ambient pressure. Hard-hat divers lost consciousness in dives deeper than 67 meters, returning to a normal condition once hoisted to shallower depth (1). In 1935 these symptoms were finally correlated with the narcotic effect of nitrogen in the breathing gas (2).

Nitrogen narcosis is generally produced when breathing O_2–N_2 mixes at a pressure higher than 4 ata (equivalent to $\approx$ 30 meters / 98 ft of depth) with signs and symptoms that include (3), (4):

- Disorientation (in space and in time).
- Memory loss.
- Mood changes/euphoria.
- Hallucinations.
- Impaired neuromuscular coordination.
- Psychomotor and intellectual decrement.

Mental capacity is more affected by narcosis than motor functions and dexterity skills (1). The associated loss of performance is proportional to the difficulty of the task (5).

Scuba divers are more exposed to the impact of narcosis because they need to control all the diving parameters at any given time during the dive. Divers using surface-supply systems are more protected by the presence of a support team who are in control of most of the diving elements (1), (5), (6).

The dive buddy may have a limited capacity to intervene because they could be affected by narcosis and because a diver under narcosis can become aggressive and irrational.

Narcosis also promotes some degree of amnesia, causing divers to forget instructions given during the briefing and interfering with their ability to recall key elements of the dive (7). In severe narcosis, this amnesia can last for several hours after the return to the surface, and extreme sleepiness is very common (6).

For divers tasked with data collection, narcosis-induced amnesia can jeopardize the job results by losing crucial information. To minimize this problem, divers should record the information on an appropriate support. This could be a notepad or, for more complex data, some kind of electronic device (underwater computer tablets are available). Alternatively, a communication system with topside personnel can transfer the burden of recording data to the surface team.

Some neurological alterations following exposure to the high partial pressure of nitrogen can persist for up to 30 minutes after surfacing; breathing 100% oxygen quickly reverses the symptoms (8).

A series of tests performed in a hyperbaric chamber at about 30 meters (≈ 100 ft) of simulated depth showed a drop in performance on both the mental and dexterity level, with normal levels of performance returning only once the divers were back at shallower depth during the 3 meter (≈ 10 ft) decompression stop (5).

Some drugs, particularly those that cause dizziness, such as some anti-seasickness medications, can increase the impact of nitrogen narcosis (9).

High PCO_2 in the blood can also trigger CNS narcosis with a depressant effect on ventilation, leading to further CO_2 build-up and a vicious positive feedback loop (10).

The presence of other stressors, including poor visibility, cold, fatigue, and anxiety, also increases the effects of narcosis (1), (6), (7), (8).

The deeper the dive, the higher the partial pressure of nitrogen and the more likely narcosis will develop. This induced altered mental state can lead to risky behaviors during the dive, increasing the likelihood of accidents (9). Diving below 30 meters ($\approx$ 100 ft) is associated with a 3.5-fold increase in incidents involving narcosis. The Australian Diving Fatalities Database (Project Sticky Beak) estimates that nitrogen narcosis contributes to about 9% of diving fatalities. At the global level, narcosis could account for about 3.6% of total diving fatalities (8).

Narcosis is not immediate but develops once a threshold exposure time has been reached. The deeper the dive, the shorter the onset time for narcosis. Once narcosis is fully developed, the impairment remains constant for that depth with no further performance detriment (5).

Rapid compression also facilitates narcosis (1), (6). For this reason, divers should avoid descending too fast, mainly when the descent has limited reference points, such as in blue diving, night diving, and in low visibility waters.

The susceptibility of divers to nitrogen narcosis is highly variable between individuals, and between dives for the same diver (1), (8). This variability makes a risk assessment for potential narcosis difficult. For safety's sake, any dives below 4 ata should be considered prone to creating some degree of narcosis, and the diving operations should be planned accordingly, avoiding over-tasking.

Some resiliency to the effects of nitrogen narcosis has been shown by skilled and experienced divers (1), (6); motivation can help in staying focused even under the effects of narcosis (9). Slowing down the operations and receiving specific training and overlearning of the job to be performed help in reducing the impact of narcosis (7), (8). It is to be noted that there is no scientific evidence for any effective biological adaption to nitrogen narcosis following repetitive exposures (1).

A series of strategies can be adopted to reduce the impact of narcosis on performance and safety (7):

- Minimize the need to memorize instructions by using written checklists.
- Overlearn tasks and emergency procedures.
- The diver should be familiar with the onset of narcosis and be able to estimate the realistic performance achievable under any given intensity of narcosis.
- Be able to remain focused on the task.
- Use technological support such as an alarm indicating that the planned depth and bottom time have been reached (some diving computers provide such alarm settings).

The physiological causes of nitrogen narcosis are not totally understood yet, but a few theories have been developed (1), (3), (4), (8), (9):

- *Meyer-Overton hypothesis*: The narcotic effect of inert gases is due to their solubility in lipids. This causes the lipid layers of the neuronal cellular membrane to expand above a specific limit that interferes with their functioning and causes narcosis.
- *Quastel-metabolic*: Interference with the metabolism of the brain cells.
- *Hydrates*: Formation of clathrates stabilized by proteins and causing narcosis by increasing the impedance of nerve tissues.
- *Icebergs hypothesis*: Similar to the hydrates hypothesis. In this case, an area of highly ordered water molecules sur-

rounds the gas molecule dissolved into the neuronal cell stiffening the lipid membrane and lowering the cell's conductance, thus affecting electrical signal transmission between neurons.

Lipid solubility seems to be the key factor explaining the different narcotic potentials of other gases, from argon (the most narcotic) to helium, which does not show narcotic effects until very high pressures above 40 atm. The likely involvement of changes in neurotransmitters and receptors in narcosis could eventually allow for the development of a pharmacological treatment to reduce its impact (4).

Inert gas narcosis is not a trivial risk because it impairs mental functions and increases the risk of errors and mishaps that can lead to accidents. Its variability makes it challenging to develop a consistent risk-mitigation procedure. Divers should be aware that any dive below 4 ata can be affected by narcosis. Maintaining good focus on the task at hand and having good situational awareness may help reduce the impact of narcosis. On the other hand, exposure to other stressors, particularly reduced visibility and cold, may increase the effects of narcosis.

High-pressure neurological syndrome

In the late 1960s, the British Navy was experimenting with deep dives in a hyperbaric chamber at an equivalent depth of around 250 meters (800 ft) using Heliox (a blend of oxygen and helium) as a breathing medium to avoid both oxygen toxicity (the O_2 % was set to create a partial pressure within safety limits) and nitrogen narcosis (helium is considered to have very low narcotic capacity, at least until extreme pressures are reached). During the dives, the divers observed and reported unusual signs and symptoms, including loss of mental acumen, reduction in manual dexterity, tremors, and, in some more extreme cases, dizziness, nausea, and vomiting. Similar signs were observed in animal models with epilepsy-like convulsions at the extreme depth. The phenomenon was named high-pressure neurological syndrome (HPNS) (11).

HPNS is induced by the direct effect of the high-pressure environment on the nervous system affecting divers' breathing Heliox or Trimix (a blend composed of oxygen, helium, and nitrogen) at a pressure above 13 absolute atmospheres (equivalent to depth over 120 meters / 390 ft) and is exacerbated by fast compression rates. The syndrome is characterized by a series of alterations and disorders of motor, sensory, vegetative, metabolic, and cognitive functions, including short- and long-term memory disturbances due to CNS systemic hyperexcitability combined with a reduction in the conduction velocity of axons and depression of synaptic activity. The first signs of HPNS include tremors of distal extremities, dizziness, nausea, and moderate alteration of cognitive function. Tremors include postural shaking (3–7 Hz) and activity tremors (8–12 Hz) that progressively affect the trunk, neck, and face. Exposure to oscillatory stimuli at the high biological range (> 25 Hz), such as those generated by fluorescent lights and video monitors, and pulsating noise may facilitate the development of HPNS (12), (13), (14). EEG anomalies are often present, lasting up to 12 hours after the compression stops (15). Anomalous eye movements (opsoclonus) were detected in experimental hyperbaric chamber compressions once the threshold of 180 meters (590 ft) of equivalent depth was reached (16).

EEG alterations show a reduction in alpha waves and an increase in the slower theta and delta waves. At compression equivalent to 170–180 meters (558 – 590 ft), the EEG alterations resemble microsleep. A degree of acclimation is observed after a few days at depth, but a return to fully normal cognitive function is often achieved only after final decompression (12).

In long saturation dives (where the divers live within a hyperbaric chamber pressurized at a depth equivalent to the one at which the divers will operate and to which they will be transported by using diving bells), alteration of the sleeping pattern is observed, with longer superficial stages (I and II) and shorter deep stages (III and IV) (12). Mood disturbance and sleep loss were reported in saturation dives at 260 meters in open sea and dry chamber tests (17).

Due to the significant individual variation in HPNS sensitivity, some genetic mechanisms may be present (18).

HPNS effects are proportionate to the speed and magnitude of compression; slowing the compression speed and introducing stops reduces HPNS (15), (18). Tests in a hyperbaric chamber showed that divers exposed to a staged compression responded better, with reduced and delayed HPNS symptoms than divers exposed to a linear, even if slower, compression profile (16). Deeper than 330 meters (1,082 ft), symptoms have been experienced regardless of compression speed (18).

Once the divers have been saturated to a given depth, it is possible to undergo quick compression from about 50–120 meters (164 – 394 ft) deeper without inducing HPNS (15), (19).

HPNS is evident when breathing a binary mixture of helium and oxygen (Heliox). Adding nitrogen or hydrogen, which act as narcotic gases only at very high pressure, to the mix reduces HPNS, and dives have been performed to 450–700 meters (1,476 – 2,296 ft) (3), (4), (18). In the "Atlantis series" of simulated dives at the Duke University hyperbaric facility, the use of Trimix (5% nitrogen, 0.5% oxygen, and the remainder helium) through the dive showed a reduction in HPNS symptoms, with the divers remaining able to perform in pressure equivalent to 600 meters (1,968 ft) (11), (20). Adding 50% hydrogen to the mix allowed dives to 500 meters (1,640 ft) without significant HPNS symptoms (18).

When diving at extreme depths, even hydrogen may interfere with the CNS, as indicated by the psychotic-like disorders experienced by divers involved in the Comex "Hydra" experiment series, with simulated dives to 700 (2,296 ft) meters using a breathing medium composed of all four gases (27% H_2, 65%, He, 7% N_2 and 0.56% O_2) for a total time of 42 days, of which 15 were for compression (1), (20). In an offshore test dive, the divers added 47% hydrogen to a Heliox mixture. They successfully connected a pipeline at a depth of 520 meters (1,706 ft) with a performance similar to that of 150–200 meters (492 – 656 ft) using Heliox (21).

In a hyperbaric chamber test, six divers were compressed to 450 meters (1,476 ft) for 38 hours, with a reduction in speed every 10 meters (33 ft) and stops of 150 minutes every 100 meters (328 ft). Heliox was used to 200 meters (656 ft) (PO_2 0.4 bar), and hydrogen was added with a final mix at 450 meters (1,476 ft) of 54–56% H_2, 43–45% He, and 1% O_2. EEG changes in alfa waves were observed between 100 and 300 meters (128 and 984 ft), but no tremors were observed at maximum depth (22).

Using 5% N_2, Trimix divers were compressed to 460 meters (1,509 ft) in 12 hours and 20 minutes. After one day of acclimation, the overall performance of the divers improved, although it remained below that of surface-level performance until the divers were decompressed to 300 meters (984 ft). A further test dive used 10% N_2 Trimix for a 42-day chamber dive to a maximum depth of 660 meters (2,165 ft). Mental functions were severely impaired at the maximum depth, and sleep was poor quality. HPNS symptoms appeared at 420 meters (1,377 ft) but subsided after 24 hours, with the final compression to 660 meters (2,165 ft) achieved in less than five days. From these tests, the effectiveness of using Trimix instead of Heliox to improve performance is doubtful (17).

Other tests included compressing divers breathing Heliox to a maximum equivalent depth of 300, 420, and 540 meters (984, 1,377, and 1,771 ft). Slowing the compression rate and providing intervals in the compression allowed them to reach 420 meters (1,377 ft) in 2 days, with the divers showing very mild or absent HPNS. During the first 540-meter dive, HPNS was manifest with nausea and vomiting; in the next dive to the same depth but with a slower compression rate, HPNS was not present. Adding 10% N_2 to the mix in a 660-meter dive caused severe narcosis and HPNS. A series of metabolic alterations were observed, coupled with intense feelings of cold, requiring the hyperbaric chamber to be heated to 31.7°C to be comfortable at 540 meters (1,771 ft) equivalent pressure using Heliox. Cardiovascular effects at depth were no longer present once the divers were decompressed at the surface. Still, cases of DCS of variable severity were experienced, mainly in the shallower phase of the decompression following linear profiles. Overall, a worsening in performance was observed with increased depth (23).

It is supposed that the sum of the narcotic potency of each gas in the breathing medium causes psychotic-like episodes of HPNS. The narcotic potency of gases considered "inert" because they do not participate in metabolic reactions is correlated with their lipid solubility. The mechanism generating the narcotic effect is not entirely clear yet, but the "critical volume model" states that narcosis occurs when the volume of a hydrophobic cell region is caused to expand beyond a particular critical value by the absorption of an inert substance (14):

$$E = V_i \times X_i \times P_i / V_m$$

E = fractional expansion (to have psychotic effects its mean value must be ≥ 0.0453 ± 0.0032%)

V_i = Partial molar volume of gas in a given solvent

V_m = Molar volume of a given solvent (for diving consideration V_m is equal to 640 ml)

X_i = Mole fraction solubility of the gas in the given solvent at 1 atm partial pressure

P_i = Gas partial pressure

The expansion caused by the absorption of a given inert gas is therefore correlated with the amount of gas that dissolves into the lipid cell area, the solubility of this gas and its partial pressure. The latter increases with the increasing ambient pressure that, for divers, is correlated with the depth.

Considering a Heliox mix, the theoretical maximum depth achievable before reaching a critical "E" value is in the range of 930–1,000 meters (3,051 – 3,280 ft) (14).

Increasing GABA (gamma-aminobutyric acid) and treating it with an NMDA (N-methyl-D-aspartate) antagonist in animal models reduced the effect of HPNS, suggesting the potential for drug treatments for divers exposed to HPNS risk (18).

In general, no long-term permanent effects of HPNS have been observed (18), but very deep saturation diving (200–500 meters / 656 – 1,640 ft) for a prolonged time, as in the case of commercial divers routinely employed in offshore operations, may cause long-term neurological alterations, in particular in the sensory system often associated with abnormal

EEGs, paresthesia and difficulties in concentration. A history of DCS was also common in the analyzed divers, with 95% of the population (40 Norwegian commercial divers) having experienced type 1 and type 2 DCS at some point during their careers (24).

A limited number of recreational divers have experienced some symptoms of HPNS during deep bounce dives with fast compression to depths of around 200 meters (656 ft); limiting time at maximum depth and performing a fast ascent to the first decompression stop are strategies used to reduce the HPNS symptoms in these dives (20).

Most divers will never be exposed to extreme environmental conditions to cause an appreciable risk of HPNS. Individuals involved in such ultra-deep operations are professionals operating at the cutting edge of technology and benefitting from solid support in terms of infrastructure and assistance.

Long-term effects are a risk factor for divers performing very deep and very long saturation dives; mitigation strategies include limiting exposure, continuous monitoring of the physiological parameters during the operations, and careful post-dive medical evaluation.

Oxygen toxicity

While oxygen is vital for our survival, when breathed under pressure, it may cause inflammation and potential damage to our tissues, adversely affecting the CNS.

The toxic effects of oxygen at high pressure can be divided into two categories (25):

- *Bert effect*: Impacts the CNS. It is named after Paul Bert, the French physiologist of the 19th century credited for the first studies on DCS that in 1878 observed convulsions in larks exposed to 15–20 ata of air. Usually, CNS toxicity develops at a pressure above 3 ata, but if the exposure is prolonged, it may happen even at lower pressure. Convulsions of tonic-clonic type are often associated with CNS oxygen toxicity. Reduced levels of GABA are also often linked with the occurrence of seizures. Other factors, including high partial pressure of CO_2 in the breathing medium, fatigue, cold, and stress, may facilitate the onset of CNS toxicity.
- *Smith effect*: Impacts the lungs, causing pulmonary toxicity. It is named after J. Lorain Smith, who in 1899 while studying the Bert effect in rats noted fatal pneumonia after four days of exposure to 73% O_2 at 1 ata, with the first symptoms developing after about 10 hours.

CNS toxicity – Bert effect

Exposure to high pressure O_2 causes various neurological symptoms, including blurred/tunnel vision, tinnitus, and twitching; the severity of the symptoms varies greatly between individuals and between exposures, highlighting the importance of environmental and personal factors in the development of CNS toxicity (26).

Exposure to high-pressure O_2 can trigger sudden convulsions without premonitory symptoms; PO_2 of 1.8 ata should be considered an absolute limit (6). In divers breathing PO_2 of 2.0 ata, convulsions developed after 10 to 50 minutes of exposure (27). During the tonic-clonic seizure, breath-holding is common (28). This effect can be extremely dangerous for scuba divers because it could lead to lung over-expansion and potential AGE (arterial gas embolism).

Increased physical activity levels, reduced visual input, dark environmental conditions, and increased partial pressure of CO_2 allow for faster onset of CNS toxicity (26).

NOAA has developed tables and algorithms to identify time limits for oxygen exposure based on the PO_2 (29). In the NOAA tables the maximum acceptable PO_2 is 1.6 ata with an associated maximum exposure time of 45 minutes. If more than one dive (in a 24-hour interval) has reached or exceeded the limits of a single exposure, then a minimum surface time of 2 hours is required before any further dive. Spending at least 12 hours at normoxic level will reset the series. The suggested limits are for light activity; a more conservative approach is needed in case of heavy work and stressful conditions.

An "oxygen clock" allows for the quantification of %CNS of the maximum total allowed for any given exposure:

$$\%CNS = t_x / t_m$$

t_x = Actual exposure time

t_m = Maximum allowed exposure time

Breathing oxygen at high pressure facilitates the production of free radicals that affect several biological mechanisms, including neurological function (28). These radicals cause lipid peroxidation, inhibit nucleic acids and protein synthesis, and deactivate cellular enzymes (25). The primary neural target for seizure is still unknown, making identifying the mechanisms leading to CNS toxicity unclear (26).

In general, CNS toxicity causes no residual neurological damage once the PO_2 has been reduced (26); however, if the exposure to high-pressure oxygen continues beyond the point of seizure, then irreversible neurological damage and death may occur, following what is called "John Bean effect" (28).

CNS toxicity is a severe risk and requires careful assessment. The critical factor for its mitigation is to respect the maximum operative depth (MOD) based on limiting PO_2 to 1.6 ata or, even more conservatively, to 1.4 ata. Nitrox divers can reach such limits at relatively moderate depths if breathing highly enriched mixtures; therefore, they should be very careful in monitoring their depth. Mixed gas divers who use high-oxygen mixes for decompression should ensure that the gas switch to such mixtures is done at the correct depth and well within the relative MOD.

Pulmonary toxicity

Breathing oxygen at a pressure above 0.5 atm may cause some degree of pulmonary inflammation leading to a reduction in vital capacity (VC). A decrease of 2% is considered acceptable during diving, and 10% or more is accepted during emergency hyperbaric treatment. The reduction in VC is reversible, and a drop of up to 30% is recovered within 1–2 weeks. In air diving, to reach 0.5 ata of oxygen partial pressure, the diver has to dive below 15 meters ($\approx$ 50 ft); in Nitrox diving, such partial pressure is reached at even shallower depths. From these considerations, some reduction in VC is likely to develop in most dives (30).

Another way to calculate pulmonary oxygen toxicity is by considering the unit pulmonary toxic dose (UPTD). This toxic effect is equivalent to exposure to 100% O_2 for one minute at a pressure of 1 ata (30).

All combinations of PO_2 and time, which have a toxicity of 1 UPTD, fall along a curve with asymptotes at 0 time and 0.5 ata (Fig. 7.5.1) (31).

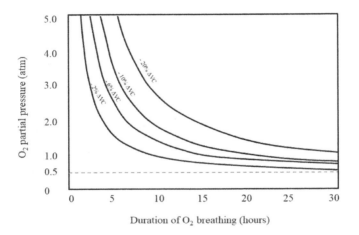

Fig. 7.5.1. Reduction % of pulmonary capacity related to O_2 partial pressure and breathing time.

It is possible to calculate the UPTD for any given constant PO_2 using the following formula (32):

$$UPTD = t_x \times \left(\frac{0.5}{PO2-0.5}\right) - \frac{5}{6}$$

t_x = Time of exposure in minutes

PO_2 = Partial pressure of oxygen in the breathing medium in ata

Pulmonary O_2 toxicity, with airway resistance increasing up to

30%, has been reported in individuals exposed to PO_2 0.83–2.0 ata for 6 to 74 hours; symptoms also developed after 6 to 14 hours at 1 ata PO_2. Increasing PO_2 to 2 ata caused symptoms to develop in 3 to 6 hours. A large variability in tolerance has been observed within individuals; intermittent exposure to O_2 seems to enhance tolerance (33). When using a high O_2% mixture for decompression, "air breaks" should be taken every 20 minutes to limit oxygen toxicity (29).

The variation in pulmonary vital capacity (DVC) is related to oxygen exposure in the following way (33):

$$\% \text{ DVC} = -0.011 \times (PO_2 - 0.5) \times t_x$$

PO_2 = Partial pressure of oxygen in the breathing medium in ata

t_x = Time of exposure in minutes

Due to the long exposure needed to develop degenerative lung changes, pulmonary O_2 toxicity is usually not an issue for scuba divers performing relatively short dives (6).

Negative impact on the lungs can become relevant in prolonged exposure to high levels (above 0.5 ata) of oxygen, such as during extended decompression stops using high O_2%, hyperbaric chamber treatments, and long/multiple rebreather dives. In practical terms, UPTD tracking is essential only on multiple (> 3) days of prolonged exposure (29).

In an experimental series of dives using 100% O_2 as the breathing medium at a depth of 6 meters, with two brief excursions (less than 15 minutes) to 12 meters, minor pulmonary toxicity was observed after 4 hours of exposure; the symptoms developed earlier when the divers were doing physical tasks than when at rest (34).

Mechanical effects of hyperbaric breathing

The increased density of the breathing gas in the lungs has three primary effects (10):

1. The inertia of the gas molecules flowing through the airways increases and may affect the distribution of ventilation. Due to the relatively small mass of the gas involved, this effect is usually limited.
2. Diffusion within the gas phase is inversely proportional to the gas density, so higher density reduces the relative mixing of the inspired gas within the alveolar region.
3. The increased gas density causes increased airway resistance, leading to a rise in the workload required to achieve a given ventilation rate. This can cause CO_2 retention at greater pressure as the diver reduces ventilation to avoid the fatigue of the respiratory muscles.

Maximum voluntary ventilation decreases approximately as a square root function of the breathing gas density; at 90 meters of depth, the drop can reach 75% if compared with the ventilation at sea level. The expiratory flow becomes effort-independent; that is, it cannot be increased by increasing the work of the respiratory muscles, and the diver can become unable to ventilate correctly, with further accumulation of CO_2 (35).

In deep diving, the increased gas density can play a very relevant role in respiratory effort. To mitigate this impact, the regulators should be of very high quality and able to provide a large gas flow with minimal resistance. The use of Trimix in deep dives not only allows the PO_2 and N_2 to be maintained within acceptable limits but also reduces the respiratory effort thanks to the low density of helium. Being able to control the breathing pace is also very important.

Decompression risk

The main risk factors for DCS (decompression sickness) can be divided into three categories (36):

1. *Diver specific*: Age, gender, fitness, BMI (body mass index), PFO (patent foramen ovalis), previous DCS.
2. *Dive related*: Depth, bottom time, ascent protocol, single or multiple dives, temperature, fatigue.
3. *Post-dive related*: Ascent to altitude, exercise, and environmental conditions.

On some of these parameters, the divers have a degree of control and should act accordingly to reduce the DCS risk. Divers should aim to develop and maintain good aerobic fitness. Following a conservative approach in terms of limiting maximum depth and bottom time also reduces the risk of incurring decompression-related problems. Respecting minimum surface interval before moving to altitude and limiting post-dive work is also a good risk-reduction strategy.

Basics of decompression theory

All other factors being equal, deeper dives expose the diver to a higher risk of DCS. The following section provides some critical elements of decompression theory and practice to define better the concepts associated with DCS risk. The information supplied is only an overview of the theory of decompression. If you would like more detailed information on decompression models, other references are available such as the books by Asser Salama (37) and Mark Powell (38). An extensive mathematical analysis of decompression theory can be found in the work of Bruce Wienke (39).

For risk assessment, the critical point is that any decompression theory is based on models of the human body. The so-called "tissues" or "compartments" are mathematical simulations that allow for the development of algorithms to forecast the behavior of the inert gas during the dive and the following decompression phase. The limit of such models is that they cannot include specific physiological characteristics of the individual and are therefore targeted at an "average diver" in terms of gas exchange.

One family of such models is the dissolved-gas models. In these models, the inert gas considered for the calculation is the one dissolved in the tissues only. Another family is the dual-phase group of models. In these models, the inert gas is considered both when dissolved in the tissues and as micro-bubbles. More recent probabilistic models do not use any theoretical tissue but are instead based on a statistical analysis of DCS occurrence over large numbers of dives. The model will generate decompression schedules for various risk levels to be compared with the chosen dive plan to calculate the probability of DCS (38), (37).

Inert gas saturation

Henry's law states that the amount of a gas that dissolves in a liquid is directly proportional to its partial pressure above the liquid.

The concentration of a gas in the liquid phase (C) can be calculated as follows (40):

$$C_{liquid} = (\alpha_{liquid} \times P_{liquid}) / (K \times T)$$

α = Ostwald solubility coefficient for the liquid

P = Gas partial pressure (tension) in the liquid

K = Boltzmann constant

T = Absolute temperature (°K)

When we breathe air at atmospheric pressure, an equilibrium between dissolved nitrogen in the tissues and its partial pressure in the atmosphere is maintained; we are saturated with nitrogen, and our tissues will not intake more gas. This equilibrium is offset when the environmental pressure increases, such as when diving. The deeper and longer we dive, the more nitrogen (considering a binary mix such as air or Nitrox) is absorbed (29). Therefore, this gas does not participate in metabolic reactions and is not consumed by any biological process; it will simply accumulate within the tissues. After a length of time that depends on the depth and a variety of physiological parameters, the tissues will be fully saturated with nitrogen, and no further intake of inert gas will happen (41).

The gas saturation is reached in tissues via the circulation of blood as the tissues seek to equalize their tensions with the partial pressures in the breathed mix. Equilibrium is reached first in the alveoli, then in blood and tissues. The inert gas partial pressure in the alveoli and in the arterial blood is assumed to be equivalent, as the exchange rate is very fast, so an equilibrium is reached almost instantly. The kinetic of this gas exchange controls the tissues' saturation and supersaturation during decompression (40).

The factors determining how quickly the tissues reach equilibrium are (42):

- Magnitude of blood perfusion.
- Solubility of the gas in the tissue relative to its solubility in the blood.
- Gas diffusion rate in the tissue.
- Tissue temperature (influencing gas solubility, diffusion rates, and regional perfusion).
- Tissue PCO_2 (influencing regional perfusion).
- Local energy consumption (which is related to workload influencing regional perfusion).

Tissue temperature is one of the main parameters affecting DCS risk. Being cold or warm modifies the peripheral circulation and the tissues' perfusion interacting with gas exchange. Being warm at depth and cold during the decompression phase is a situation that enhances DCS risk (43). In this case, the perfusion is greater at depth, and more gas can dissolve into the tissues; being cold during the decompression slows down the perfusion leading to reduced off-gassing. An example is if the diver uses an active warming garment (such as an electrically heated vest under a drysuit) during the bottom phase of the dive, and then the heating system fails (perhaps running out of battery) during the decompression phase.

Some analyses of DCS rates in divers using hot-water suits show that being warm at the bottom increases DCS risk, outweighing any benefit of being warm during the decompression phase. However, this is only one contributing risk factor, as the typology of the dive profile is the main controlling risk-factor for DCS (44).

Tissues model

Considering all human body tissues and their complex interactions in detail would be almost impossible. Therefore, decompression theories are based on simplifying the system using a limited number of hypothetical tissues called compartments. Each of these tissues is characterized by its half-time. This is the time needed for the given tissue to intake half the difference between its inert gas content found at equilibrium with the surface pressure and the gas content the tissue would have if saturated at the pressure of the current depth; complete equilibrium (saturation) is considered to have been reached after six half-times (Fig. 7.5.2) (45).

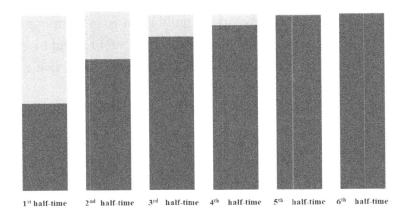

1ˢᵗ half-time   2ⁿᵈ half-time   3ʳᵈ half-time   4ᵗʰ half-time   5ᵗʰ half-time   6ᵗʰ half-time

Fig. 7.5.2. Progressive tissue saturation. After six half-times, any given tissue will be totally saturated, and it will not intake any more inert gas.

In the original work by Buhlmann, 16 compartments were considered with half-times for nitrogen ranging from 2.65 to 635 minutes; these were defined as "fast" and "slow" tissues depending on the magnitude of their half-time. Fast tissues will be saturated quickly and also will complete off-gassing quickly. Well-vascularized tissues are fast. Tissues where blood circulation is poor are slow. In this model, inner ear tissues have nitrogen half-times of 146 to 238 minutes. The skin and muscles have half-time values from 37 to 79 minutes. Finally, joints and bones are slower tissues, with half-times ranging from 304 to 635 minutes (46).

During the ascent, the environmental pressure will drop; if the tension (which is the internal pressure of the dissolved gas in the tissue) within a given tissue exceeds the ambient pressure value, then a supersaturation status develops. The difference between the tissue tension and the ambient pressure is called the gradient. If a critical threshold of supersaturation is exceeded, a temporary imbalance of the dissolved-gas-liquid equilibrium is created, resulting in an expansion of the gas phase. If the system starts without any gas phase, it is unstable, and the only way to reach a new thermodynamic equilibrium is by forming and expanding a gas phase (40). This means that bubbles will be generated within the tissues and blood. To limit the DCS risk, such bubbles should remain below a defined threshold (37).

Once the ambient pressure drops below the sum of the partial pressures of all the gasses dissolved in the tissues, then a status of supersaturation develops (37), (41), (47):

$$\Sigma\, P_{tis\,j} - P_{amb} > 0 \text{ for } J = 1, \ldots, n$$

$\Sigma\, P_{tis\,j}$ = Partial pressure of dissolved gas in the tissue

P_{amb} = Ambient pressure

Gas supersaturation is defined in terms of the total dissolved gas tension in the tissue and not in terms of any single gas; this is important because when breathing any mixture with O_2, this will be metabolized, thus lowering the overall supersaturation of the tissue. This is defined as the "oxygen window," and its relevance for decompression theory is described below (40).

If tissue tension remains below a defined threshold, the nitrogen will be carried to the lungs by the blood flow and released as part of the gas exchange within the alveoli. Upon emersion, bubbles are common in venous blood (80% of divers show some degree of bubbles), and these are usually eliminated by the lungs (pulmonary filter) without any appreciable consequence. In some cases, bubbles may form at the beginning of the venous circulation as vascular gas emboli (VGE). Under normal conditions, VGEs pass into the right side of the heart and are then eliminated by the pulmonary filter. If too many or too large, bubbles are created the pulmonary filter can be bypassed, and the bubbles may enter the arterial flow, causing a blockage in the smallest vessels, producing tissue damage, and leading to DCS. Decompression procedures aim to limit bubble formation, thus containing the risk of DCS (41), (48), (49). A rapid decompression can cause the dissolved gas in the tissues to undergo to a phase disequilibrium leading to the formation of bubbles and potential DCS (40).

In repetitive dives (i.e., more than one in a 24-hour period), bubbles are more likely to form, and this is the reason why multiple ascents are likely the single biggest risk-factor for DCS (42).

To measure the level of supersaturation of a given tissue, the "tissue ratio" value is used (40):

$$T_R = \Sigma\, P_{tissue} \,/\, P_{ambient}$$

T_R is given by the total dissolved gas tension rather than being based on a single component. To have phase disequilibrium, it is necessary to have supersaturation in all the gaseous components.

In other words, the tissue ratio represents the level of super-saturation of a tissue. The supersaturation level indicates how much higher the tissue tension is than that of the surrounding environment.

Faster tissues tolerate higher overpressure because their faster gas clearance rate means that high supersaturation will not last too long (45).

To prevent DCS, a widely applied method is to perform "staged decompression," that is, stopping the ascent at defined depths for defined times to progressively reduce the tissue tension, limiting bubble formation. Depths and times will be calculated by algorithms based on models of the tissues that implicitly (gas content models) or explicitly (bubbles models) aim to minimize bubble formation by controlling tissue gas supersaturation (47).

Gas exchanges within the tissues follow what is called an exponential function. An exponential function is a function that "accelerates" through time, beginning with low values and rapidly reaching higher values once a given threshold is reached. Various natural phenomena follow such trajectories, including bacteria growth, compound interest, radioactive decay, and, of course, tissue saturation (50).

In some models, such as the Haldane model, gas intake and off-gassing are both exponential and symmetrical (37). In other models, even if the gas intake and off-gassing are influenced by the same parameters, the overall degassing process is much slower than the ingassing (42). In a "linear-exponential" model the exponential ingassing kinetic (fast) is coupled with a linear (slow) off-gassing kinetic. As a result, the model is asymmetric, with longer decompression times (51).

Whatever the model, the diving tables represent its output, considering each dive as a "square dive" – that is, a dive where the maximum depth is reached at the beginning of the dive and all the dive time is spent at this depth until a continuous ascent to the surface is initiated.

Dive computers can handle more complex profiles that include multi-depth stages of variable durations.

Perfusion models

These models consider the gas uptake (ingassing) to be primarily influenced by tissue perfusion (the greater the blood flow through the tissue, the faster the equilibrium is reached) and by the solubility of the gas in the tissue (the greater the solubility the slower the equilibrium is reached, and more gas is dissolved) (42):

$$[P_T N_2]^t = [P_T N_2]^0 + (PaN_2 - [P_T N_2]^0) \times (1 - e^{-q\alpha_B /a_T})$$

$[P_T N_2]^t$ = Partial pressure of nitrogen in the tissue at time t

$[P_T N_2]^0$ = Partial pressure of nitrogen in the tissue at the beginning

PaN_2 = Arterial partial pressure of nitrogen

q = Blood supply to the tissue

α_B = Solubility of nitrogen in the blood

a_T = Solubility of nitrogen in tissues

In perfusion-limited models, the inert gas tension in bubble-free tissue changes at a rate proportional to the difference (gradient) between arterial and tissue gas tension (40).

The accuracy of these models is somewhat limited because the factors listed above are interrelated, and some tissues have intermittent perfusion (42).

Haldane's model

"Haldane's model" is one of the most-used "perfusion limited models" and is based on three key assumptions (37), (47):

1. *Multiple parallel compartments (tissues)*: Haldane modeled nitrogen intake and its release in the body, considering several non-communicating (parallel) perfusion-limited compartments in which gas uptake and washout are symmetrical. Each compartment has its half-time based on the assumption that different tissues receive different blood flow (different degrees of perfusion) and have different solubility for nitrogen.

2. *Tolerable degree of supersaturation*: From observation on animals and humans (caisson workers), Haldane originally defined a 2:1 ratio as the maximum allowed tissue supersaturation. In the original model, greater supersaturation was tolerated at depth, but subsequent models reduced the extent to which the tolerable supersaturation increases with depth. The supersaturation ratio is also changed in more modern models.

3. *Maximize gradient*: The classical Haldanian decompression schedule allows for an initial rapid decompression which progressively slows as the surface approaches. The decompression is slowed as successively slower half-time compartments control the safe ascent. The most effective decompression schedule is obtained maximizing the tissue-alveolar gas partial pressure gradient for inert gas washout.

Shallow stops and deep stops

Decompression models are based on gas-liquid equilibrium phases following thermodynamic principles. Decompression acting over a gas-liquid system must result in an expansion of the gas phase following Boyle's law. Suppose no gas phase is present at the beginning of the decompression. In that case, the system is unstable, and bubbles can form at any point within the supersaturated liquid in an attempt to re-establish thermodynamic equilibrium (40).

In the so-called "classic deterministic gas content models," decompression is planned to maintain the tissues' supersaturation below a specific value. For a given tissue "k," the equations controlling its saturation values are (41):

$$S_{Ptis\,j,k} \leq M_k$$

$$M_k = a_k D + M_{0k}$$

$$S_{Ptis\,j,k} = \text{Tissue supersaturation}$$

$$D = \text{Ambient pressure expressed as equivalent water depth}$$

M_k = Maximum allowed tissue pressure at D

M_{0k} = Maximum allowed tissue pressure at surface

a_k, M_{0k} = Parameters determined experimentally

The shortest decompression time is thus obtained when the partial pressure gradient between the model tissues and alveolar gas are maximized to optimize gas washout. As the ascent progresses, tissues with progressively longer half-times (slower tissues) will become the leading tissues for the decompression lengthening the stops at shallower depths (41).

In the so-called "bubble models," the DCS risk is assessed considering tissues' perfusion and the number and size of bubbles. These factors can be minimized by doing the first decompression stops at greater depth than the initial stops prescribed by the classical gas content model (41).

A deep stop is commonly defined as a stop performed at half the difference between the maximum depth of the dive and the depth of the planned first shallow decompression stop. In the varying permeability models based on dual-phase theory (gas and dissolved phase), deep stops allow for the shortening of the shallower stops, resulting in an equal or shorter total decompression time (52).

Initial deep stops aim to reduce tissue gas supersaturation by forming fewer bubbles than at shallower initial stops. Bubbles that form at a deep stop remain more compressed and have lower gas influx from the surrounding tissues because of the reduced bubble surface area and lower diffusion gradient between tissue and bubble. This is important because bubble formation, even if asymptomatic, substantially slows gas washout by lowering the partial pressure gradient for tissue-to-blood gas exchange because a fraction of the dissolved gas in the tissue is now in the bubble (41).

The relation between the pressure inside the bubble (P_{bub}) and the tissue supersaturation is (41):

$$P_{bub} = P_{amb} + P_{st} + M$$

P_{amb} = Ambient pressure

P_{st} = Surface tension

M = Mechanical pressure exerted by the displaced tissue

Bubbles grow if the tissue gas supersaturation is:

$$(S_{ptis\,j} - P_{amb}) > (P_{st} + M).$$

Bubbles can grow only if the gas tension outside the bubble exceeds the gas tension inside the bubble, allowing gas to migrate inside the bubble. Increased curvature of the bubble surface (due to a reduced radius) elevates the gas tension requirements for the bubble to grow. If the bubble's radius remains below a critical value (which depends on the partial pressure gradient and the surface tension), the bubble will dissolve back into solution (40).

At a shallow decompression stop, the supersaturation is greater than at a deep stop, allowing for the formation of more bubbles that will also grow faster. On the other hand, the increased gradient between tissues and blood that develops at a shallower depth (due to the reduced alveolar and arterial partial pressure of the inert gas compared with that of the tissues) allows for faster washout. Once the inert gas washout has reduced the tissue inert gas pressure below that inside the bubble, the bubble will shrink. This benefit is reduced by the diffusion of the inert gas from the tissues into the bubbles, leading to a reduced pressure gradient. This latter effect is greater for shallower stops than for deeper stops (41).

If bubbles form in the tissue, the gradient for inert gas wash-out is significantly reduced because the inert gas pressure inside the bubble is only slightly higher than the ambient pressure and lower than that in the tissue. The inert gas will therefore diffuse from the tissue into the bubble, expanding it (42).

To compare the impact of deep or shallow stops on DCS risk, the US Navy conducted a study involving 390 man-dives in a wet hyperbaric chamber with a simulated depth of 52 meters (170 ft). The incidence of DCS was three cases in 192 dives that followed a shallow stops decompression schedule and 11 cases in 198 dives that followed a deep stops decompression schedule; VGE count was also higher after the deep stop trials. Redistribution of decompression time from shallow to deep stops leads to higher DCS risk and increased VGE detection. The study indicates that reducing inert gas pressure more rapidly by following a shallow stop decompression schedule is more advantageous in reducing DCS risk than following deep stops decompression aimed to minimize bubble formation and growth. During deep stops, the washout in slower compartments is strongly reduced (due to the reduced inert gas gradient between inspired gas and tissue), and further inert gas intake may happen (41).

Experimental air dives were performed at 20 meters ($\approx$65 ft) for 40 minutes bottom time, followed by an ascent to 10 meters ($\approx$33 ft) for deep stops or to 4 meters ($\approx$13 ft) for shallow stops. The 10-meter stop was for 4 minutes and was followed by a 3-minute stop at 4 meters. For the shallow stop dive, a 7-minute stop at 4 meters was performed. The total ascent time for both deep stop and shallow stop dives was, therefore, the same (7 minutes). Post-dive Doppler bubbles detection showed that a deep stop partially replacing a shallow one increases bubble grade. It seems that the dissolved-gas model is dominant for the chosen dive profile with a negligible effect of free-gas in bubble formation (52).

The addition of deep stops to be safe should also require an increase in time at the shallow stop to offset the gas load of the slower tissues during the deep stop. The overall decompression time will therefore be longer (53).

M-values

The M-value is defined as the maximum "M" value of the absolute pressure of inert gas (nitrogen or helium) that a hypothetical tissue can tolerate at any given stop depth without symptoms of DCS; it is the limit for the maximum tolerable pressure gradient between inert gas tissue tension and ambient pressure. Faster half-time compartments tolerate higher supersaturation levels than slow ones (40), (54). This is because the supersaturation will last for less time in the faster tissues than in the slower tissues, thus reducing the physiological stress on the faster tissues and allowing for better tolerance.

In a typical "bounce dive," which is a relatively deep dive with a short bottom time, the faster tissues are the leading ones, being at or near saturation at the bottom depth. The slower tissues are only partially loaded. The fast tissues will control the initial ascent with the first stop determined for when the inert gas loading in the leading tissue is equal to or near its M-value (40), (53).

The graph in Fig. 7.5.3 shows the trend of M-values against tissue tension and ambient pressure (both as absolute). The M-value line represents the established limit for the tolerated overpressure gradient above the ambient pressure line. Two models of M-values are considered: Workman and Buhlmann (54).

Workman M-values: These M-values are in linear relation with depth and are numerically represented by the slope-intercept form of a linear equation. M_0 is the intercept value at zero depth (at sea-surface pressure), ΔM is the slope of the linear equation and represents the change in M-value with changes in depth pressure.

Buhlmann M-values: In this case, the linear equation intercepts a zero-pressure value. This is for mathematical reasons only. In general, the Buhlmann equation is of the type:

$$y = a + bx$$

$$a = \text{intercept at } P_{ambient}\ 0$$

$$b = 1/\text{slope}.$$

The resulting algorithm is based on considering 12 or 16 pairs of M-values for an equivalent number of compartments (ZH-12 or ZH-16).

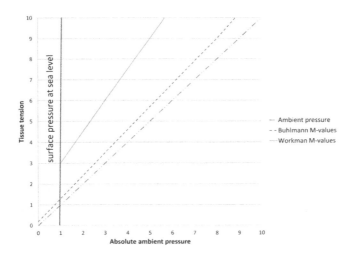

Fig. 7.5.3. Buhlmann and Workman M-value trends against ambient pressure (depth) and tissue tension.

The ZH-16 is divided into three subsets (A, B, C). The A set is for research only and has no application in diving. The B set is used in tables (where square dives are considered); the C set is used by the dive computer and aims to calculate more complex dive profiles (55).

Non-decompression M-values identify the tissues' tension limits that allow for immediate resurfacing at any time during the dive. Decompression M-values have a slope parameter that determines the change in M-value with a change in ambient pressure. Faster half-time tissues have a greater slope than slower half-time tissues tolerating more significant overpressure. A slope > 1 indicates that the compartment will tolerate greater overpressure gradients with increasing depth; a slope = 1 indicates that overpressure tolerance is independent of depth; a slope < 1 is not possible because this would indicate an intolerance to ambient (sea level) pressure that is illogical (54).

In Workman's equation the M-value line has a steeper gradient than Buhlmann's, with higher supersaturation allowed and reduced margin for safety (56).

In Fig. 7.5.3, the area between the ambient pressure line and the M-value line is the decompression zone; here, over-pressure is generated, allowing for tissue degassing. When breathing a high-PO_2 gas, a compartment can commence off-gassing even if its total inert gas partial pressure is below the ambient pressure. The decompression is controlled by the tissue that is closer to the M-value line (that represents the limit of supersaturation above which DCS risk is strongly increased); faster tissues will be the leading ones at the beginning of the decompression with slower tissues taking their role in sequence (54).

Gradient factor

Pushing the decompression to the limit of the M-values could result in an unacceptably high risk of DCS. A method for adding a degree of safety is to consider the "gradient factor" (GF). This factor defines the amount of inert gas supersaturation in the leading compartment from 0% (no supersaturation, thus no degassing) to 100% (supersaturation equal to the M-value of the tissue). GF can vary through the decompression. Its lowest value (GF-low) defines the deepest stop, and its maximum value (GF-high) identifies the accepted surfacing value of supersaturation (56).

Two examples of GF are presented in Fig. 7.5.4 (45):

- *15/85*: In this case, a deep stop is considered (GF-low 15), during which slow and intermediate tissues will intake gas; meanwhile, fast tissues will be off-gassing. A deep stop aims to reduce the micro-bubbles during the deepest phase of the ascent in an attempt to limit larger bubble formation that is considered to be aided by the presence of micro-bubbles acting as condensation seeds. Acceptable supersaturation at the surface (GF-high 85) is elevated, and therefore the safety buffer is reduced.
- *30/70*: Degassing during the ascent phase is reduced with a shallower first stop. Upon surfacing, the tissue supersaturation is 70% of the M-value. This profile is more conservative and requires a longer decompression time.

More recent research indicates that a low GF-low, which means deeper stops, is ineffective in reducing DCS risk. Symmetrical GFs, meaning equal value for GF-low and GF-high between 60/60 and 90/90, are considered safer regarding DCS risk mitigation. The values should be chosen based on the state of health of the diver (57), (58).

Changing GF values can extend or reduce the overall length of the decompression and also has a strong impact on the level of risk of DCS. Because several dive computers allow the user to fix the GF limits, it is important to clearly understand the factors affecting the decompression to define reliable safety margins.

As often happens in risk assessment, there is a trade-off between different risks. Longer decompressions reduce the DCS risk but expose the divers to higher environmental stressors during the prolonged decompression phase, requiring more gas. A reduced decompression period increases the risk of DCS but, under specific circumstances, could reduce the overall risk, limiting the divers' exposure to potentially hostile environmental conditions. As always, risk acceptance is personal and different divers may prefer different risk management strategies.

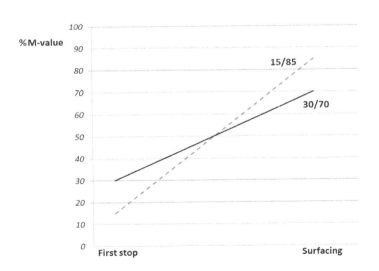

Fig. 7.5.4. Different M values will lead to different lengths of deep stops and/or shallow stops.

Oxygen window

The total tension of gasses in any given tissue is the result of the partial pressure of the different gas components. When breathing air, such partial pressures will include nitrogen, carbon dioxide, oxygen, and water vapor (59).

Gas in solution moves by diffusion from an area of higher partial pressure to an area of lower partial pressure. The diffusion rate for any given gas depends only on the partial pressure gradient of this gas (60).

The oxygen window is the inherent gas undersaturation of tissues due to the metabolic use of O_2. It varies with tissue metabolic rate and inspired PO_2 (40).

For a given quantity of O_2 being consumed, an equivalent quantity of CO_2 (80% of the used oxygen) is produced. Still, most of it is dissolved as bicarbonate in the blood and thus removed from the overall tissue gas partial pressure. The oxygen window opens when O_2 is removed from the arterial blood, but it is only partially replaced by CO_2 in the venous blood, leading to a drop in the overall gas tension (48), (60).

The non-metabolic gas (i.e., N_2 in air breathing) can move from the tissues into the venous blood, occupying the space left available by the drop in total gas tension due to the opening of the oxygen window (60).

Breathing gas with high PO_2 enhances the PO_2 gradient between arterial blood (considered in instantaneous equilibrium with the PO_2 in the alveoli) and tissues enlarging the oxygen window. Therefore, the inert gas elimination gradient is increased (48), (51).

Due to the shape of the oxygen saturation curve in arterial blood, when the arterial oxygen partial pressure exceeds 1600 mmHg, the oxygen window has reached its maximum value of 1400 mmHg; above this point, any further increase in PO_2 will not increase the oxygen window (Fig. 7.5.5). Oxygen toxicity limits the actual breathable PO_2 to much lower values (60).

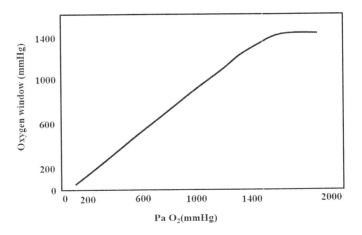

Fig. 7.5.5. Oxygen window against partial pressure of O_2

Higher PO_2 in the arterial blood allows more inert gas to dissolve, increasing gas washout. Inert gas can also be removed from already formed bubbles, reducing their volume (48).

Considering the effects of the oxygen window on inert gas bubbles, we can establish a relationship between the different partial pressures (59):

$$P_w = P_B - (P_{tisN_2} + P_{tisO_2} + P_{tisCO_2} + P_{tisU} + P_{H_2O})$$

P_w = Oxygen window

P_B = Barometric pressure

P_{tis} = Partial pressure of the given gas in the tissue (nitrogen N_2, oxygen O_2, carbon dioxide CO_2, other gases U and water vapor H_2O)

It is supposed that P_{tisN_2} is equal to the arterial partial pressure of nitrogen P_{AN_2} that is also equal to: $P_B - P_{AO_2} - P_{ACO_2} - P_{H_2O}$

Assuming $P_{tisU} = 0$ and that P_{O_2} and P_{CO_2} in the bubble equal their counterparts in the tissue and that total pressure in the bubble equals P_B:

$$P_w = P_B - (P_B - P_{AO_2} - P_{ACO_2} - P_{H_2O} + P_{tisO_2} + P_{tisCO_2} + P_{H_2O}) =$$

$$= P_B - P_B + P_{AO_2} + P_{ACO_2} - P_{tisO_2} - P_{tisCO_2} = P_{AO_2} + P_{ACO_2} - P_{tisO_2} - P_{tisCO_2}$$

O_2, CO_2, and H_2O equilibrate easily between the inside and outside of the bubble. P_{N_2} equals the total pressure inside the bubble minus the partial pressure of O_2, CO_2, and H_2O. P_{N_2} in blood and tissue is set by the blood/gas exchange of N_2 in the lungs, where P_{N_2} is lower than in the bubbles because O_2 in the alveolar gas is higher than in the tissues.

$$Pw = P_{bubbleN_2} - P_{AN_2}$$

Outgassing of N_2 caused by the oxygen window tends to increase P_{O_2}, P_{CO_2} and P_{H_2O}, but these gases permeate so rapidly that they do not build up pressure in the bubble, leading to a volume readjustment after any pressure change.

Long-term effects of deep diving on the skeletal system

A peculiar avascular bone necrosis called "dysbaric osteonecrosis" (DON) has been observed in individuals exposed to hyperbaric conditions for relatively long periods, such as tunnel workers who usually perform their job in a pressurized environment (the pressurization is needed to overcome the hydraulic load of the surrounding water table allowing the tunnel to stay dry until a proper water-tight sealing is established) and divers (61), (62), (63).

DON causes necrotic lesions in the fatty marrow containing shafts of the long bones and ball socket joints of hips and shoulders, leading to osteoarthritic changes (62), (64). The main affected bones are the femur, tibia, and humerus (61).

The causes of DON are not totally clear yet, although it is supposed that ischemic conditions are involved. It is plausible that DON is linked to the occurrence of micro-embolisms with disruption of the blood flow at the end of long bones (65). The location of DON supports this hypothesis, the most common sites for necrotic damage being the femoral shaft, head of the humerus, and head of the femur, all characterized by reduced venous drainage and, therefore, more exposure to blood stasis (61).

Decompression-induced physiological changes, including bubble formation, are generally accepted as causative mechanisms for DON, even if bubbles alone should not be sufficient, and other predisposing factors ought to be involved (62).

The aggregation of intravascular nitrogen emboli and the formation of inert gas bubbles in the bone marrow or in fat cells – causing a bone compartment syndrome or rupture of fat cells followed by fat embolism – can be causes of DON (66). Increased hypercoagulability due to increased levels of serum plasminogen activator inhibitor plays a key role in DON occurrence (65). Injured marrow adipocytes can release fat, thromboplastin, and other vasoactive substances, triggering intravascular coagulation (61). Fat droplets released into the bloodstream may result in catastrophic physical embolism and vascular obstruction (65). Levels of plasminogen activator inhibitor (PAT-1) above 38.0 mg/ml were predictors of DON, resulting in thrombus formation and contributing to the development of ischemia (62).

DON is often associated with Type-1 DCS, but the level of correlation is unclear (61), (66). Lipid degeneration has been linked to rapid decompression, with rupture of adipocytes releasing their contents to form large coalescent intracellular aggregates of fat bubbles that, combined with gas bubbles, may cause extravascular compression on blood vessels at juxta-articular areas of long bones (65). Rapidly expanding inert gas in the adipose tissue of the bone marrow can cause injury, triggering local and systemic intravascular coagulation (61). Even a small increase in intravascular pressure gradient above the systemic venous pressure may cause fat embolism (65). The risk of DON increases with longer bottom time and with deeper dives (64). Maximum diving depth below 35 meters ($\approx$115 ft) was a predictor for DON (62). Even a single exposure to fast decompression can trigger DON (67). Deviation from safe decompression procedures and former DCS injuries are the main factors involved in DON. Other risk factors are habitual alcohol intake and use of steroids (61).

Juxta-articular lesions represent 20% of DON lesions for divers and can lead to disabling arthritis, particularly of the femur head. Clinical symptoms include joint pain and can develop months or even years after exposure to hyperbaric conditions, making DON diagnosis even more difficult. Progression of

DON has been observed even after more than ten years without further hyperbaric exposure (61).

An investigation of 56 male divers showed a 55% rate of bone lesions, with a prevalence in proximal humerus and femur (62). In another study, DON incidence of 3% was identified in German military divers comparable with that of British (1.7%) and US Navy (2%) divers. A higher incidence of DON was detected in commercial and fishermen divers with up to 50% for Japanese fishermen with a history of DCS (66). DON incidence seems negligible in recreational divers, with only four cases reported worldwide (67). Screening of 198 compressed-air workers with three years of hyperbaric exposure between 1994 and 1997 showed a DON incidence of 15.2%; 63% of the lesions were on the knee joint at the proximal end of the tibia, 15% were at the hip joint at the proximal end of the femur (68). In a screening of 611 US Navy divers, the incidence of DON was quantified as (63):

- Saturation divers   3.1%
- Divers First Class   2.9%
- Helium divers   3.2%

Overall military divers are less prone to DON than commercial or professional fishermen, likely due to stricter controls on dive profiles and decompression schedules (66).

The DON risk perception among recreational divers is very limited or absent (67). Conservative profiles and the use of oxygen during decompression should reduce DON risk (64).

The impact of free radicals on enhancing cell death has possible amplifying effects on DON, and the use of free-radical scavenging agents has been proposed as a pharmacological approach (65). The use of anti-coagulants can also contribute to mitigating DON (62).

Long-term effects of DCS on the central nervous system

DCS can cause acute neurological dysfunction involving speech, hearing, and visual deficits, with permanent damage mainly to the spinal nerves. Bubbles associated with DCS may cause pathophysiological effects in different ways (69):

- *Indirectly*: Activation of biochemical pathways.
- *Directly*: Blood vessels blockage leading to ischemic hypoxia.
- *Mechanically*: Stimulation of nerves pathways.

Most neurological damage from DCS affects the spinal cord rather than the brain, mainly the white matter, where bubble formation has been observed to lead to neuron damage. Accumulation of damage over time may lead to long-term neurological deficit. For example, memory loss was associated with mixed-gas bounce dives performed by offshore commercial divers. Whether these issues happen only following DCS or whether repetitive exposure to hyperbaric conditions may also cause some sort of long-term neurological deficit is not clear. Currently, there is no evidence that diving without severe acute DCS causes any permanent neurological deficit (69).

Cardiovascular risk

The hyperbaric environment causes significant stress on the cardiovascular system with increased end-diastolic and systolic volumes and reduced ejection fraction. Enhanced total peripheral resistance caused by endothelial dysfunction increases cardiac work (36).

Several studies show that even a single dive may impair cardiac performance for up to two hours after surfacing, suggesting a right ventricular overload and an impairment of both right and left ventricular diastolic function (70).

The microcirculatory endothelial function shows signs of impairment soon after diving, with a transient enhancement at 24 hours after diving before finally returning to pre-dive levels. In particular, a reduction in flow-mediated dilation (FMD) was observed after a single dive for 30 minutes at 30 meters (100 ft); FMD returned to pre-dive values after three days at the surface with no further dives. It is observed that FMD is compromised by diving, even in the absence of DCS and with limited bubbles. No chronic effects are believed to be associated with this transient reduction in FMD. Endothelial function is also affected by increased hydrostatic pressure and oxidative stress during diving (48). The pre-dive ingestion of antioxidants, such as large doses of vitamin C, partially prevents this endothelial dysfunction with faster post-dive recovery of FMD (70).

The impairment of vascular function and vascular inflammation might be just a link in the chain of pathological changes triggered by DCS. An increase in microparticles (originating from cells fragments) triggering vascular changes, including elevation of vascular permeability, has been observed in divers. The increase in vascular permeability leads to hypovolemia and is commonly associated with DCS (48).

The endothelium may also be the source of micronuclei that allow for the formation of bubbles that will then enter the blood flow, enhancing the risk of DCS (36). Venous bubble can damage the pulmonary endothelium, which may result in pulmonary vasoconstriction, reducing the blood flow through the alveoli (70).

Gear damage

Deep diving is stressful not only for divers but also for diving gear. The increased ambient pressure makes flooding and even implosion more probable. The walls and lids of waterproof housing may inflect, compromising the integrity of water-tight seals. Under very high hydrostatic loads, housing and other air-filled gear may suddenly implode. An implosion of a battery pack can be dangerous for its mechanical impact and because some batteries, such as lithium-based batteries, may catch fire if exposed to water. External battery packs should be within reach of the diver and easy to jettison if needed.

One very exposed area is where cables enter water-tight containers. For example, the electric cable linking the head with the battery pack of an underwater light. The diver should avoid bending the cable close to its penetration point and prevent extreme stress on the cable by not pulling it.

In contrast, the increase in pressure may help the sealing of O-rings when correctly in place and well lubricated.

To limit the risk of damaging the gear, it is important to avoid using it below the maximum allowable depth and to always check the integrity of any seal.

When diving very deep, the environmental pressure can be so elevated that pneumatic tools (that work using a controlled flow of air) may not be fully functional because the hydrostatic load overcomes the pressure of the air source.

Risk identification and mitigation strategies

The risks associated with deep diving affect both the diver and the equipment, stemming from being exposed to a hyperbaric environment that poses high levels of physical stress. Even if some of the risks cannot be avoided, they can be mitigated by correct planning, appropriate procedures, and by using adequate diving gear.

- *Nitrogen narcosis*: There is a risk that nitrogen which is inert at sea-level pressure, may interfere with some neurological functions when breathed at hyperbaric pressure. Narcosis is very erratic regarding activation threshold and impact, even for the same diver under the same conditions, making accurate risk assessment difficult. Reducing the percentage of nitrogen in the mix (by using Nitrox or Trimix, depending on the planned maximum depths) and/or limiting the operative depth and dive time may reduce the onset of narcosis. Overlearning and the use of pre-arranged guidelines may mitigate the impact of narcosis, allowing divers to maintain a sufficient level of operative capacity.
- *Oxygen toxicity*: Breathing oxygen at hyperbaric pressure may cause CNS toxicity and lung inflammation. The best risk mitigation is to respect the MOD for the breathing gas used to maintain PO_2 below a defined threshold (usually 1.4 ata). Limiting exposure time also reduces the risk of pulmonary inflammation, that, in any case, is not a high-risk factor for scuba divers, given that the timeframe of a typical dive is shorter than the length of exposure needed to develop oxygen toxicity in the lungs.
- *DCS*: Multiple factors are linked to increased risk of DCS. The main factors are depth, length of the dive, and ascent speed. Limiting these factors strongly reduces the overall DCS risk.
- *DON*: Dysbaric osteonecrosis affects mostly divers exposed to extreme hyperbaric conditions and represents a long-

term permanent medical issue. The risk management of DON includes limiting the exposure to such extreme depths.

- *Permanent CNS damage*: DCS events can cause permanent damage to the CNS, affecting both higher mental functions and motor nerves. The risk mitigation is the same as for DCS – that is, following conservative dive profiles. Once a diver has experienced DCS, they are exposed to a higher risk of further DCS and potentially permanent neurological damage. In this case, a medical assessment is required to quantify the damage and identify the limit for future exposure.

- *Cardiovascular risk*: Diving is a physically demanding activity that requires a healthy cardiovascular system. To mitigate the associated risk, periodic medical checkups should be planned, and an active and healthy lifestyle should be followed.

Risk	Affected elements	Mitigation/avoidance strategies
Nitrogen narcosis	Divers	• Limit maximum depth. • Reduce the % of inert gas in the breathing gas.
DCS	Divers	• Follow conservative dive profiles. • Ascend slowly.
CNS oxygen toxicity	Divers	• Check oxygen % in the breathing gas. • Plan and respect MOD.
Lung oxygen toxicity	Divers	• Limit exposure to hyperbaric O_2.
Long-term CNS damage	Divers	• Avoid DCS. • Conservative dive profiles.
HPNS/DON	Divers	• Avoid extreme depth.
Cardiovascular damage	Divers	• Maintain fitness and good cardiovascular status. • Avoid over-exertion.
Gear implosion/flooding	Dive gear	• Respect MOD for the gear. • Lubricate O-rings and seals.

Lessons learned

- Deeper dives expose divers to an overall higher risk.
- Gases inert at ambient pressure have a strong physiological impact when breathed at depth.
- Nitrogen can affect the CNS, leading to narcosis, and will also dissolve in the tissues at depth, requiring specific procedures to avoid DCS.
- Diving imposes stress on the cardiovascular and respiratory systems, especially in deep dives.

- Long-term effects of deep diving are variable but can be relevant under specific circumstances, such as in saturation dives and in multiple deep bounce dives.
- Exposure to high pressure will increase the risk of gear implosion and damage.

References

1. **Bennet, P. and Rostain, J.C.** Inert gas narcosis. [book auth.] Bennet and Elliott. *Physiology and medicine of diving.* 2003.

2. **Behnke, A.R., Thomson, R.R. and Motle, E.P.** The psychologic effects from breathing air at 4 atm pressure. *American Journal of Physiology.* 1935, Vol. 112, pp. 554–558.

3. **Rostain, J.C. and Balon, N.** Recent neurochemical basis of inert gas narcosis and pressure effects. *UHM.* 2006, Vol. 33, 3, pp. 197–204.

4. *Nitrogen narcosis, the HPNS, and trimix.* **Rostain, J.C. and Balon, N.** 2004. P. Bennet Symposium.

5. **Kiessling, R.J. and Maah, G.H.** *Performance impairment as a function of nitrogen narcosis.* s.l. : NEDU, 1960. Research Report 3-60.

6. **Miles, S. and Mackay, D.E.** *Underwater medicine.* s.l. : Granada Publishing, 1976.

7. **Fowler, B.** Under influence: A performance guide to managing narcosis. 1991, Vol. 3.

8. **Clark, E.** Moving in extreme environments: Inert gas narcosis and underwater activities. *Estreme Physiology and Medicine.* 2015, Vol. 4, 1.

9. **Strauss, M.B. and Askenov, I.** *Diving Science.* s.l. : Human Kinetics, 2004.

10. **Hlastala, M. and Berger, A.** *Physiology of respiration.* Oxford : Oxford University Press, 2001.

11. **Bennett, P. and Schafstall, H.** The value of trimix 5 to conyrol HPNS. [book auth.] Y. and Shida, K. Lin. *Man in the sea.* San Pedro, CA : Best Publishing, 1990.

12. **Talpalar, A.** High pressure neurological syndrome. *Revue Neurologique.* 2007, Vol. 45, 10, pp. 631–636.

13. **Talpalar, A. and Grossman, Y.** CNS manifestations of HPNS: Revisited. *UHM.* 2006, Vol. 33, 3, pp. 205–210.

14. **Abraini, J., David, H., Vallee, N. and Risso, J.J.** Theoretical considerations on the ultimate depth that could be reached by saturation human divers. *Mecical Gas Research.* 2017, Vol. 6, 2, pp. 119–121.

15. **Bacharach, A.** *The high pressure nervous syndrome during human deep saturation and excursion diving.* Bethesda, MD : Naval Medical Research Institute, 1973.

16. **Torok, Z.** The compression strategy in the Alverstoke Deep Dives Series. [book auth.] Y. and Shida, K. Lin. *Man in the sea.* San Pedro, CA : Best Publishing, 1990.

17. **Logie, R. and Baddeley, A.** A trimix saturation dive to 660 metres: Studies of cognitive performance, mood and sleep quality. *Ergonomics.* 1982, Vol. 26, 4, pp. 359–374.

18. **Kangal, M. and Murphy-Lavoie, H.** High pressure nervous syndrome. *NCBI Bookshelf.*

19. **Russell, P., Ragnar, V. and Lembersten, C.** Development and evaluation of compression procedures form deep operational diving. [book auth.] Y. and Shida, K. Lin. *Man in the sea.* San Pedro, CA : Best Publishing, 1990.

20. **Kot, J.** Extremely deep recreational dives: The risk for carbon dioxide (CO2) retention and high pressure neurological syndrome (HPNS). *International Maritime Health.* 2012, Vol. 63, 1, pp. 49–55.

21. **Gardette, B., Lemaire, C., Rostrain, J. and Fructus, X.** The French Deep Diving Scientific Program on oxygen-helium, trimix and oxygen-hydrogen gas mixtures. [book auth.] Y. and Shida, K. Lin. *Man in the sea.* San Pedro, CA : Best Publishing, 1990.

22. **Rostain, J., Gardette-Chauffour, M., Lemaire, C. and Naquet, R.** Effects of a H2-He-O2 mixture on the HPNS up to 450 msw. *UBR.* 1988, Vol. 15, 4.

23. **Hempleman, H., Florio, J., Garrand, M., Harris, D., Hayes, P., Hennessy, T., Nichols, G., Torok, Z. and Winsborough, M.** UK deep diving trials. *Philosophical Transactions of the Royal Society of London.* 1984, Vol. 304, 118, pp. 119–141.

24. **Todnem, K., Nyland, H., Skeidsvoll, H., Svihus, R., Rinck, P., Kambestad, B.K., Riise, T. and Aarli, J.** Neurological long term consequences of deep diving. *British Journal of Industrial Medicine.* 1991, Vol. 48, pp. 258–266.

25. **Patel, D., Goel, A., Agarwal, S., Garg, P. and Lakhani, K.** Oxygen toxicity. *JIACM.* 2003, Vol. 4, 3, pp. 234–237.

26. **Bittreman, N.** CNS toxicity. *UHM.* 2004, Vol. 31, 1, pp. 63–72.

27. **Ledingrad, I.** *Hyperbaric oxygenation.* 1964.

28. **Jain, K.** *Textbook of hyperbaric medicine.* 5th edition.

29. **NOAA.** *NOAA diving manual.* 5th edition.

30. **Tetzlaff, K. and Thorsen, E.** Breathing at depth: Physiologic and clinical aspects of diving while breathing compressed air. *Clinics in Chest Medicine.* 2005, Vol. 26, 3, pp. 355–380.

31. **Bardin, H. and Lambertsen, G.J.** *A quantitative method for calculating cumulative pulmonary oxygen toxicity: Use of the unit pulmonary toxicity dose (UPTD).* Philadelphia, PA : Institute for Environmental Medicine; University of Pennsylvania, 1970.

32. **Baker, C.** *Oxygen toxicity calculations.* s.l. : Sheerwater.

33. **Harbin, L., Homer, D., Weatherspy, P.K. and Flynn, E.T.** *Predicting pulmonary O2 toxicity: A new look at the pulmonary toxicity dose.* s.l. : Naval Medical Research and Development Command.

34. **Butler, K.** *Central nervous system oxygen toxicity in closed-circuit scuba divers III.* s.l. : NEDU, 1986.

35. **Mitchell, S., Cronje, F., Meintjes, J. and Britz, H.** Fatal respiratory failure during a "technical" rebreather dive at extreme pressure. *Aviation, Space and Environmental Medicine.* 2007, Vol. 78, 2, pp. 81–86.

36. *Exercise and decompression.* **Richardson, R.** s.l. : Lang, Brubakk, 2009. The future of diving: 100 years of Haldane and beyond.

37. **Salama, A.** *Deep into deco.* s.l. : Best Publishing Company, 2015.

38. **Powell, M.** *Deco for divers.* s.l. : Aquapress, 2014.

39. **Wienke, B.** *Diving physics with bubble mechanics and decompression theory in depth.* s.l. : Best Publishing Company, 2008.

40. **Tikusis, P. and Gerth, W.** Decompression theory. *Bennett and Elliott's Physiology and Medicine of Diving.* 5th edition. 2003.

41. **Doolette, D., Gerth, W. and Gault, K.** *Redistribution of decompression stop time from shallow to deep stops increases incidence of DCS in air decompression dives.* s.l. : NEDU, 2011.

42. **Des, G.** *Decompression theory.* s.l. : Royal Australian Navy.

43. **Vann, R.D., Butler, F.K., Mitchell, S.J. and Moon, R.E.** Decompression illness. *Lancett.* 2011, Vol. 377, pp. 153–164.

44. **Toner, C. and Ball, R.** *The effect of temperature on decompression sickness risk: A critical review.* 2004. NRMC 2004-003.

45. *Gradient factors.* **Pollock, N.** 2015, Alert Diver Magazine.

46. **Buhlmann, A.** *Decompression and decompression sickness.* s.l. : Springer Verlag, 1984.

47. *Haldane still rules.* **Doolette, D.** s.l. : Lang, Brubakk, 2009. The future of diving: 100 years of haldane and beyond.

48. **Balestra, C. and Germonpre, P. (eds).** *The science of diving: Things your instructor never told you.* Saarbrucken, Germany : LAP Lambert Acdemic Publishing, 2014.

49. **Griffiths, L.** *A simple guide to decompression illness.* s.l. : Aquapress, 2010.

50. **Anderson, M.** *The physics of scuba diving.* Nottingham : Nottingham University Press, 2011.

51. **Hamilton, R. and Thalmann, E.** Decompression practice. *Bennett and Elliott's physiology and medicine of diving.* 5th edition. 2003.

52. **Schellart, N., Corstius, J.J., Germonpre, P. and Sterk, W.** Bubble formation after a 20m dive: Deep stop vs. shallow stop decompression profiles. *Aviation, Space and Environmental Medicine.* 2008, Vol. 79, pp. 488–494.

53. **Baker, E.** *Clearing up the confusion about "deep stops".*

54. —. *Understanding M-values.*

55. **Wild, W.** *Dive computers.* Berlin : GmbH, 2014.

56. **Anttila, M.** *Gradient factors.* s.l. : Dive Rite.

57. *Optimisation of gradient factor selection in military divers.* **De Ridder, S., Pattyn, N., Neyt, X. and Germonpre, P.** Prague : EUBS 2022, 2022.

58. **Longobardi, P.** Gradient factors: Come ottimizzarli. *Fondazione Mistral.* [Online] [Cited: December 20, 2022.] https://fondazionemistral.com/novita/gradient-factors-come-ottimizzarli/.

59. *The oxygen window and decompression bubbles: Estimate and significance.* **Van Liew, H., Conkin, J. and Burkard, M.** September, 1993, Aviation, Space and Environmental Medicine, pp. 859–865.

60. **Brian, E.** *The effect of hyperbaric oxygen on the oxygen window.* s.l. : GUE, 2004.

61. **Uguen, R., Pougnet, R., Uguen, A., Lodde, B. and Dewitte, J.D.** Dysbaric osteonecrosis among professional divers: A literature review. *UHM.* 2001, Vol. 41, 6, pp. 580–590.

62. **Miyashi, K., Kamo, Y., Ihara, H., Naka, T., Hirakawa, M. and Sugioka, Y.** Risk factors for dysbaric osteonecrosis. *Rheumatology.* 2006, Vol. 45, pp. 855–858.

63. **Harvey, C.A. and Sphar, R.L.** *Dysbaric osteonecrosis in divers.* s.l. : Naval Submarine Medical Research Laboratory, 1976. Report 832.

64. *Oxygen decompression may prevent dysbaric osteonecrosis in compressed air tunnelling.* **Ronson, L.** 2008. 3rd Conference US-Japan on Aerospace, Diving Physiology and Technology.

65. **Mahato, K.** Short update on dysbaric osteonecrosis: Concepts and decompression management. *Journal of the Bangladesh Society of Physiology.* 2015, Vol. 10, 2, pp. 76–81.

66. **Bolte, H., Koch, A., Tetzlaff, K., Bettinghausen, E., Heller, M. and Reuter, R.** Detection of dysbaric osteonecrosis in military divers using MRI. *European Radiology.* 2005, Vol. 15, pp. 368–375.

67. **Laden, M. and Grout, P.** Aseptic bone necrosis in an amateur scuba diver. *British Journal of Sport Medicine.* 2004, Vol. 38.

68. **Chen, W., Chen, S., Chan, W., Sun, H. and Lin, M.** *A prescriptive study of compressed air working environment and dysbaric osteonecrosis.* 1998. EUBS.

69. *Does diving destroy the brain?* **Daniels, S.** s.l. : Lang, Brubakk, 2009. The future of diving: 100 years of Haldane and beyond.

70. *Exercise, endothelium and diving phisiology.* **Dujic, Z.** s.l. : Lang, Brubakk, 2009. The future of diving: 100 years of Haldane and beyond.

7.6. HYPOXIA, HYPOXEMIA, AND CO$_2$

Chapter highlights

Hypoxia and hypoxemia are related. Hypoxia refers to decreased partial pressure of oxygen in the breathing gas. Decreased partial pressure of oxygen in blood is hypoxemia.

Oxygen is the gas needed for metabolic energy production. If its partial pressure drops below certain levels, then hypoxemia develops. The brain is the organ that requires most of the available oxygen to function and can be permanently damaged by even short periods of hypoxemia.

Hypoxemia may develop due to behavioral attitudes and as a consequence of physiological problems that affect the exchange of oxygen at the alveolar or cellular level. Divers are also exposed to the risk of hypoxia following dysfunction of their breathing systems; this may include O$_2$ sensors failure in rebreathers or the use of hypoxic mixes at the wrong depth.

Hypercapnia develops when the partial pressure of CO$_2$ in the blood and tissues rises to levels considered toxic for the human organism. Even small percentages of CO$_2$ contamination can have strong physiological consequences, leading to loss of consciousness or even death.

Precursor symptoms of CO_2 toxicity are variable, and often the individual cannot identify any anomaly until it is too late.

It has been noted that increasing CO_2 in the organism lowers the threshold for CNS oxygen toxicity due to the influence of CO_2 on cerebral blood flow.

Divers can develop habits that enhance the likelihood of hypercapnia; if this is associated with reduced sensitivity to increased levels of CO_2, the risk of CNS oxygen toxicity is strongly increased.

Introduction

Oxygen is the key element for metabolic energy production. Within the cells, carbohydrates, proteins, and fats are used to produce the energy-storage compound adenosine triphosphate (ATP); this oxidative reaction (known as aerobic metabolism) consumes O_2 and releases CO_2. Under insufficient O_2 availability, energy can still be produced by glycolysis (anaerobic metabolism), but its efficiency is less than one-tenth of that of aerobic metabolism; moreover, the byproduct of this anaerobic reaction is lactic acid, which is more difficult to eliminate than CO_2 (1). One molecule of glucose can generate 38 molecules of ATP through aerobic metabolism, but the same molecule can produce only 2 ATP molecules (via lactic acid production) in the absence of O_2 (anaerobic). The basal metabolic consumption of oxygen is about 200 ml/minute, but under a high workload, it can reach 3 liters/minute (2).

A diver who is working hard, for example, swimming against a strong current, may need a very high volume of oxygen and will produce a proportionally high volume of CO_2 that needs to be disposed of; this will lead to faster breathing and reduced duration of the gas reserve. An accurate evaluation of the level of work to be performed during the dive is needed to assess the associated risk of running out of breathing gas. Over-exertion is one of the main risks to which a working diver can be exposed.

One average adult breathing air at sea level has the following total levels of dissolved O_2 (2):

- *Lungs*: 450 ml
- *Blood*: 850 ml
- *Body fluids*: 50 ml
- *Myoglobin in muscles*: 200 ml

Dry air at nominal 760 mmHg has PO_2 159 mmHg; once inspired, some dilution occurs, and PO_2 drops to 149 mmHg; further dilution in the alveoli brings the PO_2 to 105 mmHg. Arterial PO_2 is about 100 mmHg, and venous blood has a PO_2 of about 40 mmHg. The difference in PO_2 between arterial blood and alveoli allows oxygen to flow from the alveoli into the surrounding capillaries (2).

Oxygen dissolves in blood according to Henry's law, and at normal arterial PO_2 of 100 mmHg, only 0.3 ml O_2 are dissolved in a dl of blood. This quantity is insufficient for sustaining metabolic demands; instead, a more efficient medium for transporting O_2 is hemoglobin, a complex molecule composed primarily of four polypeptide chains containing iron able to bind to O_2. A gram of fully saturated hemoglobin can carry 1.34–1.36 ml O_2. In a healthy individual breathing normal air at sea level, the hemoglobin approaches saturation. Considering both the dissolved O_2 molecules and those carried by the hemoglobin, the total O_2 content in arterial blood is about 20 ml/dl (1).

Hypoxemia

The brain, liver, and kidneys require the highest circulating O_2 for their metabolic needs. They are the first organs to be affected by hypoxemia, which is a drop in arterial PO_2 below 50–60 mmHg. At PO_2 of less than 40 mmHg, mental performance is severely impaired (2).

Becoming even slightly hypoxemic strongly increases the risk of fatal outcomes in divers because of its impact on mental capacity, leading to incapacitation of the diver, who becomes unable to react to the situation.

The typology of hypoxemia depends on the causes which have led to a reduction of the available oxygen supply to the organs (1), (2):

Hypoxemic hypoxemia

Includes all the conditions leading to a reduction in arterial PO_2; it is the most common in diving, and its leading causes are:

- *Inadequate oxygen supply*: Results from a decrease of PO_2 in the breathing gas.

Example: This can result from a diver using a hypoxic mix above its safe minimum depth or using a rebreather with a malfunctioning O_2 injection system. Both situations cause a reduction in PO_2 and the onset of hypoxia in the breathing medium.

- *Alveolar hypoventilation*: The amount of gas flowing in and out of the alveoli is reduced, and there is an associated CO_2 retention.

Example: This may happen in very deep dives due to the strongly increased density of the breathing gas, in drowning syndromes, and in extended breath-holding dives.

- *Ventilation-perfusion inequality and shunt*: Blood is not sufficiently oxygenated within the alveoli, and once it moves into the systemic circulation, it causes a drop in the available oxygen supply.

Example: Diving-related causes of this situation are pulmonary trauma/DCS, near drowning, and pulmonary O_2 toxicity.

- *Diffusion defect*: Slowed diffusion of oxygen through a thickened alveolar-capillary barrier.

Example: Can be the result of near-drowning or pulmonary O_2 toxicity.

Ischemic hypoxemia

The amount of O_2 delivered to any tissue equals the amount of blood perfusion multiplied by the differential between arterial and venous oxygen partial pressure. A reduction in blood perfusion leads to a PO_2 drop in tissues, meaning the O_2 used by metabolic activity is not sufficiently replenished.

Example: Syncope of ascent (inadequate cardiac output),

pulmonary barotrauma/DCS with associated emboli, and envenomation by marine life forms are some causes of such hypoxia in divers.

The human body has developed physiological mechanisms to react to hypoxic conditions. A reduction in arterial PO_2 stimulates chemoreceptors in the carotid artery to increase the body's respiratory rate. The activity of these organs increases when PO_2 falls to 50–60 mmHg and reaches its maximum at 20–35 mmHg. Further reduction in arterial PO_2 can cause decreased chemoreceptor stimulation, likely amplifying the detrimental effect of severe hypoxemia. Ventilation will accordingly increase, but severe hypoxemia will cause severe hypoxemic depression of the CNS, leading to decreased ventilation (1).

Divers in a hypoxemic state will be severely impaired and likely unable to act promptly, further aggravating their perilous situation. Accurate and reliable monitoring of the breathing mix is of the utmost importance to ensure that the correct levels of O_2 are maintained at every point during the dive. In open-circuit dives, this is guaranteed by pre-dive gas analysis and by respecting operative depths (mixes with less than 21% O_2 have to be used only below depths that ensure a minimal safe PO_2); in closed-circuit diving, the oxygen sensors must be calibrated and checked.

Diving equipment impact on hypoxia

The main risk of hypoxia is due to having the wrong O_2% in the breathing gas, leading to insufficient PO_2 to sustain life at the given environmental pressure.

The leading causes of such reduced PO_2 include:

- *Wrong gas switch at depth when using hypoxic mixes*: In this case, a cylinder that was to be used during a deeper phase of the dive is instead used at too shallow a depth to allow sufficient PO_2 considering the O_2% of the mix.
- *Loss of oxygen % in the stored gas*: This may happen when mixes are left for a long time within a cylinder that undergoes internal rusting. The oxidation reactions leading to rust formation will consume oxygen, and the overall O_2 content may drop to levels unsuitable for breathing.
- *Inadequate O_2 flow in CCR*: This is typical of constant flow CCR where the O_2 flux is calibrated based on the assumed metabolic needs of the diver. If the actual metabolic consumption of oxygen exceeds the planned rate, the mix can become hypoxic.
- *Oxygen dilution in CCR*: This may happen if the gas in the counter lungs becomes too diluted.
- *O_2 supply failure in CCR*: This can be due to solenoid malfunction, wrong sensor readings, or the O_2 cylinder being left closed.

These risks can be mitigated by an attentive pre-dive check, including breathing gas analysis, consistent use of checklists, and scheduled equipment maintenance.

CO_2 toxicity

The normal PCO_2 in the atmosphere at sea level varies between 0.23 and 0.30 mmHg. Our body produces CO_2 as a byproduct of cell metabolism in almost stoichiometric equilibrium with the used oxygen; the oxygen uptake and CO_2 production ratio is about 0.8 under normal circumstances, meaning that 10 volumes of O_2 are delivered to the cells for every 8 volumes of CO_2 produced. As a result, the PCO_2 in arterial blood is about 40 mmHg, compared with 46 mmHg in the venous blood. These values are not affected by any change in the surrounding environmental pressure and only result from metabolic reactions. About 200 ml CO_2 is produced every minute, and if this is not eliminated by respiration, PCO_2 will climb at a rate of 3–6 mmHg every minute in the arterial blood (1), (2). Under intense physical activity, CO_2 production can be significantly elevated, up to 4 liters/minute, and, if not properly removed, can lead to toxic effects. In some experiments using ergometer tests, an endpoint for CO_2 poisoning was found to be 71 mmHg (3).

At normal arterial PO_2, about 4% of the total blood CO_2 content is stored as carbamino compounds (bound to hemoglobin), accounting for 40% of the CO_2 exchange in the lungs. The vast majority of CO_2 storage is as bicarbonate, accounting for 90% of the total blood storage of CO_2 (1).

In normal healthy subjects, alveolar ventilation is regulated to maintain PCO_2 within the alveoli and the arterial blood at around 40 mmHg (4).

Within the physiological PCO_2 range of 25–50 mmHg, there is a linear relation between PCO_2 and CO_2 content (1).

CO_2 is the primary stimulus to respiration, acting on chemoreceptors located in the brain (medulla) and in the aortic bodies, and can trigger increased respiratory drive more quickly than a decrease in serum oxygen levels. These receptors react to an increase in arterial CO_2 and acidosis. The peripheral receptors (aortic) respond primarily to hypoxemia (low blood O_2 concentration) (2). The ventilation rate is susceptible to even small increases in arterial PCO_2 (1). If a diver breathes CO_2-contaminated gas while performing physical activity, the breathing rate can become very elevated, particularly when the inspired PCO_2 reaches 20 mmHg or more (5). This high breathing rate is not sustainable for long, and the diver will become exhausted. If hypoxia adds to hypercapnia, the resulting increase in ventilation is greater than the two separate effects simply added together (1).

When diving, the respiratory system is mechanically challenged by increased breathing effort, and as a result, the alveolar PCO_2 may increase, following two main mechanisms (6), (7):

1. *CO_2 retention*: A tendency to hypoventilate results in a mismatch between metabolic production and removal of CO_2 during the submerged activity. This trait is more prevalent in experienced and working divers.
2. *CO_2 building up*: This occurs due to impaired performance of the scrubber in closed- and semi-closed-circuit rebreathers, leading to an increase of CO_2 within the respiratory loop.

Diver's CO_2 retention is likely the result of increased static lung load caused by the surrounding increased hydrostatic pressure, increased gas density, increased metabolic production, and behavioral attitude such as skip-breathing (4).

Adding helium to the breathing mix reduces its density, allowing for a higher threshold for the flow speed within the lungs before becoming turbulent, causing enhanced respiratory resistance (8). The use of Trimix, therefore, has a positive effect on reducing the overall breathing effort, especially during deep dives.

At rest, a diver can tolerate an inspired PCO_2 up to 30 mmHg (equivalent to 4% CO_2 at sea level pressure); once the physical activity level increases, such tolerance decreases. A diver can produce up to 2 liters/minute of CO_2 for more than 30 minutes of intense activity and up to 3 liters/minute during short bursts of extreme effort (2). If this CO_2 is not promptly eliminated, toxicity may develop.

Increased PCO_2 reduces hemoglobin O_2 affinity by directly and competitively binding with hemoglobin and by the release of H+ following CO_2 hydration reaction that will also bind with hemoglobin, further limiting its availability for O_2 transport (1).

Alveolar and arterial PCO_2 are considered the same due to the fast equilibrium between alveolar gas and CO_2 dissolved in the circulating blood in the alveoli capillaries. A rise in CO_2 tension can be due to an increase in metabolic CO_2 production, or a reduction of alveolar ventilation, or a combination of the two (9):

$$P_A CO_2 = (VCO_2 / V_A) \times K$$

$$P_A CO_2 = \text{Alveolar/arterial } PCO_2$$

$$VCO_2 = \text{Metabolic } CO_2$$

$$V_A = \text{Alveolar ventilation}$$

$$K = \text{Constant}$$

A complete relation for the arterial/alveolar PCO_2 includes the inspired CO_2 pressure and the presence of dead space,(that are spaces of reduced ventilation where CO_2 accumuates) (5):

$$P_ACO_2 = P_ICO_2 + 863 \ (VCO_2 \ / \ V_A) \times (1 - V_D/V_T)$$

P_ACO_2 = Alveolar/arterial PCO_2

P_ICO_2 = Inspired PCO_2

863 = Corrective factor from STPD to BTPS

STPD = Standard temperature ($0°C$), pressure (1 atm), and dry (no water vapor) conditions

BTPS= Body temperature ($37°C$), pressure (1 atm), and saturated (water vapor) conditions

VCO_2 = Metabolic CO_2

V_A = Alveolar ventilation

V_D = Dead space volume

V_T = Tidal volume

Dead spaces are present in some parts of the diving gear, including the snorkel and the internal volume of diving helmets and full-face masks. For example, in a series of tests, the use of a full-face mask with no oro-nasal cup (that aims to reduce the dead space) showed an increase in ventilation up to 12% when performing a 100-watt equivalent exercise compared with a full-face provided with an oro-nasal cup (10).

CCR divers are exposed to higher respiratory effort than open-circuit divers due to the design of the breathing loop that does not have any facility for reducing the breathing effort, compared to an open circuit, where once the second stage is initiated, a slight overpressure enhances the gas flow (8).

Although hypercapnia (excess CO_2 in the blood) stimulates respiration and thus helps self-regulatory mechanisms, a sudden rise in PCO_2 may bypass premonitory signs, leading to sudden unconsciousness. Even a relatively small percentage of CO_2 in the breathing gas can generate an unacceptably high PCO_2 at depth (2).

This represents a serious risk in rebreather diving, where a failure in the CO_2 absorption system (scrubber) may cause a sudden spike in PCO_2 within the breathing loop, leading to sudden loss of consciousness and likely drowning. For open-circuit divers, a contaminated cylinder can be a source of CO_2 in the breathing medium.

Increase in the alveolar/arterial PCO_2 can lower the threshold of PO_2 for CNS toxicity effects (4). Increased PCO_2 causes cerebral vasodilatation that increases the blood flow through the neural tissues, leading to increased PO_2 in the brain tissues (3), (11), (12). At hyperbaric pressure, CO_2 may also increase the production of nitric oxide (NO), which also causes cerebral vasodilatation, further promoting higher PO_2 flow in the brain (12). A diver with a PCO_2 that is equal to or below the value equivalent to 2% CO_2 in the breathing medium at surface pressure (nominal 1 ata) and who dives within the US-Navy single-depth oxygen exposure limits will not significantly increase the risk of CNS toxicity (5).

In divers, there is a tendency to hypoventilate when under exercise; this can lead to the development of hypercapnia, increasing the risk for CO_2-adverse reactions, including CNS toxicity (4), (6), (7). In some individuals, this tendency is also associated with a general low sensitivity to CO_2, enhancing the risk of oxygen toxicity mainly when breathing mixes with high PO_2 such as Nitrox (11). A threshold of 25 mmHg has been identified as the minimum detectable PCO_2 for the average diver (12).

There are no clear-cut indicators for approaching PCO_2 limits; the diver has to rely on subjective sensations that can include increased rate/depth of breath, hunger for air, dizziness, headache, and a warm feeling; these symptoms have strong variation both inter-individual and intra-individual (6), (12).

Some symptoms have been associated with specific threshold levels in PCO_2 (7):

- Altered mental status $51 < PCO_2 < 52$ mmHg
- Tunnel vision and headache $60 < PCO_2 < 66$ mmHg
- Nausea and panicky sensation $PCO_2 > 61$ mmHg

These symptoms are not consistently experienced, making a clear and assured correlation of symptoms with limits of PCO_2 impossible.

When the inspired PCO_2 is around 15 mmHg (equivalent to 2% at 1 ata), maximal work capacity is reduced, especially if the increase in CO_2 is associated with augmented respiratory resistance. Breathing CO_2 equivalent to 6% at 1 ata or above 51 mmHg causes impaired mental processes, and if breathing resistance is suddenly increased, this can result in immediate loss of consciousness (5), (7).

Respiratory sensitivity to CO_2 is reduced in the presence of increased resistance to breathing; once CO_2 toxicity has developed, active ventilation becomes ineffective, leading to exhaustion of respiratory muscles with further increase of PCO_2 and finally unconsciousness (9). In one experimental study, it was observed that only 34% of the subjects were able to detect an inspired PCO_2 below or equal to 27 mmHg; after some specific training, this rose to 90% (6).

Divers who both tend to hypoventilate and have reduced sensitivity to increased levels of CO_2 are at most risk for CNS toxicity. The so-called CO_2 retainers have an end-tidal $CO_2 > 69$ mmHg when inhaling PCO_2 of 42 mmHg, and this can be even more relevant in deep dives where high levels of CO_2 can go unnoticed due to the high level of tissue oxygenation linked to the high PO_2 in the breathing mix (12).

Overall, it is important to avoid even modest CO_2 contamination of the breathing gas. For example, inhaling just 2% CO_2 requires an increase in ventilation of 61% to maintain the alveolar/arterial PCO_2 within 40 mmHg; when breathing under pressure, the increase in ventilation is limited by a series of factors (gas density, hydrostatic loads, equipment resistance) and therefore PCO_2 in the organism can reach dangerous levels (7).

The principal risks of CO_2 toxicity in diving are (2):

- *Failure of the scrubber in the rebreather*: This will cause CO_2 levels in the breathing loop to rise above tolerable limits.
- *CO_2 build-up in equipment dead spaces*: This can affect diving helmets that are not adequately ventilated or can be due to improper gear, such as too long and too narrow snorkels.
- *Inadequate ventilation*: This can result from some pathology affecting the lungs' ventilatory capacity or can be a consequence of bad practices such as skip-breathing in an attempt to save breathing gas.
- *Gas contamination*: CO_2 could be present in the breathing gas due to contamination during the filling procedures.

- *Physiological issues*: Some individuals tend to retain higher levels of CO_2.

Risk identification and mitigation strategy

The development of hypoxia and CO_2 poisoning leads to extremely dangerous conditions for the divers with potentially fatal outcomes. The real impact is likely underestimated due to the difficulties in identifying CO_2 poisoning in post-mortem investigation (8). Therefore, assessing the risk and identifying reliable and practical mitigation procedures is mandatory.

Another risk is associated with breathing a gas mix that does not include any oxygen, for example, from cylinders used to fill a drysuit with argon. These cylinders must be clearly marked as "non-breathable," Under no circumstances should they be connected to a regulator with a second stage.

Risk	Affected elements	Mitigation/avoidance strategies
Hypoxic gas	Divers mostly at shallow depth	• Analyze O_2 content before using the gas. • Identify the operative depth for the gas. • Clearly mark cylinders' content and their operative depth.
Anoxic gas	Divers	• Never connect second-stage regulator to cylinders that do not contain breathable gas.
Reduced O_2 level in the gas	Divers	• Analyze O_2 content before using the gas. • Always use "fresh" cylinders.
Loss of O_2 feed in CCR	Divers	• Bring and use bailout. • Regular maintenance. • Monitor O_2 values in the breathing loop.
CO_2 contamination	Divers	• Use reliable compressors for filling.
CO_2 build-up	Divers	• Use proper breathing gear. • Avoid breath-skipping. • Avoid over-exertion.
Sudden CO_2 increase in CCR	Divers	• Proper packaging of chemical scrubber to avoid "channeling."

Lessons learned

- Divers under high workload need a large amount of oxygen to satisfy their metabolic needs. If respiration cannot match such demands, then hypoxemia may develop.
- The diving environment and the diving breathing gear put stress on the respiratory system, and this, in turn, enhances the risk of hypoxemia and hypercapnia.
- Even small CO_2 contamination of the breathing gas could cause strong respiratory distress and unsafe buildup of CO_2 partial pressure at alveolar and cellular levels.
- Higher levels of CO_2 reduce the threshold for CNS oxygen toxicity, increasing the risk for the divers, especially if hyperoxic mixes (Nitrox) or high PO_2 are used.
- Increase of PCO_2 can go unnoticed by the divers until dangerous levels are reached with potential sudden loss of consciousness or CNS oxygen toxicity.

References

1. **Hlastala, M. and Berger, A.** *Physiology of respiration.* Oxford : Oxford University Press, 2001.

2. **Edmonds, C., Bennett, M., Lippman, J. and Mitchell, S.** *Diving and Subaquatic Medicine.* 5th edition. s.l. : CRC Press, 2016.

3. **Donald, K.** *Oxygen and the diver.* 1992.

4. **Pendergast, D.R., Lindholm, P., Wylegala, J., Warakander, D. and Lundgren, G.** Effects of respiratory muscle training on respiratory CO2 sensitivity in scuba divers. *UHB.* 2006, Vol. 33, 6.

5. **Knafel, E.** *Physiologic basis for CO2 limits within semi-closed and closed-circuit underwater breathing apparatus.* s.l. : NEDU, 2000.

6. **Eynan, M., Daskalovic, Y., Arieli, Y., Arieli, R., Shpak, A., Eilender, E. and Kerem, D.** Training improves divers' ability to detect increased CO2. *Aviation Space and Environmental Medicine.* 2003, Vol. 74.

7. **Shykoff, B. and Warkander, D.** Exercise carbon dioxide (CO2) retention with inhaled CO2 and breathing resistance. *UHM.* 2012, Vol. 39, 4.

8. **Kot, J.** Extremely deep recreational dives: The risk for carbon dioxide (CO2) retention and high pressure neurological syndrome (HPNS). *International Maritime Health.* 2012, Vol. 63, 1, pp. 49–55.

9. **Mitchell, S., Cronje, F., Meintjes, J. and Britz, H.** Fatal respiratory failure during a "technical" rebreather dive at extreme

pressure. *Aviation, Space and Environmental Medicine.* 2007, Vol. 78, 2, pp. 81–86.

10. **Warkander, C. and Lundgren, D.** Dead space in the breathing apparatus; interaction with ventilation. *Ergonomics.* 1995, Vol. 38, 9.

11. **Arieli, R., Ariely, Y., Maskalovic, Y., Eyanan, M. and Abramovich, A.** CNS oxygen toxicity in closed-circuit diving: Signs and symptoms before loss of consciusness. *Aviation Space and Environmental Medicine.* 2006, Vol. 77, 11, pp. 1153–1158.

12. **Eynan, R., Arieli, R. and Adir, Y.** Response to CO2 in novice closed-circuit apparatus divers and after one year of active oxygen diving at shallow depths. *Applied Physiology.* 1985, Vol. 98, 5.

7.7. FATIGUE

Chapter highlights

Fatigue is a state of extreme tiredness due to the over-coming of our resistance. Being fatigued strongly impairs mental and physical performance and is one of the leading causes of accidents and mishaps.

The diving environment can cause fatigue in a relatively short time because of its characteristics, such as cold, water resistance against the diver's movement, and increased respiratory effort.

The impact of fatigue on cognitive function can be compared to that of alcohol; a fatigued diver will have reduced situational awareness and will be slower in reacting to unforeseen events.

Sleep deprivation and de-synchronization of the circadian rhythm are the primary sources of fatigue. This can affect divers traveling through multiple time zones to reach their destination.

Good rest before diving is mandatory to ensure safe and enjoyable dives. Post-dive fatigue is frequently associated with lengthy or strenuous dives and following extended decompression; using Nitrox may be beneficial in reducing the decompression obligations. Indeed, reduced fatigue has often been reported by divers using Nitrox.

Introduction

We are all humans, so we have some unavoidable physical limits. One of these is that we are affected by fatigue when the working load overcomes our capacity. When operating in demanding environments, such as during diving, our body is pushed more quickly to its natural limits, and fatigue may settle within a relatively short time.

A feeling of tiredness is not necessarily correlated with loss of performance; motivation can offset fatigue, at least temporarily. Fatigue can generally correlate with the number of duty hours irrespective of the amount of work done (1).

For divers to properly assess their fatigue risk, the overall "on duty" time should be considered, not only the actual dive time. For example, divers often spend long hours traveling to their dive destination, and additional time is spent preparing their gear. All of this will add to the general level of fatigue. On the other hand, the usually strong motivation and excitement linked to diving will often partially offset fatigue, allowing for good performance. Despite this, a limit will be reached sooner or later, and some rest will eventually be needed.

Fatigue is a physiological reaction to protect our body from overworking and potential injuries. It is almost impossible to measure its impact accurately, and it is also very difficult for us to be aware of even our fatigue (2).

It should be noted that psychological factors influence physical fatigue, and the reaching of the exertion threshold is often due to a psychological boundary rather than a physiological limit (1).

Fatigue can affect performance by overuse of the available resources, a loss of effort in activating such available resources, or a combination of the two. Motivation seems to offset fatigue up to a certain level, and well-learned/simpler tasks are more resilient to fatigue than newly acquired skills and more complex cognitive performance (3). Vigilance is also negatively affected by fatigue, with impairment in attention and reaction times to stimuli becoming irregular. Alternating different tasks reduces the onset of fatigue (1).

Divers need to be continuously vigilant of multiple parameters during the dive; repeating these same tasks can build up fatigue in multiple dives. For this reason, appropriate breaks should be planned between the dives, and, in case of several days of diving activity, some days off should also be considered.

Fatigue strongly affects safety; it is estimated that around 80% of transportation accidents are due to fatigue-induced human errors, mainly occurring between 3 am and 7 am when the physiological levels of arousal are at their minimum (4). In seafarers, 33% of personal injuries and between 11% and 23% of collisions and groundings are linked to fatigue, with an up to 50% reduction in situational awareness (5).

US Navy divers indicate that fatigue is the second most common cause of diving accidents (6). A fatigued diver is less alert and can make mistakes that otherwise would have been avoided.

In general, fatigued individuals tend to develop a significant degree of negligence, and an increase in their willingness to take chances and cut corners to avoid further effort, even if this leads to riskier behavior (1).

Circadian rhythms have been identified in various biological functions, including body temperature and mental efficiency. These cycles are often linked together, such as peaks in body temperature and performance. If a desynchronization of the cycles happens, then a feeling of malady and a drop in efficiency may result. Individual differences account for different habits, with some people being more efficient early in the morning and others late at night (7).

Fatigue has more of an impact during the nadir of the circadian rhythm (2–8 am) than when the cycle is at its peak (6–10 pm) (3). Complex operations, such as flying an aircraft, show the worst decrement in performance between 3 and 6 am (2). The importance of biological rhythms is highlighted by the average individual requiring up to seven days to adjust to working night shifts (6). In a study of night-shift workers, 20% reported falling asleep on the job, with a concurrent increased risk of accidents (8).

Jetlag can also affect the circadian rhythm; for this reason, a diver who has traveled through multiple time zones should be aware of their potentially reduced capacity due to the temporary offsetting of the circadian cycles and the need to adapt to new environmental conditions, such as when changing climate zones (2), (8), (9). The main impact of jetlag is within the first two days of arrival in the new time zone (7). Following the natural cycles of the arrival zone as soon as possible allows for a faster resetting of the biological clock. The average speed of adjustment is about one day for each hour of time change.

Divers should consider the impact of jetlag on their biological cycles, allowing for time to re-synchronize the internal clock before beginning complex and demanding underwater operations (10).

Causes of fatigue

Fatigue can be divided into three main typologies (6), (11):

1. *Acute fatigue*: Produced by a single episode of physical exertion and/or sleep loss. An individual usually recovers from this type of fatigue within a single period of undisturbed sleep.
2. *Cumulative fatigue*: Caused by multiple days (three or more) of working above comfort level and/or sleep loss (sleeping less than six hours) over consecutive nights. Multiple days of rest and full-sleep nights are required to recover from this type of fatigue.
3. *Chronic fatigue*: Fatigue that does not recover with rest and often indicates an underlying medical condition.

Sleep deprivation is the main impact factor on the onset of fatigue and subsequent loss of performance. Acute sleep loss with fewer than four hours of rest per night causes a quick deterioration of an individual's performance and an increase in lapses which become common after 16 hours of continuous wakefulness. A sleep deprivation study observed that sleeping less than the ideal 8.2 hours/night (but not less than 7 hours/night) allowed an individual to maintain good performance levels for over 14 consecutive days (11). After 24 hours without sleep, a reduction of 25% in performance is likely to happen (9). Sleep quality can be affected by noise, motion, and other environmental factors, so even if an individual sleeps an adequate number of hours, a sense of fatigue may develop if the quality of this sleep is poor (5). Constant sleep deprivation cannot be compensated for, even if napping can reduce the rate of fatigue-related mishaps by up to 50%. The use of stimulants to offset fatigue should be carefully limited and controlled (2), (6), (12).

Divers on live-aboard vessels can be exposed to low-quality sleeping environments due to the vessel's motion, noise, and crowded sleeping quarters. If possible, divers should be allowed to rest onshore properly after some days at sea. This should be considered when planning for complex operations requiring multiple days of diving.

The onshore breaks will also positively affect morale, allowing the divers to rejoin family members and friends. Such leaves were employed during the long and demanding operations required to salvage the submarine USS Squalus (13).

Longer working hours clearly cause more fatigue and require adequate periods of rest. Recovery from an 84-hour working week (12 hours/day for seven consecutive days) takes around three days (11).

Professional divers can be exposed to long working hours due to the requirements of organizing a diving operation (organizational meetings, preparing the material, loading and offloading, early departures, etc.). Still, recreational divers should also be aware that diving after a strenuous working week may expose them to a higher risk of fatigue-induced errors.

Environmental stressors such as cold, noise, extreme motion, and multi-tasking make fatigue more evident (5), (12).

As divers, we are exposed to several of such stressors: diving in cold water causes significant losses of heat, increasing the feeling of fatigue; when diving from a boat, we are subjected to high levels of motion and/or noise from the engines; and multi-tasking is quite common during a dive, being necessary to monitor a variety of elements. Therefore, it is mandatory to be well-rested before any diving activity to offset and delay the impact of the stressors as much as possible.

Impact of fatigue

The effects of fatigue have been likened to those of alcohol (9), (12). More complex actions that require particular sets of skills will see a general deterioration in performance. Tunnel vision may develop, disintegrating the overall pattern of action into separate components and losing the operator's reliability (1).

Fatigue impairs both mental and physical capacity (6):

- *Cognitive effects*: Loss of situational awareness and decision-making capacity with reduced ability to cope with rapid changes in the operative environment.
- *Behavioral effects*: Increased irritability and decreased tolerance of stressors, with a tendency toward forgetfulness.
- *Communication effects*: Speech is less expressive and articulate; the individual can struggle to understand even simple messages.
- *Motor skills effects*: Loss of coordination, poor timing in actions.
- *Physical effects*: feeling colder than normal, experiencing a sense of starvation, or, on the other extreme, not feeling the hunger stimulus. One can also feel extremely weak and dizzy.

These effects can be highly debilitating for divers who must be mentally and physically in good shape to perform with proficiency and safety. A tired diver will be more exposed to the risk of mishaps, team communication will be reduced, and the impact of the physical stressors associated with the diving environment will be increased.

Increased susceptibility to nitrogen narcosis and cold and increased risk of mishaps due to impaired mental ability and motor skills have been linked to fatigue in divers (6). Tests show that diving can alter the cognitive function of divers, with increased mental fatigue, sustained attention reduction, and response time (14).

In divers, post-dive fatigue is sometimes reported and can be related to one or a combination of the following diving events (15):

- Heavy physical activity during the dive.
- Thermal stress due to cold water.
- Decompression stress.
- Exposure to high PO_2 as demonstrated during hyperbaric chamber trials.
- Anxiety.
- Seasickness.

During a dive, up to 700 ml of blood is shifted from the peripheral circulation to the core in response to the increased ambient pressure, cold-induced vasoconstriction, and buoyancy effects on blood circulation. This increased blood flow is sensed as elevated blood pressure by the kidneys, which in an attempt to lower the pressure, causes increased urine production (diuresis). In the post-dive phase, the dehydration attributed to diuresis and the return of the blood to a normal distribution may cause a sense of sudden fatigue (15).

Extreme diving situations, such as saturation dives, expose divers to very high stress and fatigue levels. A study in hyperbaric chamber simulated saturation dives to 150, 180, and 230 meters of depth for about 16 days of total time showed alterations to the sleeping patterns of participants, with a decrease in the deep sleep stages, increased number of wakes, and a general sense of fatigue (16).

Nitrox and fatigue

Nitrox has often been associated with reported reduced fatigue by divers, but no medical explanation is available. On the contrary, the increased oxidative effect of breathing oxygen-enriched gas ought to be a source of fatigue (17).

Tests in hyperbaric chambers and during actual dives are inconclusive regarding the effectiveness of breathing Nitrox for reducing post-dive fatigue. In some cases, no difference between using air and Nitrox was noted; in other situations, an increase in fatigue after breathing high-percent oxygen gas was reported (15), (17). The only objective result is an increase in alertness in Nitrox divers (18). A study involving 12 divers breathing a 40% O_2 Nitrox mix showed a reduction in gas consumption rate when performing strenuous exercises compared to breathing air (19).

An advantage of using Nitrox is the extended no-deco time compared to air; this in turn will reduce decompression-related stress and nitrogen narcosis. These positive effects could be related to the feeling of reduced fatigue reported by several Nitrox divers.

Risk identification and mitigation strategies

As divers, we must be careful of fatigue's impact on our capacities, particularly regarding loss of situational awareness and reduced ability to react in emergencies. Adequate rest periods should be clearly identified and respected within multi-day diving plans.

Risk	Affected elements	Mitigation/avoidance strategies
Acute fatigue	Divers and surface crew	• Reduce workload. • Allow for a period of undisturbed sleep.
Cumulative fatigue	Divers and surface crew	• Reduce workload. • Increase available daily sleeping time. • Allow for a few days of rest.
Chronic fatigue	Divers and surface crew	• Look for medical advice.
Loss of circadian rhythms	Divers and surface crew	• Allow time for adaptation to the new time zone. • Avoid frequent changes in shifts (night-shifter should stay on nights and day-shifter on mornings if feasible).
Post-dive fatigue	Divers	• Reduce workload. • Use Nitrox. • Limit decompression time. • Allow for recovery periods.
Low quality of sleep	Divers and surface crew	• Create a quiet environment for sleeping. • Schedule onshore days during extended operations at sea.
Loss of focus	Divers and surface crew	• Overlearning of skills. • Enforce checklists to reduce slips and lapses. • Cross-checking.

Lessons learned

- Being fatigued strongly affects performance with reduced mental and physical capacity.
- Divers are exposed to environmental stressors, such as cold water and the resistance of moving through a dense medium, that can enhance fatigue.
- Breathing Nitrox seems to offset fatigue partially, but no scientific explanation of this effect is available.
- Adequate rest should be part of any dive plan, especially when planning multiple and/or intense dives.
- To partially offset the loss of attention due to fatigue, over-learning of skills, use of checklists, and reciprocal monitoring should be enforced.

References

1. **Holding, D.** Fatigue. [book auth.] G. Hockey. *Stress and fatigue in human performance.* New York : John Wiley and Sons, 1983.

2. **Beaty, D.** *The naked pilot: The human factor in aircraft accidents.* s.l. : Airlife, 1995.

3. **Staal, M.** *Stress, cognition and human performance: A literature review and conceptual framework.* Washington, DC : NASA, 2004.

4. **USCG.** *Team coordination training student guide.* s.l. : USCG, 1998.

5. **Smith, A., Allen, P. and Waddsworth, E.** *Seafarer fatigue.* Cardiff : The Cardiff Research Programme, Centre for

Occupational and Health Psychology, Cardiff University, 2006.

6. **O'Connor, E.** *A Navy diving supervisor's guide to the non-technical skills required for safe and productive diving operations.* Panama City, FL : NEDU, 2005.

7. **Palmer, J.D.** *The living clock.* Oxford : Oxford University Press, 2002.

8. **Kryger, M. and Zee, P.** *Sleep-wake cycle: Its physiology and impact on health.* s.l. : National Sleep Foundation, 2006.

9. **Murphy, J.** *Fatigue management during operations: A commander's guide.* Canberra, Australia : Australian Defence Force, 2002.

10. **Lock, G.** *Under Pressure.* 2019.

11. **Spencer, M.B., Roberts, K.A. and Folkard, S.** *The development of a fatigue/risk index for shiftworkers.* s.l. : HSE, 2006. Reasearch Report 446.

12. **Gregory, D. and Shanahan, P.** *The human element: A guide to human behavior in the shipping industry.* s.l. : RCA-TSO Crown Copyright, 2010.

13. **Maas, P.** *The terrible hours.* 2001.

14. **Pourhashemi, S., Sahraei, H., Meftahi, G., Hatef, B. and Gholipour, B.** The effect of 20 minutes scuba diving on cognitive function of professional scuba divers. *Asian Journal of Sports Medicine.* 2016, Vol. 7, 3, pp. 1–5.

15. *Air, nitrox and fatigue.* **Nochetto, M.** 2014, Alert Diver.

16. **Seo, Y., Matsumoto, K., Mohri, M., Matsuoka, S. and Park, K.** Changes in sleep patterns during He-O2 saturation

dives. *Psychiatry and Clinical Neurosciences.* 1998, Vol. 52, 2, pp. 141–142.

17. **Florian, J.** *Rapid recovery: Research fights cardio, muscolar fatigue in Navy divers.* s.l. : NEDU, 2015.

18. **Lafele, P., Balestra, C., Hemelryck, W., Donda, N., Sakr, A., Tahem, A., Maroni, S. and Germonpre, P.** Evaluation of critical flicker fusion frequency and perceived fatigue in divers after air and enriched air Nitrox diving. *DHM.* 2010, Vol. 40, 3, pp. 114–118.

19. *Influence of elevated oxygen fraction on breathing gas consumption during physical workload in shallow water submersion.* **Schipke, J., Moeller, F., Jacobi, E., Muth, T. and Hoffman, U.** Tel Aviv : s.n., 2019. EUBS 2019.

8. CHECKLISTS

Chapter highlights

Checklists were developed in aviation to reduce the memory workload of the cockpit crew.

Several structured methods for completing a checklist offer varying degrees of redundancy.

Written checklists strongly facilitate the correct execution of complex operations, acting as a step-by-step guide.

As with other human actions, checklists are not immune from potential errors, and preventive behaviors should be adopted. The most important is to avoid distraction while calling out the checklist items.

Divers can strongly benefit from pre-dive checklists, whose use has been shown to reduce the incidence of mistakes.

Introduction

The idea of using checklists to assist in complex operations was first developed in 1935 following the fatal crash of an experimental model of a new Boeing bomber (that became the famous B-17) due to a command lock left in place by the pilots, preventing the elevators and rudder from functioning once airborne. The introduced checklist aimed to reduce the task load on the pilots, who, in this way, would not need to rely on their memory to check the multitude of systems required for controlling multi-engine aircraft that had become far more complex than the first simple single-engine planes used in early aviation (1).

The main objectives of adopting a checklist are (2):

- Aiding the operator in configuring the system.
- Presenting standard procedures to be followed.
- Providing a logical and convenient sequence of operations.
- Allowing mutual supervision by cross-checking.
- Sharing awareness of status at team level.
- Optimizing team workload and roles.

Time pressure, environmental, physiological, and psychological stressors, and the inherent fallibility of human memory often can cause the overlooking of critical operative steps, leading to potential failure modes and possible accidents. Moreover, a level of complacency may foster a cavalier attitude in skipping controls and procedures on the false assumption that because this behavior has not caused harm in the past, it is acceptable. This decisional bias is often called "normalization of the deviance," meaning that violating standard procedures becomes a habit by our thinking that a course of action was correct even if, in reality, it was not. We succeeded only by several factors that somehow mitigated our wrong decision (3).

The development of checklists protects against these dangers, requiring the operator to follow a structured procedure of controls and actions (4).

Divers are exposed to an elevated stress level operating in a complex environment and relying on a series of artificial life-support systems that must be set appropriately and correctly used to ensure survival in such potentially hostile situations. Using checklists can strongly reduce the load on the memory and allows for a more consistent approach to standardized controls and procedures.

Typology of checklists

There are different typologies of checklists; each will work better in specific scenarios than others (5):

- *Generic list*: Items are grouped into categories with no specific order within the list.

A typical use of this model is the equipment checklist; the various gear is checked off without any specific preference of order. A diver can use this checklist when assembling and/or packing the diving gear. For example, fins, diving suit, hood, gloves, and mask could be grouped in one section of the checklist; regulators, BCD, dive computer, weigh system, and cylinders could be in another section, and so on. The idea is to have items grouped together based on their logical belonging to a category. This will make following the checklist easier.

- *Sequential*: The order, sequence, and flow of items are relevant for the outcome.

This is used as procedural checklist. A diver can use this model when assembling the diving gear because a logical sequence of actions should be followed. For example, the BCD must usually be connected to the cylinder before the regulators.

- *Iterative*: Items, tasks, and criteria require repeated review.

Divers can use this style during the pre-dive cross-checks that require dive buddies to verify each other's configurations before entering the water. With this method, the checklist is repeated twice with enhanced redundancy.

- *Diagnostic*: Follows a flowchart style.

This can be used by divers to troubleshoot diving gear or to manage unusual and/or complex situations, such as during a first aid assessment.

Another important distinction is between checklists used during normal operations and checklists used during emergencies and/or systems malfunctions (2), (6), (7), (8), (9):

- *Normal checklist*: Describes a series of actions to be performed under normal operational conditions. The checklist provides guidance for standard configurations as a sequential framework aimed at optimizing workload, enhancing teamwork, and allowing for cross-checking and quality control. These checklists are effective when a series of conditions are respected, including:

  o Time is not critical.
  o The series of tasks is too long to be committed to memory.
  o The environment physically allows the use of the checklist.

A normal checklist can be used by divers as a guide in assembling the diving gear (mostly if more complex configurations are needed and/or the divers do not have much experience), conducting the pre-dive checks and final assessment at the surface, and/or the safety drills in shallow water before proceeding with the descent. In all these situations time is not critical, the checklist can be physically used, for example, in the form of a slate, and tasks can be followed with a pre-planned sequence that does not need to be recalled from memory. A typical use of this type of checklist is when preparing a rebreather for a dive; a series of steps are provided by the manufacturer to be followed (10), (11).

- *Emergency checklist*: Used during system malfunction and/ or emergency situations as a memory prompt to ensure that all critical actions follow a standardized response sequence.

An emergency checklist enhances team performance and coordination under high workload and stressful conditions. When time is critical, emergency procedures should be embedded in the procedural memory of the operators. The checklist is used after the actions are performed to confirm their correctness. If time is not critical, these checklists can be developed as a flowchart or decision tree to be followed step-by-step. Creating an effective emergency checklist involves considering its accessibility and readability, providing critical elements in a concise form, responding to specific problems, and assisting in managing the overall system. Finally, it should be recognized that they will be used under high-stress conditions. Despite our best efforts, emergency checklists will always have limitations, as it is impossible to design checklists that can address every possible situation.

In an underwater diving emergency, time is limited, and the divers cannot follow a formal written checklist. In this case, overlearning procedures can be a fundamental step in ensuring quick and correct reactions, possibly prompted by a mnemonic used to remember the correct sequence of actions. In less time-demanding situations, such as when gear failure is detected during the pre-dive checks, an emergency checklist could be used to thoroughly troubleshoot the system to identify and fix the problem.

Training checklists

During training, expanded checklists can be used as a supplement to provide explanations and details of the various steps. These are not intended to be used during operations (2).

With divers following an instruction course, detailed checklists could be provided to explain critical steps better and reinforce the learning process.

Electronic checklists

Checklists can be simply printed on paper or can be part of a more complex computer-aided system. Electronic checklists generally avoid skipping some steps because the computer will not allow the operator to continue through the checklist unless each step is completed. However, electronic systems have their limits, including relatively small displays and potential electronic failures (2), (7).

Electronic checklists are often used with rebreathers, which require the diver to go through a specific series of controls to activate the electronics and prepare the unit for diving. The system provides a form of interlock, preventing the diver from starting the dive with omitted checklist steps.

Structure of checklists

Due to the limits of human working memory, the sequences of items to be remembered should be divided into blocks following a sensible logic and appropriate path. Critical items should be checked first and could be repeated later in the checklist to add redundancy. Pictorial and spatial organization of the checklist provides additional pointers in case of checklist interruption (2).

For example, checking that the cylinders are full and their valves open could be the first step of a pre-dive checklist. The final (redundant) step could be gas availability – a critical element (e.g., see Table 8.1).

Cylinder pressure value		
O₂ % value		
MOD		
Valves open		
Manifold position	open	closed
Primary regulator in working order		
Secondary regulator in working order		
BCD inflator connected and in working order		
Primary light		
Secondary light		
Primary reel		
Secondary reel		
SMB		
Valves open		
Manifold position	open	closed

Table 8.1. Example of a checklist for a double-cylinder configuration. The position of the valves is checked twice, at the beginning and the end of the list (the latter being the most critical point).

Longer checklists should be divided into multiple shorter lists, and the tasks should be grouped by the systems to be checked with the different sections clearly separated (8).

Multiple pre-dive checklists could address several areas that require attention, such as:

- Gear assemblage and configuration.
- Gas management (analysis and labeling of all cylinders, verification of gas availability based on the planned dive and estimated breathing rates, gas redundancy at personal and team levels).
- Environmental consideration (ingress and egress areas safely accessible, weather forecast, absence of potential hazards).

The checklist may require jumping to other pieces of information depending on the specific situation to be addressed (7) and may also have some decision points to guide the operators to specific sections of the checklist based on the exact situation they are facing at the moment (9).

This kind of checklist can be used in gear troubleshooting: finding an anomaly can prompt the use of specific secondary checklists for solving that malfunction.

The use of specific typography and symbols can enhance the readability of the checklist; the format should also make it easy for the operator to follow each step (7).

For checklists to be used underwater, it is important to consider that the illumination could be poor and that colors will fade with depth due to the water's absorption of the longer light wavelengths. Using bold fonts with high contrast between them and the background should be preferred.

Too long and too detailed checklists become excessively time-consuming, leading to complacency and potential skipping of steps (2). The checklist length is also critical during emergencies where the operators are already under high workload and time pressure (4), (7).

A diving emergency checklist could be designed as a flowchart facilitating the divers to quickly assess the most critical points (e.g., see Fig. 8.1). Pictorials can also enhance the memory retention of essential elements.

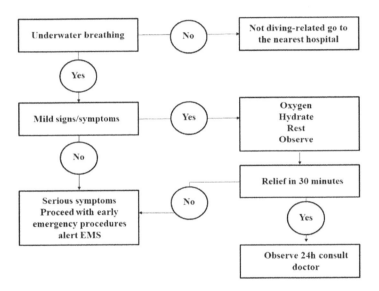

Fig. 8.1. Example of a simplified flowchart for diving medical emergencies. (This is for demonstration purposes only. It is NOT intended to be used during an actual emergency. Proper training is needed to manage medical emergencies).

A checklist should have a section where the operator physically checks off the items; studies show that the error rate of checklists with this section is 3×10^{-3} compared with 1×10^{-2} for checklists without it (2). This shows that a checklist where the items are marked is ten times less prone to errors than one that does not allow for physically marking each step.

The structure of the checklists, in particular the wording used, should consider the presence of linguistic and/or cultural differences within the team to reduce the risk of misunderstanding, especially during emergencies (7).

Special attention should also be given to acronyms that can change over time or vary even when indicating the same thing. For example, the buoyancy control device in English-speaking countries can be abbreviated to BC (buoyancy compensator) or BCD (buoyancy control device). Measurement units should be clearly indicated: for example, in Europe, the gauge pressure is usually in bar and the volume of the cylinders in liters; in the USA, the pressure is measured in psi, and the volume of the cylinders in ft^3 at the nominal filling pressure.

A "completion call" step should conclude the checklist. This ensures that all the steps in the checklist have been completed and prompts the operator to take the following action (8).

Using a checklist

Most checklists follow the same strategy in their use (2):

- Reading/hearing the checklist item.
- Accomplish the required action.
- Respond to the outcome of the action performed.

There are two main methods for performing a checklist that are often used in combination depending on the specific checklist in question (2):

- *Challenge-response*: The operators configure the system and then use the checklist to verify that the configuration is correct. Operator "A" calls the checklist item, both operators "A and B" verify the configuration, and then operator "B" calls the verified status of the item. With this method, there is a double redundancy generated by using the checklist as a configuration verification tool and by the cross-checking between the operators.

  This method could be used during the pre-dive checklist with the two diving buddies working together and cross-checking their equipment. If consistently used, this approach strongly reduces the risk of omitted steps in configuring the diving gear.

- *Do-list*: The checklist is used as a guide for a step-by-step configuration of the system. Operator "A" calls for an item, operator "B" sets the item and announces the new status of the system. This method does not have the redundancy of the challenge-response method, and if a step is skipped, a mistake could go unnoticed.

  This is the method used when following an electronic checklist. In this case, the electronic prompt acts as operator "A" and the diver as operator "B" in setting the system accordingly. The presence of interlocks can prevent the operator from skipping a step.

The most common method is the challenge-response, which has full redundancy. The response should describe the actual status of the item checked and not be a simple "checked" message. Ideally, the checklist execution should be decoupled from other critical operations, and adequate time should be allowed as a buffer for recovery from checklist delays (8).

For example, a diver checking the availability of breathable gas should read the actual pressure indicated by the gauge and verify that the cylinders are open, breathing briefly through the regulators.

Problems with checklists

Despite the essential simplicity of using checklists, a series of major aviation accidents were nonetheless due to their misuse (2). Especially when under stress, instructions on the checklists can be confusing for an inexperienced operator, and if complex operations are required, such as performing calculations, errors are likely (9).

Example: If a diver needs to recalculate the diving profile because of overstay at depth, exceeded maximum depth, or loss of some decompressive gas, the mental workload is much heavier than doing the calculation on land, also aggravated by the divers feeling under stress. In this case, having some already planned contingency dive profiles available, rather than just a checklist indicating the steps for calculation, can reduce the workload and the likelihood of errors.

During an abnormal situation, it is not uncommon to mis-interpret the cues and therefore use the wrong checklist (9). Emergency checklists are also rarely used – their main use is during training, and consequently, the potential for their mis-use is higher (2). Moreover, some emergencies require a greater degree of adaptation, and therefore following a rigid step-by-step procedure can be ineffective or inappropriate (6). In fast-developing emergencies, there could be no time to access and use a checklist (9). In this case, robust overlearning of emergency procedures reduces the risk of inappropriate actions.

Standard checklists that are routinely repeated may induce lapses in the operator, who may not notice deviance or become complacent, omitting real cross-checking and/or recalling the items from memory, skipping the checklist to save time (2).

Example: During the pre-dive checks, the divers should be focused on this operation, avoiding distractions and taking the time needed. Rushing a checklist could easily lead to the omission of a step.

Standard checklists should not be called on during critical phases because the operators are already under a high workload, and the cues that normally prompt the beginning of the checklists could go unnoticed; emergency checklists are an exception, being designed for use under very stressful conditions (2), (8).

Example: In a diving-related emergency, time is usually very limited, and using a formal checklist could be unfeasible. In this case, mnemonic prompts could facilitate the recall of overlearned procedures.

Interruption of the sequence of a checklist will likely cause steps to be missed upon resuming. Ideally, the checklist should be restarted from the beginning. This is another reason for having relatively short checklists (2).

Example: The divers should conduct the checks calmly and steadily, allowing their attention to be totally focused on the actions performed. Rushing a pre-dive checklist seconds before jumping from a boat is not good practice and will likely lead to errors.

Any change to a given checklist requires time to be fully mentally "absorbed"; otherwise, it is likely that under stress, the operator will revert to an older model which is more deeply embedded in memory, with the potential for errors as a result (2).

Example: Divers using new diving protocols or modified configurations requiring a different checklist should be given time to become acclimated to the latest procedures and checks.

It is important that the checklist is considered a helpful tool and not a nuisance by the operators. Otherwise, a series of behavioral biases, including complacency and boredom, will reduce or void its efficacy (8).

Example: The use of checklists should be introduced early on during training sessions so that these are accepted as a regular part of diving activity. It is also important to foster a safety culture within the team, supporting using checklists as important tools.

Over-reliance on checklists can lead to omitting other best safety practices (6).

Example: A diver should always be aware of the correct procedures to apply; the checklist should only be used as a memory aid to help trigger well-learned procedures, not as a substitute for proper knowledge.

The use of checklists in the diving community

In the diving community, checklists are still very limited despite evidence of their utility in reducing the probability of errors. A pre-dive team approach allows for effective cross-checking of diving gear configuration, gas management, and emergency procedures and could strongly avoid or mitigate accidents (12).

The checklist is particularly relevant when using more complex diving gear such as rebreathers. Several authors suggest that pre-dive and post-dive checklists should be enforced at all times (13), (14), (15), (16). The use of integrated electronic checklists can be of help in preventing divers from diving with a unit that has not been thoroughly readied (17), (18), (19).

Forgetting or omitting adequate pre-dive preparation can lead to diving mishaps. To assess the efficacy of pre-dive checklists in reducing diving issues a trial on 1,043 divers completing a total of 2,041 dives was conducted. Only 6.6% of the divers reported regular use of checklists during their standard diving activity. The divers were divided into two groups: an active group required to go through a formal pre-dive checklist and a control group who did not use a checklist. Using the checklist reduced major mishaps (including rapid ascent, lost buddy and being low/out of air) by 36% and minor issues by 26% (20).

Another study conducted in 2012 on 426 divers completing 840 dives in 30 location-days revealed that 21% did not use any checklists, 71% used some form of mnemonic checklist, and 8% routinely used a written checklist. An analysis of the reported diving mishaps highlighted that only written checklists reduced mishap incidence; mnemonic checklists were ineffective (21).

Lessons learned

- Checklists are a powerful tool to assist divers in following standardized procedures and controls.
- In emergencies, there may not be enough time to follow a checklist; emergency procedures should be overlearned.
- When going through a checklist, the diver should focus, avoiding distractions that compromise attention.
- If a checklist is interrupted, it should be started again from the beginning.
- The challenge-response style offers higher redundancy and should be preferred by the diving team.

References

1. **Ludders, W. and McMillan, M.** *Errors in veterinary anesthesia.* New York : John Wiley & Sons, 2017.

2. **Degani, A. and Wiener, E.** *Human factors of fight-deck checklists: The normal checklist.* Washington, DC : NASA, 1990. Report 177549.

3. **Lock, G.** *Under pressure.* 2019.

4. **Gawande, A.** *The checklist manifesto: How to get things right.* New York City : Metropolitan Books, 2009.

5. **Trust, Health Research and Educational.** *Checklists to improve patient safety.* Chicago, IL : HRET.

6. **Clay-Williams R. and Colligan, L.** Back to basics: Checklists in aviation and healthcare. *BMJ Quality & Safety.* 2015, Vol. 24, pp. 428–431.

7. *Design guidance for emergency and abnormal checklists in aviation.* **Burian, B.** 2006. Human factors and ergonomics society annual meeting proceedings.

8. **Deagani, A. and Wiener, E.** Cockpit checklists: Concept, design and use. *Human Factors.* 1993, Vol. 35, 2, pp. 28–43.

9. *Aeronautical emergency and abnormal checklists.* **Burian, B.** San Francisco, CA : s.n., 2006. Proceedings of the humanfactor and ergonomics society 50th meeting.

10. **Bozanic, J.** *Mastering rebreathers.* 2013.

11. **Lombardi, M.** *Closed circuit open sourced.* s.l. : CReate Space, 2019.

12. *Checklists.* **Lock, G.** 2014, X-ray Magazine, Vol. 61.

13. *Rebreather fatality investigation.* **Vann, R., Pollock, N. and Denoble, P.** s.l. : AAUS, 2007. Diving for Science 2007.

14. **Kesling, D.** Operational considerations for the use of closed-circuit rebreathers in scientific diving research. [book auth.] N.W., Sellers, S.H. and Godgrey, J.M. Pollock. *Rebreathers and scientific diving.* Catalina Island, CA : s.n., 2015.

15. **Short, P.** Technical diving community. [book auth.] D.R., Denoble, P.S. and Pollock, N.W. Vann. Orlando, FL : s.n., 2012.

16. **Heinerth, J.** Five golden rules: shifting the culture of rebreather divingto reduce accidents. [book auth.] D.R., Denoble, P.S. and Pollock, N.W. Vann. Orlando, FL : s.n., 2012.

17. **Fletcher, S.** *Assesment of manual operations and emergency procedures for closed-circuit rebreathers.* Cranfield : Cranfield University, 2011.

18. **Tetlow, D.R. and Jenkins, S.** The use of fault-tree analysis to visualize the importance of human factors for safe diving with closed-circuit rebreathers (CCR). *International Journal of the Society for Underwater Technology.* 2005, Vol. 26, 3, pp. 51–59.

19. **Stone, B.** Rebreather hazard anakysis and human factors. [book auth.] R.D., Denoble, P.S. and Pollock, N.W. Vann. *Rebreather Forum 3 .* Orlando, FL : s.n., 2012.

20. **Ranapurwala, S., Wing, S., Poole, C., Kucera, K., Marshall, S. and Denoble, P.** The effect of using pre-dive check-

lists on the incidence of diving mishaps in recreational scuba diving: A clustered randomized trial. *International Journal of Epidemiology*. 2016, Vol. 45, 1, pp. 223–231.

21. —. Mishaps and unsafe conditions in recreational scuba diving and pre-dive checklist use: A prospective control study. *Injury Epidemiology*. 2017, Vol. 4, 16.

9. FAULT TREE ANALYSIS

Chapter highlights

A fault tree analysis (FTA) is a deductive process that aims to identify the root causes leading to an unwanted event – that is, an incident/accident.

Using Boolean logic gates, it is based on a flow chart of the different intermediate events leading to a final outcome.

Different analysts can generate different paths for the FTA, considering different chains of intermediate events, but the final identified root causes should be the same.

Applying FTA to diving incidents/accidents can help identify the root causes so that they can be correctly managed to prevent the adverse outcomes from happening again.

An example of FTA of an out-of-air situation is provided and critically analyzed.

Introduction

Fault tree analysis (FTA) is the best tool for detailed root-cause analysis and probabilistic risk assessment in various complex systems. FTA was first developed in 1961 at Bell Laboratories for the "Minuteman" nuclear launch control system of the US Air Force. In 1965 Boeing and the University of Washington presented the first papers on FTA applications and methods. Currently, FTA is used by various entities working with complex systems, including the nuclear power industry (1).

FTA is a top-down deductive process that aims to identify the root causes (the "basic events") of an accident/incident (the "top event," also defined as the "unwanted event" or UE) by using a series of logic gates (AND/OR) connecting the intermediate events. It is a pictorial representation of the chain of events leading to the final output. Starting from the top event, its direct causes are identified at the next level of events. If each of these events could have caused the top event by themselves, then an "OR" logic gate is used; if all the events have to happen together, then an "AND" gate is used. The logic gates follow the laws of Boolean algebra (2), (3), (4), (5).

An "OR" gate allows for the free propagation of the failure through the fault tree; an "AND" gate instead identifies some degree of protection because two or more events must happen simultaneously for the failure to propagate (6).

The numerical value of the probability (P_{UE}) of the UE based on the type of gate used can be calculated as (1):

"OR gate": $P_{UE} = P_A + P_B - P_A \times P_B$ with A and B the basic events associated with the UE.

"AND gate": $P_{UE} = P_A \times P_B$ with A and B the basic events associated with the UE.

The events connected by an "AND gate" are considered independent, and the probability of the UE happening is much lower when an "AND gate" can be established for its basic events.

As the exposure time (that is, the component's time of exposure to potential failure) increases, the probability of failure of the given component increases exponentially, approaching $P = 1$ (certain failure) after a time specific to each component (its lifetime). This is quite intuitive, meaning that the longer our system is exposed to potentially adverse conditions, the more likely it is that some of its components will fail (1).

An application of this concept is the suggested service time for diving regulators: this usually happens at least annually, so that it is very likely the various components will be checked and replaced well before reaching their lifetime limit.

We should also consider that skills degrade over time if not periodically reassessed – they, too, have a "lifetime." For these reasons, divers should consider continuous training as a strategy to maintain proficiency in the learned skills.

As a method to increase system resilience to failure, "interlocks" can be used. These safety arrangements prevent a given system from functioning if an unsafe mode is likely to develop. Interlocks introduce "AND gates," reducing the probability that the UE will happen (1).

For example, in surface-supply a non-return valve is installed in the connection of the umbilical carrying the breathing gas to the diver's helmet. This prevents dangerous depressurization of the helmet should the umbilical be severed or detached. From an FTA perspective, using a non-return valve introduces an "AND gate" because for the helmet depressurization (the UE) to occur, it would be necessary not only for the umbilical to be detached but also for the valve to fail.

Redundancy is another method of introducing "AND gates" by duplicating critical components to increase the system's reliability. As we will see, attention should be given to avoid configurations that lead to "apparent redundancy" but which do not really increase the system's resiliency to failure (1).

For example, rebreathers use multiple oxygen cells to analyze the O_2 content in the breathing loop; a voting logic is often used, with the reading too far from the average being dismissed. Even though this adds to the redundancy, the sensors may not be "truly independent" because they use the same calibration gas, work in the same environment, and are likely sourced from the same manufacturer (7). In addition, because the cells have a lifetime – after which their readings can be faulty – at any given time, one should ideally have cells that were all installed at different stages of their lifetime to reduce the likelihood that they all fail at the same time, thus losing the adequate redundancy (8).

A "minimal cut set" (MCS) is defined as a list of necessary and sufficient conditions (basic events) for the occurrence of the top event. Usually, a minimal number of MCS contribute to the majority of the top events following the Pareto principle. Sometimes different MCS have identical characteristics, showing common vulnerability to the same causes; in this case, there is only apparent redundancy. Similarly, common cause failures (CCFs) are multiple component failures occurring simultaneously or within a relatively short interval that share a common cause; this occurrence is an important contributor to the failure of redundant identical components. CCFs include (1), (5):

- Use of identical components in critical subsystems.
- Design/material flaws.
- Common installation errors.
- Common maintenance errors.
- Common environmental susceptibility.

For example, a faulty batch of O-rings (material flaw) can cause multiple equipment failures. Wrong routing of cylinder straps (installation error) can cause cylinder detachment even if multiple straps are used. Not properly rinsing the diving gear (maintenance error) can lead to enhanced material aging and potential failure of parts. Using two identical regulators (identical components in critical subsystems), which are both prone to freezing in cold water (environmental susceptibility), does not add safety because it is very likely that if one fails due to freezing issues, the other will fail too.

The probability of the top event occurring is the expression of the cumulative probability of every single basic event that is part of its MCS. This is valid only if such probabilities are small (< 0.1). Probabilities for intermediate events are calculated considering such events as top events for the partial fault tree below them (5).

Human errors should also be included in the FTA because they are often the dominant root cause of system failure. The possibility that human actions can prevent system failure should not be included in the FTA because the analysis only aims to assess failure modes. Typical human errors causing a UE can be classified into the following five types (1):

1. Operator fails to perform the appropriate function.
2. Operator performs the function incorrectly.
3. Operator performs a function inadvertently.
4. Operator performs the wrong function.
5. Operator actions exacerbate the results of a system failure.

Some examples of each type in a diving environment are:

Type 1 error: A diver does not inflate the BCD during the descent, thus becoming unable to stop at the planned depth.

Type 2 error: A diver tries to inflate the BCD during the descent but fails.

Type 3 error: A diver dislodges the weight belt causing the belt to become loose during the dive.

Type 4 error: A diver switches to the wrong gas during a dive.

Type 5 error: A diver with a free-flowing regulator fails to close the correct valve on the cylinder.

Fault tree analysis applied to scuba diving.

An example of an FTA for a scuba incident is given in Fig. 9.1. An out-of-air top event is analyzed, encompassing divers using a single cylinder with a single regulator and octopus. Interestingly, the basic events leading to the incident are mostly human-induced errors.

Adding an independent backup breathing gas source, such as a pony tank with regulator, and/or using a twin cylinder configuration with manifold would have strongly reduced the likelihood of the top event because an "AND gate" would have been introduced requiring both (primary and secondary) systems to fail at the same time to have an out-of-gas situation. Quantification of such probabilities indicates that an out-of-gas situation when using a redundant independent gas source is ten times less likely than when using an octopus (6).

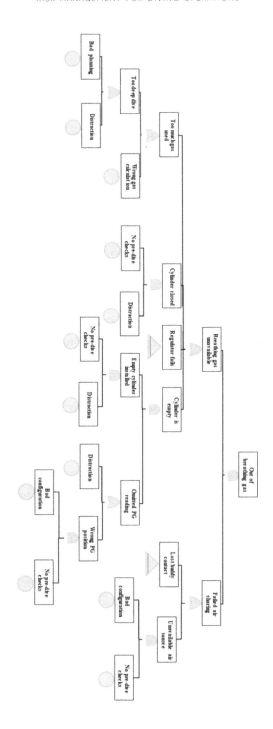

Fig. 9.1. Example of a fault tree analysis diagram for an "out-of-gas" situation.

Analysis of the fault tree

The following is a step-by-step analysis of the fault tree elements and their relation as causes leading to the top event.

Out-of-gas: This is the top UE causing the diver to be deprived of breathing gas. It could result in a fatal outcome. A series of events leading to the UE are described in the various levels of the fault tree as follows:

- *Empty cylinder*: This can be caused by three independent events:
  - *Poor gas monitoring*: The diver fails to control the SPG during the dive or to check the cylinder pressure as part of the pre-dive checks. The basic event for this is *poor training*. The diver should know that controlling the breathing gas reserve is a key element for the safety of the dive.
  - *Wrong planning*: This may include a mistaken estimate of the gas consumption, the use of a too-small cylinder, or diving too deep. All these causes can be linked to *poor training*.
  - *Increased gas consumption*: This can be caused by over-exertion or over-breathing the regulator when under stress. Both causes originated from poor training because well-trained divers should be able to control their stress levels and manage their efforts underwater to avoid excessive gas consumption. Even going too deep is another source of potentially running out of gas due to the increased breathing rate linked to higher environmental pressure.

- *Regulator failure*: This can be caused by two independent events:

  o *First stage fails*: The failure of the first stage can be caused by *mechanical failure* or *freezing*. *Mechanical failure* has a basic event in *poor maintenance*. The regulators need to be regularly serviced. *Freezing* can be caused by diving in too cold waters and using a regulator not fit for cold water. These events are due to *poor technical knowledge* and *poor environmental assessment*; both have *poor training* as their basic event.

  o *Second stage fails*: This can be caused by three independent events. *Freezing* follows the same chain of events as the first stage failure. *LP hose failure* is caused by *poor maintenance*. The diver should always assess the state of the hoses with particular attention to any crack or anomalous bend of the hose. *Mechanical failure* of the second stage indicates a lack of proper maintenance/servicing; therefore, its basic event is *poor maintenance*.

Fault trees have a degree of subjectivity because they are based on the experience and skill of the analyst who will define the chain of events leading to the top event.

Analysts may design different pathways, but the identified basic events should be the same or equivalent.

In this example, other intermediate events could have been considered, such as improper connection of the first stage on the cylinder valve, a leaking valve, a disconnected mouthpiece from the second stage, etc. What is important is that the identified root causes are the same or equivalent. Moreover, it is interesting to highlight that a relatively small number of basic events are common causes of failure. If the probability of the events is to be calculated, then this should be accounted for, avoiding duplicating the probability of the same event.

FTA can be applied to identify the basic events of various scuba accidents, helping to assess for possible corrective procedures; it is to be noted that in the case of multiple independent failures, the applicability of FTA is strongly reduced.

Lessons learned

- Fault tree analysis is a tool to analyze the chain of events leading to a failure.
- Multiple intermediate causes can be reduced to a few basic root causes.
- Acting on this limited number of basic events could prevent many negative final outcomes.
- Human errors are often found within the basic events leading to system failure.
- Fault tree analysis strongly relies on the experience and skill of the analyst to define the chain of events leading to the accident/incident.

References

1. **Ericson, C.** *Fault tree analysis primer.* Charleston, NC : s.n., 2011.

2. **Belland, J.** *Fault tree training: Course notes.* s.l. : Isograph Ltd., 2015.

3. *Fault tree analysis: What is it?*

4. *Fault tree analysis.* **Andrews, J.** 1998. Proceedings of the 16th International System Safety Conference.

5. **Vesely, W.** *Fault tree handbook with aerospace applications.* Washington, DC : NASA, 2002.

6. **Tetlow, S.** *Formal risk identification in professional scuba (FRIPS).* s.l. : HSE, 2006.

7. **Jones, N.** PO2 sensor redundancy. [book auth.] R.D., Denoble, P.S. and Pollock, N.W. Vann. Orlando, FL : s.n., 2012.

8. **Life, Deep.** *How rebreathers kill people.* 2016.

10. DIVING INCIDENTS AND ACCIDENTS

Chapter highlights

Despite our best efforts, there can never be a 100% guarantee of an accident-free activity. Proper training, good situational awareness, and correct decision-making can strongly reduce the likelihood of accidents occurring and ameliorate their consequences if they do.

Most diving accidents share a few common causes that, if correctly identified and avoided, would have prevented the escalation of the problem.

Errors in gas management and buoyancy control issues are the two leading causes of injuries and fatalities.

Consistent use of pre-dive checks, rehearsal of emergency procedures, and good dive planning are the key elements for incident prevention.

Human errors are almost invariably the real cause of equipment failure; poor maintenance, mistakes in assembling the gear, and lack of skills are the most common errors.

Panic generates fatal situations that a calm and confident diver could have otherwise managed.

Introduction

Divers must operate in potentially hostile environments using life-support systems that allow underwater survival. These systems are fairly reliable but may fail under certain conditions, as with any other system. Most of the time, human interaction with the system is the source of the problem, creating unsafe conditions and leading to incidents or accidents.

A diving incident is defined as any error/event that reduces the safety of a dive. If damage to material or injury to the divers follows, we define this as a diving accident (1), (2). Our goal as divers should be to implement all the reasonable procedures needed to reduce the likelihood of an accident.

Human factors play a determinant role in diving mishaps, highlighting the importance of sound knowledge, training, and experience to respond to unforeseen circumstances and avoid escalating the problems that lead to an accident (3).

Causes of diving incidents and accidents

Lack of experience/knowledge, disregard for safety practices, complacency (mostly among experienced divers), panic, and health issues are the leading causes of diving accidents. However, all mishaps in water are potentially dangerous due to the hostile nature of the environment and the highly reduced timeframe for any effective intervention (4).

The errors identified in an analysis of 1,000 scuba diving incidents were classified into five main categories, as follows (see also Fig. 10.1) (1):

1. Knowledge-based   30.8%
2. Rule-based   28.3%
3. Latent   16.9%
4. Skill based   16.0%
5. Technical (mix of knowledge and rule-based) 8.0%

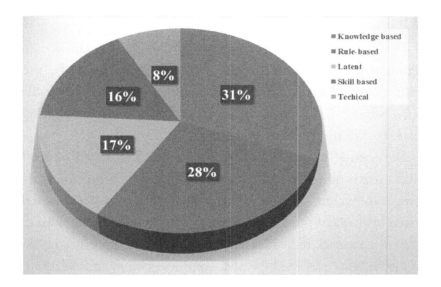

Fig. 10.1. Typology of most common errors in an analysis of 1,000 diving accidents.

Latent errors were mistakes not immediately associated with the event but considered to be an influencing factor for the future event to take place. For example, missing something during a pre-dive check may cause problems during the dive.

Skill-based errors caused some harm in 75% of the cases studied, highlighting the importance of overlearning basic diving skills. Overlearning allows divers to be able to respond to emergencies even when under high stress. In this way, the response becomes almost instinctive, leading to quick and effective actions.

In another study of diving errors, failure in proper buoyancy control was the main skill-based error leading to 154 incidents, 48 of which caused some kind of injury in the form of DCS (35.4%), AGE (25.0%) and pulmonary barotraumas (20.8%). In 35.5% of the events, the power-inflator mechanism of the BCD was not correctly connected. Of the overall incidents, about 25% could have been prevented by proper pre-dive checks (5).

Performing checks before any dive should be enforced as standard procedure. Ideally, a written checklist should be used with cross-checking between the diving team. Even expert divers, if relying only on their memory, may skip necessary checks if distracted or under time pressure.

Between 1995 and 2004, the information provided by 5,046 divers performing 52,582 recreational dives in both tropical and temperate waters showed that buoyancy problems were experienced by 4.7% of the divers, mainly in terms of too fast an ascent rate (often associated with the use of drysuits). Interestingly, 88% of fast ascents recorded by dive computers went undetected by the divers, being identified only during the post-dive analysis of the recorded logs (6). This highlights the importance of monitoring the information provided by the computer, especially during critical phases of the dive, such as ascending and decompression.

A diving fatality usually involves a series of related events that create "holes" in each of the safety layers of the dive through active (caused by actions during the dive) or latent (caused by actions before the dive) errors. Often multiple factors may simultaneously influence an incident (7).

Applying the Pareto principle (a limited number of causes is linked to most accidents) to the diving risk assessment means correctly identifying and eliminating just a few causes may strongly reduce the likelihood of most accidents (see Chapter 9).

By analyzing the most common causes of diving accidents, it is possible to identify some of the paths leading to mishaps and develop accident-avoidance strategies.

Sequential events leading to accidents are defined as (8):

- *Trigger*: Event directly linked to and immediately preceding the accident.
- *Disabling agent*: Hazardous conditions associated with the trigger.
- *Disabling injury*: Direct cause of death.
- *Cause of death*: As formally assessed by the coroner.

Triggers and disabling agents are limited in typology and can be identified and managed through accurate and rigorous risk assessment during the pre-dive briefing and checks.

For example, acknowledging the presence of a strong current may lead to a change in the gas-management strategy, considering the likely increase in breathing rate due to the extra effort of swimming against the current, thus reducing the risk of an out-of-air situation.

Scuba diving incident and accident rates

An analysis of the diving fatalities in 2000–2006 by the Divers Alert Network (DAN) shows that there were 187 diving-related deaths among a population of 1,141,367 divers, providing an individual risk per annum (IRPA – representing the probability that an individual is killed during one year of exposure) of 1.6×10^{-4}. This value is comparable with that of working in mining and quarrying (1.1×10^{-4}) or construction (0.6×10^{-4})

and below that of car accidents (1.1×10^{-3}). Activities with a fatality rate greater than 1×10^{-3} are usually considered unacceptable for the general public. An IRPA between 1×10^{-3} and 1×10^{-5} is tolerated only if further reduction is cost-prohibitive or impracticable (9).

In 2002–2006 the IRPA for scuba diving in Australia was 8.5×10^{-5} for Australian divers and 1.5×10^{-5} for overseas visitors (10). A similar analysis of scuba diving accidents in the UK in 2006 provided an IRPA of 4.8×10^{-5} (11).

The annual per capita fatality rates in the period 2000–2006 for DAN America was $1.6 \times 10^{-4,}$ and for the same period, the British Sub Aqua Club (BSAC) provided a value of 1.4×10^{-4}; gas management, entrapment/entanglement and buoyancy problems were the most common causes of such accidents (12).

A further study of diving incidents in the UK from 1998–2009 considered a total of 4,799 events, of which 197 were fatalities; the fatality rate was 0.54×10^{-5} for BSAC divers and almost twice that (1.03×10^{-5}) for non-BSAC divers. Buoyancy issues were involved in 12.8% of the incidents/accidents, and out-of-gas events were linked to 8.6%. Rebreather mishaps represented 10.7% of the total, and human error was identified as the cause of failure in 73% of such rebreather issues. The authors of the study indicated that the following preventive actions could have averted most of the accidents (13):

- Pre-dive checks and proper briefings could have avoided 29% of the accidents.
- Attentive monitoring of the diving parameters could have avoided 18% of the accidents.
- Practice of critical diving skills could have avoided 16% of the accidents.

- Not exceeding proper limits could have avoided 9% of the accidents.

An investigation of fatalities among PADI divers involved in training in 1989–1998 and 1999–2008 highlighted a fatality rate of 1.16–2.82×10^{-5} of the divers and 0.3–0.7×10^{-5} of the dives studied; the majority of fatalities were during deep and night dives on advanced diving courses (14).

The American Academy of Underwater Sciences (AAUS) accidents report for scientific dives in 1998–2007 indicates 102 incidents over 1,019,159 dives; of these, 33 were confirmed cases of DCS, an incident rate of 3.24×10^{-5} (15).

An analysis of scientific diving reported 67 incidents from 1998–2005 over 766,090 dives, an incident rate of 8.7×10^{-5}; DCI represented 50% of the cases, and ear/sinus barotraumas 19% (16).

Commercial divers are often exposed to riskier environments than recreational or scientific divers, reflected in the generally higher rate of accidents. In 2010 in Belgium, the estimated fatality rate for commercial divers was 2.3×10^{-3}; similarly, in France, it was 1.1×10^{-3}, and in the UK, the HSE estimate was 2–4×10^{-4}. Fatality rates were staggeringly high at the beginning of the offshore diving business, with rates of 1.25×10^{-2} mainly for the North Sea oil industry. These very high values were likely due to a sharp increase in the number of commercial divers in the area, which went from about 400 to more than 2,000, involving hiring less qualified divers and diving supervisors (17).

From these data (see Table 10.1), the overall risk for diving emerges as relatively low (excluding the very early phase of commercial diving), but clearly must still be addressed. Using consistent procedures, training, checklists, and good gear maintenance are all critical elements of risk control and mitigation.

IRPA	Year
1.6×10^{-4}	2000–2006
8.5×10^{-5}	2002–2006
1.5×10^{-5}	2002–2006
4.8×10^{-5}	2002
0.54×10^{-5}	1998–2009
1.03×10^{-5}	1998–2009
$1.16 \times 10^{-5} - 2.82 \times 10^{-5}$	1989–2008
3.24×10^{-5}	1998–2007
8.7×10^{-5}	1998–2005
$2 \times 10^{-4} - 2.3 \times 10^{-3}$	2010

Table 10.1. IRPA range for diving accidents. Sources are given in-text.

Chain of events and causes of injury

A diving accident is almost invariably the result not of a single occurrence but of a chain of often linked events; avoiding even one of those events may interrupt the chain preventing the accident (18).

This is a very important consideration because it is often relatively easy to avoid any one of the single events. Still, managing the impact of multiple errors that build into a "snowball" effect becomes increasingly complex and sometimes impossible. Early recognition of deviations is a critical element in preventing the chain of adverse events from developing. Various causes of injury will be present depending on the diving method adopted and the specific environmental conditions. Good risk assessment of the diving conditions, both in terms of the gear to be used and the methods to be applied, will reduce the likelihood of mishaps.

In a study of 228 cases of diving fatalities, the various phases of the dive where the chain of events started have been identified as follows (see also Fig. 10.2) (19):

- Bottom   48%
- Surface post-dive   23%
- Ascent   9%
- Surface pre-dive   8%
- Early phase of dive   8%
- Not identified   4%

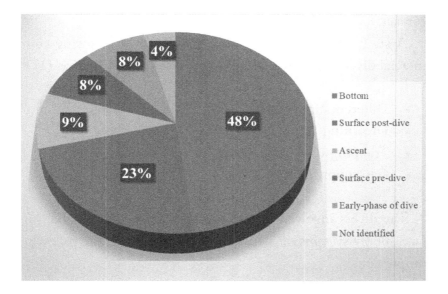

Fig. 10.2. Different phases of a dive where the chain of events leading to a fatality started.

The three main mechanisms leading to injury are rapid ascent, running out of gas, and panic (31% of the cases each).

About 31% of the victims lost consciousness underwater, and 24% lost consciousness upon resurfacing.

In most of the reported scuba fatalities in the USA, Canada, the UK, and Japan, the victims did not ditch their weights (90%), were separated from their diving buddy (86%), and/or failed to inflate the BCD (50%). Almost 50% of them were in the process of extending their diving experience when the accident occurred, with the first unsupervised open-water dive being the most dangerous in terms of potential fatalities (20).

A proper buddy system, gas monitoring, surface supervision, and assistance could have prevented many fatalities. Mastering basic self-rescue skills, such as being able to ditch the weight system, should be overlearned so that even under stress, the diver can act, reducing the risk of an accident.

A study of 577 fatalities from 1975 to 2014 involving commercial divers identified the leading causes of accidents as (17):

- Differential pressure 22%
- Drowning 12%
- Trapping 10%
- Gas-supply issues 10%

The divers involved in the accidents were using scuba, surface-supply systems, or bell/saturation systems in the following proportions:

- Scuba 44%
- Surface-supply 42%
- Saturation 14%

Of the 577 fatalities, 192 were offshore divers. For these, the causes were:

- Trapping 27%
- AGE/DCI 25%
- Gas supply issues 20%
- Helmet dislodged 19%

The diving methods for these divers were:

- Surface-supply 77%
- Bell/saturation 79%
- Scuba 36%

Trapping could be prevented by good tether/umbilical manning and by having the divers trained to free themselves from entanglement. Helmet issues could be avoided through careful pre-dive checking of the locking mechanism by well-experienced assistants.

Inshore divers accounted for 298 of the total 577 fatalities, with causes identified as:

- Differential pressure 36%
- Trapping 8%
- Contamination of gas supply 8%

The diving methods in inshore diving were:

- Scuba 51%
- Surface/supply 49%

Differential pressure is the main risk for operations near gates, intakes, and when using airlifts/pumps. Attentive pre-dive assessment of potential sources of differential pressure should be mandatory.

There were 84 fatalities among ship-maintenance divers:

- Drowning using scuba 27%
- Propeller injury 18%
- Differential pressure 13%

The diving methods for these divers were:

- Scuba 77%
- Surface-supply 23%

Most drownings using scuba when working on ship maintenance could have been prevented using helmets and surface-supply. Good communication and safety measures would have prevented propeller-related accidents. When divers are in the water, the propeller must be locked to avoid unwanted activation.

Main causes of death

A study of open-circuit scuba fatalities in 1992–2003 highlighted drowning as the leading cause of death, totaling 70% of the 947 fatalities, followed by age and cardiac-related issues, totaling 27% combined (9). An analysis of 22 deaths in Croatia in 1980–2010 highlighted similar results (21).

That drowning is the leading cause of death, as stated by the coroner, is not surprising, given that divers are underwater; what is important is to identify the root cause of an accident.

Buoyancy control issues, leading to uncontrolled ascent, accounted for 60% of the causes of accidents; insufficient breathing gas supply was the main trigger for accidents, being involved in 41% of the cases (9).

Panic was involved in 20% of the fatalities, often leading to uncontrolled emergency ascent, and AGE was the second most common disabling injury (29%), following asphyxia, which represented 33% of fatalities (8).

An analysis of diving accidents in Australia between 1972 and 2005 found similar results, with drowning representing 50% of the deaths and gas supply and buoyancy control issues being involved in 23% and 36% of the fatalities, respectively. In 66% of the cases the victim was separated from their dive buddy at a certain time during the dive; 17% of the victims were performing their first dive ever (10).

From this analysis of diving fatalities, it is clear that the main issue is not DCS but that running out of air and loss of buoyancy control are the real dangers. Training should therefore be more focused on teaching correct gas-management techniques and buoyancy skills. Gas-integrated computers that provide alarms for low-gas situations could also enhance the divers' situational awareness. Finally, regular rehearsal of some emergency drills, such as controlled emergency ascent, could also improve the divers' confidence and ability to manage an out-of-air situation, strongly reducing the likelihood of fatal consequences.

Diving equipment failure

Equipment is considered to fail when it is not performing as stated by the manufacturer though it is correctly used and maintained (22). This means that incidents caused by diver error, even if they involve a piece of equipment, should not be referred to as equipment failure. For example, loss of buoyancy caused by the diver not correctly connecting the LP hose to the power-inflator mechanism of the BCD is not an equipment failure. The system worked fine, but the operator did not apply the correct procedure.

Complex systems are more prone to operator error or malfunctions than simpler systems but have more redundancy and self-protection features. Therefore, a simpler system can be damaged more by a relatively small number of failures than a more complex one (23). An example is the use of a single regulator vs. two regulators; it is true that using two regulators increases the likelihood of having a failure in one of these two, but it also introduces a degree of redundancy, making this configuration much safer.

In a study of 1,000 diving incidents, about 10% involved equipment dysfunction, but the vast majority were due to some kind of operator error; in fact, 60% of these incidents could have been avoided by proper pre-dive checks and maintenance. It should be noted that design modifications could have prevented 55% of the incidents, highlighting a need for the diving industry to improve its quality control. The main adverse consequences were DCS and pulmonary barotrauma (22).

Some equipment-related incident trends have been identified over the years, as follows (24):

- *Weight systems*: Failure in ditching the weights can impair emergency ascent. Sudden loss of the weight system (e.g., belt detachment) can cause loss of buoyancy control.
- *BCD*: Most failures are due to diver negligence in servicing/using the BCD.
- *Cylinders*: Failure to check that the valves were correctly open.
- *Regulators*: As with BCD failures, these are mainly due to poor servicing/maintenance.

- *Pressure gauge*: A faulty gauge can lead to an erroneous estimate of the breathing gas reserve.
- *Depth gauge*: Some gauges require calibration when diving in fresh water and/or at altitude. Failing to do so may cause an incorrect measurement of the diving depth.
- *Dive computers*: Diving at the computer's model's limits can increase the DCS risk. Also, a poor understanding of the computer's features can cause problems.
- *Breathing gas*: Using the wrong gas switch has been the cause of several fatalities in tech-diving. Contaminated gas is also a potentially fatal threat.

Divers depend on their equipment to survive underwater, so scuba gear should be considered a life-support system and treated as such. Protect it from unnecessary contamination (such as sand and dirt), avoid exposure to thermal extremes, and be careful of mechanical damage.

Pre-dive checks should always be performed to ensure that the gear is correctly in place and functioning. Cross-checking the gear with a dive buddy reduces the risk of missing some steps in the pre-dive procedure. Under no circumstances should a thorough pre-dive check be skipped; even expert divers can miss potentially life-threatening situations if checks are not correctly performed.

Diving gear is exposed to very harsh conditions, so proper maintenance and servicing are mandatory to guarantee its correct operation. The servicing interval suggested by the manufacturer may need to be shortened if the gear has undergone heavy usage or has been exposed to potential damage, such as being in contact with chemicals or subjected to mechanical shock.

More complex systems, such as rebreathers, need routine specific checking and maintenance, and the divers operating the gear should be fully knowledgeable and skilled in performing the necessary checks.

Cave diving accidents

Cave diving strongly differs from open water diving in terms of risk exposure, required training, diving procedures, and equipment to be used. An analysis of the most common causes of cave diving accidents follows.

A first attempt to recognize common causes of cave diving accidents was based on the rules and procedures described by Sheck Exley (25); the result was the identification of a few common errors (26):

- Failing to use a continuous guide-line to the surface: the divers must always have direct physical contact with the exit during the dive. This is considered the golden rule of cave diving.
- Failing to use the "rule of thirds": a gas management plan should consider using one-third of the total available breathing gas for entering the cave, one-third for coming out, and the remaining one-third as a reserve for contingency. In some cases, an even stricter gas management plan might be needed.
- Failing to respect the MOD: this may cause oxygen toxicity and onset of seizure/convulsion leading to drowning.
- Failing to have the appropriate training: cave divers must have specific training which differs from that for open-water dives.

A 1997 survey of cave diving fatalities showed drowning was the main cause of death (93%), with lack of appropriate cave training and failure to use a guide-line as the two leading contributing factors. In 2006 a British study of 368 cave diving fatalities confirmed lack of training and poor use of guide-lines as the main causes of accidents for both trained and untrained cave divers; out-of-gas situations were caused by poor gas management planning in 97% of the accidents, with only 3% due to a sudden increase in breathing rates because of swimming against strong currents (26).

From 1950 to 1999, a total of 475 fatalities were recorded in the cave diving community. Data were available on some of the accidents (27):

- 143 of 190 fatalities involved non-certified cave divers.
- 256 of 426 fatalities involved failing to have a proper guide-line.
- 377 of 411 fatalities involved a total out-of-air situation.
- 106 of 236 fatalities involved divers who were using a buddy system.
- 145 of 403 fatalities involved divers who did not have any light.
- 197 of 403 fatalities involved divers who had one light only.

These data (see also Fig. 10.3) highlight the staggering number (75%) of fatalities involving non-certified divers. It is to be noted that divers with even high levels of open water certifications, including instructor rating, are involved in cave diving fatalities because they lack the specific skills needed to operate in restricted and overhead environments safely. Only trained and certified cave divers should attempt to enter a flooded cave. Of the total fatalities, 91% involved an out-of-air situation, clearly showing the paramount importance of proper gas planning and using (at least) the "rule of thirds" when diving in a cave. Once again, this is essential knowledge for any trained cave diver but is not part of open-water training. In 45% of the accidents, the divers were with dive buddies; this highlights the big difference in emergency planning and management between cave diving and open water diving: in a cave, the help that a buddy may provide is somewhat limited; for example, failing to use a proper guide-line will not be helped by using a buddy system. The key safety factors are higher redundancy in the life-support system and strong self-rescue capacity.

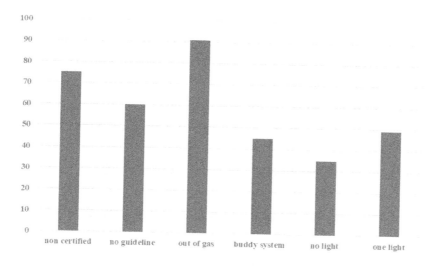

Fig. 10.3. Percentage distribution of fatalities based on the identified leading cause.

Guideline failure was involved in 50% of cave diving fatalities in the UK from 1957–1978 and in 33% of non-fatal accidents. Anxiety and panic also played a role in 12% of non-fatal accidents. In accidents involving well-experienced cave divers, complacency is considered to be the main root cause (28).

Mt. Gambier is a well-known karst area in Australia where aggressive (below 90 meters / 295 ft) cave dive profiles are common, as well as the use of air in very deep dives (60 meters / 196 ft) in cold water (11°C / 52°F). One study analyzed a total of 56,899 dives in this area from the period 2001–2012, identifying 16 DCI cases with an incidence of 0.03% compared with 0.01% of open-water recreational dives in similarly cold waters. Of all the DCI cases, 50% followed multi-day repetitive dives. Post-dive altitude traveling (above 300 meters / 985 ft) is a possible contributing factor to the onset of DCI. In several cases, O_2 was not readily available, thus increasing the consequences of decompression issues (29).

Using rebreathers allows for deeper and longer cave dives. It avoids the need for the diver to swap between multiple cylinders, thus reducing one of the main areas of potentially fatal mistakes. When using a rebreather in cave diving, the availability of adequate bailout gas is critical, and this can be achieved by using a secondary rebreather unit. The complexity of handling two rebreathers should be considered regarding risk management (30), (31).

Wreck diving accidents

Wrecks can be found in various environments, from extremely deep cold water to very shallow clear warm water. Therefore, the associated risk level is variable, as are the required skills and equipment. To plan a dive on a wreck, besides its depth, a series of parameters should be considered, including (32):

- *Visibility*: This plays a main role because in reduced or zero visibility, diving operations become extremely challenging, increasing the time needed for any step and making orientation and communication extremely difficult. Inside wrecks, visibility can quickly drop to zero if silt, accumulated within the structure, is disturbed by the diver's movement.
- *Water temperature*: This will affect the comfort of the diver but also the ingassing/off-gassing of inert gas, influencing the risk of DCI.
- *Distance from the shore*: Some wrecks are several miles offshore, requiring long traveling time. This should be assessed when considering an emergency evacuation of an injured diver.
- *Penetration*: A wreck that is relatively easy to swim around can become very challenging to penetrate, strongly increasing the risk.

In complex wreck diving operations that include penetration, the diving gear and its configuration share many characteristics with that used in cave diving. The aim is to provide the divers with high levels of redundancy for key safety elements (32).

An analysis of wreck diving accidents highlighted the following results (33):

- Wreck diving often involves deep diving (below 40 meters /131 ft) and penetration into overhead environments, both of which are very challenging situations. One might think that these were the main source of diving mishaps. However, the majority of fatalities actually happened in waters shallower than 40 meters (131 ft) and without any wreck penetration.

- Most of the accidents were due to panic-induced errors, which prevented the divers from correctly assessing the situation.
- Poor ability in basic diving skills, such as mask clearing, emergency ascent, and buddy-breathing, was often the root cause of accidents.
- Experienced divers have died because of extreme exertion and nitrogen narcosis-induced errors.
- Most of the equipment failures could have been avoided by proper pre-dive checks and good maintenance.
- Failures in proper dive planning were a leading cause of accidents.

From this information, it is possible to infer that many accidents involved divers with limited training and experience who were attracted by the thrill of visiting a wreck. As in any other underwater activity, the divers should progressively build experience over time, avoiding operations that significantly strain their capacity.

Wreck diving is performed mostly from a boat that anchors above the diving spot. For this reason, the divers must be able to return to the descent line to surface nearby the support vessel. Failure to do so may lead to lost diver situations. To reduce this risk, each diver should have appropriate signaling systems, which can vary from a simple inflatable marker to radio communication devices able to provide GPS location. The boat should also have appropriate beacon devices, especially if the diving site is in an area with heavy boat traffic and/or poor visibility, for example, due to fog (32).

Diving a wreck, even without penetration, is challenging because the diver can be distracted by the unusual environment, forgetting to monitor the basic parameters of the dive.

Moreover, psychological stress is common, especially if the divers have limited experience. The best approach to manage the risks associated with this activity is to dive with more experienced divers, following an attentive planning and briefing phase that focuses on maintaining control of the diving parameters and on following the basic safety rules.

Rebreather diving accidents

Closed-circuit rebreathers (CCR) and semi-closed-circuit rebreathers (SCR) are systems that aim to recycle (totally or in part) the breathing mix, allowing for extended diving time in terms of gas availability. These systems also generate a constant PO_2 through the dive that can be optimized to reduce the decompression needs. Their level of complexity is higher than that of open circuits (OCs), involving mechanical and electronic parts plus the use of chemicals for breathing gas treatment (CO_2 scrubbers). As a result, higher workload in managing a rebreather is required by the diver, as is specific training and experience. This section deals with fatalities that involved rebreather divers in an attempt to identify common causes and effective risk-avoidance strategies.

The rebreather technology, given its inherent complexity, is associated with a higher risk of malfunction and operator error, requiring greater levels of knowledge and training to be safely operated and maintained (34), (35), (36), (37), (38). Most CCR units are not designed for, and should not be used by, recreational divers because they require complex management skills and are intended for environments beyond their training (39). The level of attention needed by the diver using a CCR reduces the available time and cognitive resources for other tasks (40). Even professional divers can be overloaded by the requirements of controlling the CCR alongside their operational tasks, with an increased risk of accidents. To reduce the workload, a safety diver could be used to monitor the safety of the working buddy. A simple "green go" or "red no-go" HUD mounted in positions visible by both the CCR diver and their buddy will also reduce the risk of missing any system malfunction alarm (41).

Despite their technical complexity and higher workload, rebreathers represent a powerful tool in the hands of expert and well-trained divers, allowing for underwater operations that would not be possible without the use of these systems. For example, deep-water dives, diving in remote areas, and long underwater cave penetrations can all benefit from using CCRs (40), (42).

Critical areas of error have been identified in CCR-SCR set-up and usage, as follows (35):

- CO_2 scrubber not replaced or not inserted.
- Omission of O-ring seals.
- Violation in the order of tasks during the assemblage of the unit.
- Forgetting to switch on the electronics.
- Omitting O_2 cells check.
- Disregarding low-battery warning.
- Omitting positive/negative pressure tests.
- Omitting leak checks on the O_2 and diluent valves/regulators.
- Breathing from the nose during the pre-breath test.
- Shortened pre-breathe test.

- Omitting checks on the bailout gear.
- Omitting SPG checking during the dive.
- Omitting backup procedures and decompression tables for bailout situations.

Most of these omissions could have been avoided using written checklists and appropriate standardized procedures. Time pressure should also be avoided because this will increase the risk of voluntary or involuntary skipping some of the pre-dive procedures.

CO_2 buildup is one of the main risks of CCR. Limits of 5 mbar and 10 mbar as the maximum allowable partial pressure have been indicated by EU certification and by the US Navy, respectively. Scrubber lifetime is calculated considering a high workload with the production of 1.6 liter/minute (0.05 cf) of CO_2, water temperature of 4°C (39°F), and 40–100 meters (130–350 ft) of depth. In a survey of 318 divers, 41.5% reported having exceeded canister alarms and/or lifetime end dates but claimed to be able to manage the resulting hypercapnia. Of those with hypercapnia symptoms, 16% bailed out, and the others remained on the loop. In general, it seems that divers do not have an accurate conception of the high risk associated with pushing the limit of the scrubber (43).

In a "fresh" scrubber, CO_2 is almost totally absorbed until 65–70% of the absorbent lifetime is reached. At this point, CO_2 content in the breathing medium spikes quickly, up to four times higher when 100% lifetime is reached. For this reason, a CO_2 sensor may work only as an alarm of a reached dangerous threshold and not as a forecasting tool for the remaining lifetime of the scrubber. Because the chemical reaction within the absorbent is exothermic (releasing heat), thermal sensors within the canister (scrubber holder) may discriminate the still active (hot) from the spent (cold) part, providing some clue about the remaining lifetime. Lifetime is also strongly affected by water temperature, with variations of up to 75% between water at 4°C and water at 30°C (44).

Pushing the limits of the scrubber strongly enhances the risk of massive CO_2 build-up in the breathing loop because once the final lifetime has been reached, the absorbent efficiency in capturing CO_2 is quickly reduced. It is good practice to replace the scrubber well in advance of its end of lifetime, especially if cold water and/or strenuous dives are planned.

Sensitivity to CO_2, the primary stimulus to breathe, can be reduced in some individuals, both by genetic and behavioral factors, including diving. The high PO_2 usually associated with CCR diving will further reduce the ventilation stimulus, generating a vicious circle leading to hypercapnia (too much CO_2 in the body). In this case, even bailing out to OC may have reduced benefits; maintaining respiration control is important to reduce the risk of CO_2 build-up (45).

Bailout is a key safety feature, and the divers should be well-trained in using the gear. Suppose manual control of the rebreather is still operational even if the system has some failure modes. In that case, the diver should stay on the loop (use the rebreather) as long as is feasible because a change to the open-circuit bailout will require a series of actions – such as swapping from the rebreather loop to the regulator and changing the decompression plan – that may increase the overall risk (42). On the other hand, staying on the loop with the rebreather in emergencies exposes the diver to a higher workload and stress, so a prompt bailout to OC could be a better solution (46).

The ideal bailout from a CCR should be another CCR; in this way, the integrity of the life-support system and the mission is maintained, and the diver can proceed to fulfill the planned goals. This kind of bailout can be extremely complex, requiring high knowledge, skill, and situational awareness to safely perform (37).

In some CCR units, it is possible to perform the bailout through a second stage that is integrated into the mouthpiece. The advantage of such a configuration is that the diver does not need to physically remove the mouthpiece for bailing out, thus reducing the risk of flooding the loop, with loss of buoyancy, and/or inhaling water. The regulator can be directly connected to an external bailout cylinder, or this latter could be connected to a manifold that controls the onboard diluent feeding. The regulator could also be connected to the onboard diluent cylinder only. No external tanks are needed in this case, and the overall configuration is more streamlined. However, the available volume of gas in the diluent cylinder is generally less than that which would have been available carrying an external bailout tank. Moreover, the O_2 content of the diluent must allow for a safe PO_2 at any depth of the dive. With onboard and offboard bailout cylinders, using a regulator integrated with the CCR mouthpiece prevents the diver from providing bailout gas to the buddy in case of need. This should be carefully addressed during the planning, especially if a mix of CCR and OC divers are involved in the same team.

The first difficulty in dealing with CCR risk assessment is the absence of reliable data on accidents (35). From 1998 to 2010, there were about 200 rebreather fatalities, with a yearly average of about 12–15 fatalities. There is a general lack of data on the actual cause of the accidents, primarily due to the complexity of the forensic environment and non-technically skilled investigators. Collaboration between manufacturers and investigators should be fostered to promote better investigative practices (47).

Good data on the causes of any diving accident is a key parameter to develop consistent risk assessment and avoid future mishaps. Those data should come from reliable sources. Frequently, newspapers and media provide erroneous information about diving accidents, leading to further confusion, and misunderstanding.

The rebreather fatalities reported by DAN during 1998–2006 were 80, with the yearly fatality rate tripling since 1998. In the USA and Canada, the fatalities from 1998 to 2004 rose from 1% to 5%. In 30 rebreather accidents, the identified root causes were (48):

- 11 operator errors.
- 3 equipment malfunctions.
- 4 losses of buoyancy due to the flooding of the unit.
- 12 unidentified

The data shows that human factors play a key role in the accidents, accounting for 61% of the identified root causes. Rebreathers are complex and tightly coupled systems. Therefore, the risk of operator error and the consequences of such errors are magnified.

In these accidents the main identified disabling agents were loss of gas and use of wrong gas, with oxygen toxicity or hypoxia responsible for more than 50% of the disabling injuries (48). In a CCR, the gas composition in the breathing loop changes during the dive. The operator is exposed to higher risk of hypoxia or hyperoxia than OC divers in case of system failure (41).

Color-coding of the cylinders, proper labeling, and respect of MOD (maximum operative depth) should be mandatory to reduce the risk of mistakes in gas management, both for the rebreather unit and the bailout gear (49).

For a diver using a CCR, it is impossible to know the exact composition of the breathing mix, and they have to rely on the information provided by the electronics. Therefore, a high level of knowledge and training on the specific unit is required to increase awareness of potential failures of the system.

About 80–90% of fatalities involved divers diving "solo" or being separated from the rest of the team (48).

Once again, diving within a team is a crucial safety factor. A well-prepared dive buddy may identify issues affecting the other diver and act accordingly. Solo diving is a hazardous behavior even for extremely well-trained divers. Situations that could be managed at team level can quickly degenerate into a full-blown accident if the diver is alone, especially if involved in challenging dive profiles, as most rebreather dives are.

In French military divers using both CCR 100% O_2 for depths up to 7 meters (23 ft) and SCR using Nitrox or Trimix up to 80 meters (262 ft) of depth over a 30-year period (1979–2009), 153 injuries were reported with an average of five accidents a year. Overall, about 15,000 dives a year were performed, leading to an accident rate of 2.5×10^{-4} for mine clearance dives (using mostly SCR) and 3.1×10^{-4} for combat swimmer dives (using mostly CCR). The predominant errors were violations of MOD and hitting the wrong gas switch leading to gas toxicity, which accounted for 68% of the accidents. In 50% of the cases, loss of consciousness happened, with increased risk of drowning. Mechanical failure of the rebreather accounted for about 6% of the accidents (36).

The high percentage of loss of consciousness highlights the need for the buddy diver to be capable of performing rescue on the disabled companion. In rebreather dives, specific rescue sequences that may differ from the standard ones used for OC divers should be followed. Proper training and knowledge of the system are therefore mandatory.

Sometimes rebreathers are used with a full-face mask (FFM). FFMs will protect the airway in case of loss of consciousness but require more training for bailout procedures and should have a mouthpiece because using an oral-nasal mask increases the risk of flooding the loop and CO_2 build-up (31).

In an analysis of 25 years of records of O_2 toxicity accidents using CCR by the Israel Defense Forces Navy Divers, 36 accidents were investigated. A series of specific signs/symptoms were observed, often with more than one manifesting before a dive was terminated. In no case did loss of consciousness occur without some premonitory symptom, even if the time interval was too short to put in place any rescue strategy. The symptoms were (50):

- Limb convulsion/tremor.
- Difficulty in buoyancy control.
- Headache.
- Visual disturbances (one-third of the cases).
- Facial twitching (one-quarter of the cases).

The rebreather diver should be aware of the premonitory symptoms, and the dive should be promptly terminated if any of these are seen.

In US Navy divers using CCR, both 100% O_2 and mixed-gas, AGE was the most common injury, accounting for 41% of the cases. This mainly happened during training for shallow-water 100% O_2 CCR (Mk 25) when students lost control of their buoyancy and popped to the surface. Barotrauma (11%) and DCS Type 2 (10%) were the other main injuries (51).

CCR-SCR training is complex, and the students should have former OC and Nitrox certification and experience. A positive attitude toward safety and attention to detail should be fostered. Emergency skills should be overlearned, with an adequate number of training dives (35). Experienced OC divers may have a high level of confidence but a lower level of ability immediately after a CCR training, becoming more exposed to the risk of mishaps (34). Learning is a critical factor in CCR training, and the students will move through the "conscious competence model," as described by Gordon Training International. The first stage is a beginner student who has no idea of the risks associated with CCR diving; at the next level, an understanding of the system develops, but the skill level is limited, and close supervision is needed; the third step is a diver who is well aware of the risks and fully competent in their management; the last stage is an experienced CCR diver who acts almost on an instinctive level. This last group is exposed to the risk of becoming complacent (46).

Divers in training, even if under a very well-standardized and regulated environment such as that of military divers, are exposed to high levels of risk. Instructors and trainers should be well aware of such risks and put in place viable strategies for their mitigation, including a reduced student-to-instructor ratio, using extra experienced safety divers, allowing for progressive smaller steps in the training procedure, and having an emergency plan ready and in place.

In 2010 it was estimated that about 14,000 active rebreather divers worldwide performed an average of 30 dives a year each. Based on these data, the fatality rate for rebreather dives is calculated at 4.0×10^{-5}. Equipment issues in CCR diving accounted for 44% of the fatalities. The overall risk of failure in a CCR is 23 times higher than an OC based on a probability fault tree analysis. More than 50% of such failures are due to human errors, including faulty training and procedures and omitted pre-dive checks. It is to be noted that 33% of the deaths were associated with low-risk dives at depths above 40 meters (131 ft), with pre-dive checks adequately performed. A UK study showed that 30% of the fatalities involved some kind of CCR equipment failure compared with 9% for OC (52).

Out of nine CCR accidents analyzed by the UK HSE (Health and Safety Executive), human error in the form of poor assembly/maintenance, undue modifications, and wrong procedures were involved in seven of the events. In two cases, the diver was diving solo. Exceeding training depth limits and solo diving are the most common key factors linked to CCR fatalities. There is a particularly increased risk of operator error during non-normal CCR procedures requiring manual operations. Therefore, specific warnings and alarms should be used to advise the diver of critical actions without ambiguity in their interpretation (35).

Once again, these data highlight the inherent complexity of rebreather diving and the need for appropriate knowledge, training, and procedures. Proper maintenance of the system is also essential because of the more significant number of failure modes, involving both mechanical and electronic, that can affect a rebreather compared with the simpler OC.

The fatal accident rate in CCR in 2016 has been estimated at about 1%, and a strong correlation between design defects and accident rate was observed. Some "poor design" elements included faulty software resulting in a frozen display, incorrect position of the O_2 cells within the breathing loop leading to contamination and false readings, and a faulty locking system of the breathing loop hose allowing the pre-breathing surface test to pass but leading to massive flooding during the dive. Some of these issues were due to operator errors that did not have any prompt feedback or automated remediation from the system. Some designs modification, including cut-off devices, specific alarms, and constraints on minimal and maximal PO_2 set points, could strongly reduce the risk of system failure. Also, best practice should be followed in the maintenance of key elements. For example, the oxygen cells should not be replaced all at the same time because it is very likely that all the sensors will be from the same batch. Therefore if one fails due to some manufacturing defect, the others may fail simultaneously, eliminating the redundancy of having multiple O_2 cells (53).

Latent errors can affect the safety of a rebreather diver. An error in design or in preparing the system may manifest itself later during the actual use of the apparatus. Manufacturers and the diving community should actively collaborate to highlight any problem encountered when operating the system and use feedback to eliminate potential sources of malfunction.

Developing standard pre-dive check sequences is critical in reducing the risk of missing a step in the procedure. These procedures should be simple and user-friendly to be fully embraced by any CCR-SCR diver. Complacency and "normalization of the deviance" may develop if several "event-free" dives have been performed even when checks were omitted. In general, professional divers are more attentive to apply checking procedures than the occasional sport diver (41). Checklists are good tools when coupled with appropriate levels of attention, discipline, and care; for this reason, critical operations should be performed under minimal distraction (35). Diver violations and complacency have been identified as major causal factors in CCR accidents (35).

Checklists should be mandatory in supporting the diver during the pre-dive controls and procedures. Under no circumstances should the standard operative procedure be neglected; complacency is always a very risky attitude but can easily be fatal when using complex systems operating in challenging environments, as is the case for most rebreather dives.

Another source of potential issues is when the divers in the team use a mix of OC and CCR. In this mixed mode, the OC diver will be the one controlling the dive in terms of gas limits and decompression obligation. The team will also need extra training to manage emergencies with shared knowledge of the OC and CCR diving gear. In mixed mode, the CCR diver must carry an external bailout with gas readily available to the OC buddy. In a mixed platform mode, the divers use different CCRs models. When using this configuration, the divers should share a general reciprocal knowledge of the different units with a particular focus on emergency procedures and alarms (54). Unfortunately, the specific characteristics of each CCR and its electronic controls make it difficult, if not impossible, to develop a general training program that can be used with any given rebreather. A standardization of elements across different manufacturers could strongly reduce the overall risk (41), (55).

In some situations, having a mixed mode or a mixed platform diving team is needed due to operational, environmental, or economic constraints. Following appropriate procedures will allow for good safety standards and proficiency level. All the divers in the team must share a clear model of the operations and have a mutual understanding of their needs.

CCR dives are more demanding than OC dives regarding equipment set-up and maintenance, pre-dive checks, and diving procedures. The divers should have specific training and the correct mental attitude to safely dive using CCRs. From the above analysis, it's clear that human errors are the root cause of most CCR accidents, highlighting the importance of high levels of operator skill and knowledge.

Other accidents

In an analysis of 4,339 recreational diving fatalities in 1956–2011, three were associated with murder and eight with suicide. A typical scuba-murder scenario involves a diving partner denying breathing gas to the victim. Given that this is difficult to prove in court, there is a possibility that a higher number of accidents were, in fact, murders. In the case of suicide, 62% were premeditated and prepared for by the victims, who were suffering from acute depression and/or mental illness (56).

A controversial case involved a diver found stabbed in the chest within a cave. The body was recovered at 54 meters (177 ft) of depth. Following an analysis of the dive-computer data, it was estimated that the diver ran out of air after 44 minutes at 36 meters (118 ft) during the ascent phase from a maximum depth of 50 meters (164 ft). Initially, other divers in the group were suspected of murdering their partner, but further investigation cleared them, concluding that the stabbing was a self-inflicted wound in response to being trapped in the cave with no air left (57).

Lessons learned

- The majority of diving accidents can be avoided with good planning and pre-dive checks.
- Almost all diving accidents result from a series of events,

each preventable or avoidable if recognized on time and acted upon promptly, that progressively worsened the situation until it became uncontrollable.

- Only a handful of causes are at the root of most diving mishaps. Identifying such causes is a critical factor in reducing diving accidents/incidents.
- Failures in gas management and buoyancy control are the most common causes of diving accidents. Mastering these basic skills could eliminate the two most significant causes of diving fatalities.
- Nearly all equipment failures are caused by human error in management or maintenance.
- Panic and complacency play a significant role in diving accidents.
- More complex systems, such as CCR, require higher levels of skill and knowledge to be safely used.

References

1. **Acott, J.** Human error and violations in 1,000 diving incidents: A review of data from the diving incident monitoring study (DIMS). *SPUMS.* 2005, Vol. 35, 1, pp. 11–17.

2. **Navy, US.** *US Navy diving manual.* Revision VI. 2008.

3. **Lock, G.** *Under pressure.* 2019.

4. **Miles, S. and Mackay, D.E.** *Underwater medicine.* s.l. : Granada Publishing, 1976.

5. **Acott, C.** An evaluation of buoyancy jacket safety in 1,000 diving incidents. *SPUMS.* 1996, Vol. 26, 2, pp. 89–94.

6. **Buzzacott, P., Denoble, P., Dunford, R. and Vann, R.** Dive problems and risk factors for diving morbidity. *Diving and Hyperbaric Medicine.* 2009, Vol. 39, 4, pp. 205–209.

7. **Lippmann, J., Stevenson, C., McD Taylor, D., Williams, J. and Mohebbi, M.** Chain of events analysis for a scuba diving fatality. *Diving and Hyperbaric Medicine.* 2017, Vol. 47, 3, pp. 144–154.

8. **Denoble, P.J., Caruso, J.L., Dear, G. de L., Pieper, C.F., Vann, R.D.** Common causes of open-circuit recreational diving fatalities. *UHM.* 2008, Vol. 35, 6, pp. 393–406.

9. *Common factors in diving fatalities.* **Denoble, P.J., Marroni, A. and Vann, R.D.** Durham : DAN, 2010. Dan fatalities workshop.

10. *Diving deaths down under.* **Lippmann, J.** 2009. Recreational Diving Fatalities workshop proceedings.

11. **Roberts, S., Nielsen, D. and Jareen, B.** Fatalities in recreational boating and sub-aqua diving. *International Maritime Health.* 2013, Vol. 64, 4, pp. 207–214.

12. **Vann, R.D. and Lang, M.A.** *Recreational diving fatalities.* s.l. : DAN, 2011.

13. **Cumming et al.** *A review of the nature of diving in the UK and of diving fatalities.* s.l. : DAN, 2011.

14. **Richardson, B.** *Training scuba divers: A fatality and risk analysis.* s.l. : DAN, 2011.

15. **Dardeau, M., Pollock, N., McDonald, C. and Lang, M.** The incidence of decompression illness in 10 years of scientific diving. *Diving and Hyperbaric Medicine.* 2012, Vol. 42, 4, pp. 195–200.

16. *Pressure related incident rates in scientific diving.* **Dardeau, M. and McDonald, C.** s.l. : AAUS, 2007. AAUS proceedings 26th Symposium. pp. 111-115.

17. *Survey and analysis of fatal accidents in the commercial diving sector.* **Hermans, F.** 2016.

18. **Denoble, P., Marroni, A. and Vann, R.** *Annual fatalities rates and associated factors for recreational scuba diving.* s.l. : DAN, 2011.

19. *Annual diving report 2010–2013 diving fatalities: Injuries and incidents.* **Buzzacott, P.** Durham : DAN, 2015.

20. **Cyprus Federation of Underwater Activities.** *Divers' deaths.* 2010.

21. **Stemberga et al.** Dive-related fatalities among tourist and local divers in the Northern Croatian Littoral (1980–2010). *Journal of Travel Medicine.* 2013, Vol. 20, 2, pp. 101–106.

22. **Acott, C.** Equipment malfunction in 1,000 diving incidents. *SPUMS.* 1999, Vol. 29, 3, pp. 122–126.

23. **Reason, J.** *Human error.* Cambridge : Cambridge University Press, 2006.

24. **Barsky, S. and Neuman, T.** *Ivestigating recreational and commercial diving accidents.* Ventura, CA : Hammer Head Press, 2003.

25. **Exley, S.** *Basic cave diving: A blueprint for survival.* s.l. : National Speleological Society, 1984.

26. **Buzzacott, P., Zeigler, E., Denoble, P. and Vann, R.** American cave diving fatalities 1969–2007. *International Journal of Aquatic Research and Education.* 2009, Vol. 3, pp. 162–177.

27. **Bozanic, J. and Halpern, R.** *Cave diving fatalities: A summary.*

28. **Churcher, R.A. and Lloyd, O.C.** British Cave Diving Accidents. *Proceedings of the University of Bristol Spelaelogic Society.* 1980, Vol. 15, 3, pp. 161–182.

29. **Harriss et al.** A 10-year estimate of the incidence of decompression illness in a discrete group of recreational cave divers in Australia. *Diving and Hyperbaric Medicine.* 2015, Vol. 45, 3, pp. 147–153.

30. **Hires, L.** Cavediving community. [book auth.] R.D., Denoble, P.S. and Pollock, N.W. Vann. Orlando, FL : s.n., 2012.

31. **Harris, R.** Rebreathers: Overcoming obstacles in exploration. [book auth.] R.D., Denoble, P.S. and Pollock, N.W. Vann. Orlando, FL : s.n., 2012.

32. **Arena, M. and Laneve, L.** *Immersione su relitti.* Trieste : North Eastern Divers, 1999.

33. **Chowdhury, B.** *Wreck diving accident analysis 1970–1990.* s.l. : NOAA – DEMA, 1991.

34. **Tetlow, D.R. and Jenkins, S.** The use of fault-tree analysis to visualize the importance of human factors for safe diving with closed-circuit rebreathers (CCR). *International Journal of the Society for Underwater Technology.* 2005, Vol. 26, 3, pp. 51–59.

35. **Fletcher, S.** *Assesment of manual operations and emergency procedures for closed-circuit rebreathers.* Cranfield : Cranfield University, 2011.

36. **Gempp, E., Louge, P., Blatteau, J. and Hugo, M.** Descriptive epidemiology of 153 diving injuries with rebreathers

among French military divers from 1979 to 2009. *Military Medicine*. 2011, Vol. 176, pp. 446–451.

37. **Stone, B.** Rebreather hazard analysis and human factors. [book auth.] R.D., Denoble, P.S. and Pollock, N.W. Vann. Orlando, FL : s.n., 2012.

38. **Kohler, R.** Failure is not an option: The importance of using a CCR checklist. [book auth.] R.D., Denoble, P.S. and Pollock, N.W. Vann. Orlando, FL : s.n., 2012.

39. **Caney, M.** CCR communities: Recreational. [book auth.] R.D., Denoble, P.S. and Pollock, N.W. Vann. Orlando, FL : s.n., 2012.

40. **Lang, M. and McDonald, C.** Rebreather perspective: The scientific diving community. [book auth.] R.D., Denoble, P.S. and Pollock, N.W. Vann. Orlando, FL : s.n., 2012.

41. **Short, P.** Emergency procedures and managing a rebreather whilst task loaded: The implementation of rebreather technology into scientific diving projects. [book auth.] N.W., Sellers, S.H. and Godfrey, J.M. Pollock. Catalina Island, CA : s.n., 2015.

42. —. Technical diving community. [book auth.] R.D., Denoble, P.S., Pollock, N.W. Vann. Orlando, FL : s.n., 2012.

43. **Gurr, K.** Monitoring and canister limits in rebreathers. [book auth.] R.D., Denoble, P.S. and Pollock, N.W. Vann. Orlando, FL : s.n., 2012.

44. **Warkander, D.** CO2 scrubber technology: Why, how and how long. [book auth.] R.D., Denoble, P.S. and Pollock, N.W. Vann. Orlando, FL : s.n., 2012.

45. **Mitchell, S.** Physiology of rebretaher diving. [book auth.] R.D., Denoble, P.S. and Pollock N.W. Vann. Orlando, FL : s.n., 2012.

46. **Heinerth, J.** Five golden rules: Shifting the culture of rebreather diving to reduce accidents. [book auth.] R.D., Denoble, P.S. and Pollock N.W. Vann. Orlando, FL : s.n., 2012.

47. **Concannon, D.** Rebreather accident investigations. [book auth.] R.D., Denoble, P.S. and Pollock N.W. Vann. Orlando, FL : s.n., 2012.

48. *Rebreather fatality investigation.* **Vann, R., Pollock, N. and Denoble, P.** s.l. : AAUS, 2007. Diving for Science 2007.

49. **Kesling, D.E.** Operational considerations for the use of closed-circuit rebreathers in scientific diving research. [book auth.] N.W., Sellers, S.H. and Godfrey, J.M. Pollock. Catlina Island, CA : s.n., 2015.

50. **Arieli, R., Ariely, Y., Maskalovic, Y., Eyanan, M. and Abramovich, A.** CNS oxygen toxicity in closed-circuit diving: Signs and symptoms before loss of consciusness. *Aviation Space and Environmental Medicine.* 2006, Vol. 77, 11, pp. 1153–1158.

51. **Runkle, M.** Military diving. [book auth.] R.D., Denoble, P.S. and Pollock N.W. Vann. Orlando, FL : s.n., 2012.

52. **Fock, A.** Analysis of recreational closed-circuit rebreather deaths 1998–2010. *Diving and Hyperbaric Medicine.* 2013, Vol. 43, 2, pp. 78–85.

53. **Life, Deep.** *How rebreathers kill people.* 2016.

54. **Seymour, B.** Mixed mode and mixed platform diving. [book auth.] N.W., Sellers, S.H. and Godfrey, J.M. Pollock. Catalina Island, CA : s.n., 2015.

55. **Lombardi, M.** *Closed circuit open sourced.* s.l. : Create Space, 2019.

56. **Buzzacott, P. and Denoble, P.** The epidemiology of murder and suicide involving scuba diving. *International Maritime Health.* 2012, Vol. 63, 4, pp. 207–212.

57. **Petri, N., Definis-Gojanovic, M. and Andric, D.** Scuba diver with a knife in his chest: Homicide or suicide? *CMJ.* 2003, Vol. 44, 3, pp. 355–359.

11. CASE STUDIES

Chapter highlights

In this chapter, some accidents and incidents are analyzed to identify the chain of events leading to the negative outcome and potential strategies that could be used to avoid such events in the future.

The goal is to provide the reader with a procedure for analyzing diving mishaps that can be applied to specific cases.

The case studies presented here are real cases, even if some details have been omitted to protect the identity of the individuals involved.

The first case is about a team of divers becoming separated, with one performing a controlled emergency ascent. The leading cause of the incident was unclear briefing and loss of communication between the divers.

In the second case, a diver becomes lost on a deep wreck and is victim of a fatal AGE during a free ascent that becomes uncontrolled. The leading causes were inexperience in this dive and becoming separated from the dive buddy.

The third incident involves a team of cave divers who become lost. The cause was a poorly placed guide-line and loss of situational awareness.

In the fourth situation, an experienced diver is involved in a near-fatal incident following omitted pre-dive checks.

The fifth case focuses on a team of professional divers who expose themselves to a risky situation because of the professional pressure to complete the assigned job.

Introduction

Despite our best efforts, operating in such a potentially adverse and risky environment as the underwater world exposes divers to some risk, and accidents and incidents happen.

While a "zero risk" approach is not possible, we should still aim for a "zero accidents" approach that mitigates the risks so that their impact on the safety of the operators is reduced.

When an incident/accident happens, it should be used as a learning moment for the whole community so that mistakes are not repeated in the future. No blame should be put on the individuals involved.

The following case studies focus on different typologies of risk. They are used to identify the key events leading to adverse outcomes and how we can mitigate the associated risks.

All the scenarios presented are genuine cases in which the author either personally witnessed or received a reliable account of what happened. Some details, such as location and names, have been omitted to protect the identity of the individuals involved.

Diver separation

This incident involved the separation of a diver from the rest of the team during an emergency. Even if the outcomes were positive, it could have had more severe consequences. A description of the situation, an analysis of the causes, and what we can learn from the incident follow.

Situation leading to the incident

A team of three divers (A, B, C) had an operational target to deploy a device off a pier in a commercial harbor.

As a side activity, some emergency drills were planned, with diver B using the alternate air source of diver C first and then of diver A, with whom diver B was supposed to team-up for the rest of the dive until the safety stop.

The maximum depth was about 20 meters (60 ft), and the planned dive time was around 40 minutes with no decompression obligation but with a safety stop.

Divers A and C were using double cylinders with manifold (left open during the dive), diver B had a single cylinder with an octopus plus a bailout cylinder with independent regulator. Cylinders were full to their nominal capacity. All the divers were wearing drysuits and gloves. Diver C was using a thicker than usual undergarment due to the cold water and was using regulators that had just been serviced. The regulators did not have anti-freeze first stages.

The divers were well-trained, with much experience in diving in the area and performing such operations.

Navigation toward the deployment area was aided by fixed guide-lines whose orientation and characteristics were very well known to divers A and C and, to a lesser degree, to diver B.

A briefing preceded the dive with details on the operation and a general review of the standard procedures. During the briefing, it was decided that diver C would lead the team during the first phase, and then diver A would be in charge.

Though challenging, the day's environmental conditions – with low visibility (1 meter / 3 ft), cold water (1°C / 34°F), and a current – were not anomalous for the area and well within the experience and skills of the divers.

The main hazard was the passage of ferries very close to the diving zone and swift tidal currents; to mitigate the associated risk, the dive was timed, considering the tide tables and schedule of the ferry. A further risk reduction was that the descent and ascent were to be performed close to or below the pier. An SMB was part of the mandatory equipment should the diver need to surface anywhere far from the dock.

The dive was planned to begin using a well opening on the pier as an entrance point. The divers had not entered this specific well before, having routinely used another very similar one just a few meters away.

Once on the bottom of the well, at about 15 meters (50 ft) of depth, the team had difficulties locating the guide-line that was not linked to a descent line as in the well habitually used. After a few minutes of searching, the guide-line was located, and the team started moving toward the deployment area, with diver C leading, diver B in the middle, and diver A closing.

The equipment to be carried was bulky and heavy, making the progression slower than usual.

After reaching the deployment area, the team started working on the planned task, which was successfully completed at about 24 minutes of dive time.

The incident

During the return phase, as planned, diver B started an out-of-air drill with diver C acting as donor. However, there was a misunderstanding about the technique to be used. So divers B and C started a buddy-breathing drill, sharing the same regulator instead of an alternate air drill. Diver A was a few meters behind divers B and C.

After a few exchanges of the regulator, diver C experienced a free-flow. Diver C attempted to reach the cylinder's valves/manifold but was impaired by the thicker undergarment, and therefore failed to close the valves.

At this stage, diver B was already back on their breathing system, and diver A was approaching diver C.

Before contact could be made, diver C started an emergency and controlled ascent, disappearing into the murky water above.

Diver A, the new team leader at this stage, decided not to follow diver C but to return along the guide-line to the pier and perform a standard ascent together with diver B.

Diver C successfully managed to surface, swimming back to the pier where the three divers were reunited with a very unhappy supervisor.

Despite the positive outcome of the events, there was clearly a breach of safety, with a diver becoming separated from the rest of the team during an emergency situation.

The chain of events

Predisposing circumstances

- The use of thicker undergarment impaired diver C from accessing the valves on the cylinders. He/she did not check this before starting the dive at the 5-meter safety check.
- The enhanced use of the regulator, which had no anti-freezing protection during the buddy-breathing in cold water, likely caused the first stage to freeze, triggering the free-flow.
- Testing the regulators after their services could have highlighted a free-flow tendency, but this is not certain.
- Diver C was stressed from the beginning of the dive due to the initial issues in locating the guide-line; they were also tired from earlier activity.
- Delay in the dive progression due to the heavy device reduced the time buffer available to the divers to be out of the ferry maneuvering area before the vessel's arrival.

Initiating circumstances

- The free-flow started a potentially out-of-air situation.
- Diver C decided to perform an emergency ascent instead of relying on the help of diver B or diver A to fix the problem on the bottom, therefore becoming separated from the rest of the team.

Aggravating circumstances

- Loss of communication within the team prevented diver A or diver B from understanding the intentions of diver C.

- The same loss of communication caused diver A not to be aware that the out-of-air simulation drill between diver B and diver C had started.
- The sudden ascent and the poor visibility led to the loss of contact between diver C and the rest of the team.
- The presence of a ship lane posed an increased risk for a diver surfacing on the approaching route of a ship.

Mitigating circumstances

- No decompression obligation and controlled ascent velocity avoided any DCI-related issues.
- Large volume of available gas reserve avoided an out-of-air situation during the ascent.
- The experience of the divers avoided the escalation of the situation and/or panic behavior.

Analysis of the incident

Why did diver C perform an emergency ascent?

- The attempt to self-close the valves failed because diver C could not reach the valves and/or the manifold due to the bulky undergarment.
- Diver C knew that even with a free-flowing regulator, there was enough gas to perform an emergency ascent still breathing through the scuba.
- Diver C was confident in being able to swim toward the pier during the ascent, thus reducing the risk of surfacing in the potentially hazardous ferry route area.

- Diver C is used to being a very independent diver; therefore, in an emergency, their first response was to self-manage the issue.

Why did diver A decide not to follow diver C during the ascent?

- Following diver C immediately would have likely caused a separation from diver B who was also the less experienced of the team; moreover, poor visibility and current would have made it very difficult to stay in touch with the ascending diver C.
- Even if divers A and B could have managed to start the ascent together, ascending without reference in poor visibility with current would also be a source of further risk of separation between them.
- Deploying an SMB by diver A or B to signal the presence of a diver in the water and as a reference for the ascent would have required time, and diver C would have already been at the surface by the time the SMB was deployed.
- The only real risk, due to some delay in the planned runtime of the operation, was the possibility of surfacing on the route of an approaching ferry. Following diver C to the surface would have only placed divers A and B at risk without any practical advantage for diver C.
- Due to the skills, experience, and diving configuration of diver C it was highly improbable that they would fail to surface; they had an amount of breathing gas more than sufficient for the two minutes needed to reach the surface (at a normal controlled speed of 10 meters/minute – 30ft/minute) from the depth of about 20 meters (60 ft), even with a catastrophic free-flow. Moreover, they had another

regulator to use should the one in free-flow become stuck. Finally, even in an out-of-air situation, the depth was within the range of an emergency ascent.

Leading causes of the incident

- Failure of communication within the team. The divers should have signaled to each other at the beginning of the out-of-air simulation drill.
- The decision of diver C to proceed with a self-rescue (controlled emergency ascent) instead of relying on the other team members to fix the issue at the bottom.

Considering the configuration used by the divers, plenty of breathing gas was available for sharing, and all of them had the needed training and experience to do so safely and proficiently.

During the debriefing, diver C took full responsibility for the mishap, but all the divers should share responsibility:

- Diver A should have been closer to divers C and B during their out-of-air simulation drill in case of necessity.
- Diver B, who was in touch with diver C at the moment of the free-flow, should have acted more promptly, immediately providing diver C with a backup breathing gas which was available in the form of the bailout cylinder and regulator carried by diver B.

A root cause of this incident can be identified as complacency among well-experienced divers who underestimated the possibility of having issues during what was considered a pretty basic drill and operation.

The same complacency caused the team not to be focused during the briefing, misunderstanding the drill to be performed. No buddy-breathing was supposed to be performed, but only alternate air sharing.

Error typology

The kind of error committed by diver C is a rule-based mistake. They correctly applied the rule for controlled emergency ascent but in the wrong circumstances. They should have fixed the problem at the bottom, working together with the two other divers.

At a team level there was a failure in communication and in effective mutual performance monitoring, with both divers A and B being unable to foresee the probable evolution of the problem encountered by diver C.

Lessons learned

- Always maintain high situational awareness, no matter how basic the diving operation seems.
- Communication within the team is a critical factor for the safety of the divers. Always be sure that others clearly understand your intentions.
- The briefing is a critical phase of the dive planning. You should be focused on the briefing with no distractions. If something is not clear, ask questions and discuss further.

Fatal ascent

This accident, with fatal consequences, involved two divers performing a deep wreck dive. A description of the situation, an analysis of the causes, and what we can learn from the incident follow.

Situation leading to the incident

Two divers were attempting a deep dive on a wreck lying on a flat muddy bottom a few miles offshore in temperate/warm waters.

The wreck was a sail-steam-powered vessel with three masts lying in navigational position on the seafloor at 60 meters (196 ft) of depth. A shot-line was connected to one of the masts.

The two divers knew each other, but they did not regularly dive together and were paired by the diving instructor just for this dive. Diver A was a well-experienced diver, although not very attentive to the buddy-system; diver B was recently certified for deep technical diving and had a history of some dive-related anxiety.

The weather conditions were acceptable, but water visibility was poor, as common in the area due to a large inflow of silty water from a river along the shore.

The diving platform was a large RIB, and multiple divers were diving simultaneously, divided into pairs.

The incident

The dive started as planned, with divers A and B descending along a shot-line fixed to one of the masts. The plan was to swim along the vessel's main deck without attempting any penetration.

After a few minutes, the divers became separated. Diver A did a quick search for the other diver but, unable to re-establish contact, proceeded alone, continuing the dive until the planned bottom time was reached, and then ascended along the shot-line, performing the required deco-stops.

Shortly after this, diver B surfaced, clearly in distress and losing consciousness soon after. The diving instructor on the RIB jumped into the water to rescue diver B who was carried onboard. As other divers were decompressing along the shot-line, the instructor decided to wait for them; finally, with all the divers onboard, the RIB zoomed for the harbor. Diver B was declared dead on arrival by EMS personnel.

We can only speculate what happened to diver B, with some clues from the data logged in the diving computer.

It seems that after the separation, diver B started to look for the ascent line but missed the correct mast. After a few minutes of hovering above one of the other masts, the diver started a free ascent, quickly losing control of the ascent speed and surfacing without the required decompression.

The chain of events

Predisposing circumstances

- Divers A and B were paired for a challenging dive without previous experience diving together.
- Diver A had a habit of poor buddy supervision.
- Diver B was recently certified with a history of diving-related anxiety.

Initiating circumstances

- Diver A and B became separated.
- Diver B was unable to return to the ascent line and attempted a free ascent.

Aggravating circumstances

- Diver B did not deploy an SMB.
- Water visibility was poor, making a controlled ascent without reference even more challenging and likely enhancing stress and anxiety.
- Waiting for other divers to complete the deco-stops caused a delay in providing proper advanced life-support to diver B.

Mitigating circumstances

- The diver instructor on the RIB brought diver B still alive onboard the boat.

Analysis of the incident

Why did diver B lose control of the situation?

- Becoming separated from your diving buddy in poor visibility on a deep wreck is a challenging and stressful situation for anyone; that diver B was anxiety-prone likely worsened the problem.
- The limited experience of diver B prevented them from maintaining good situational awareness, missing the ascent line, and not managing a difficult free ascent.

Main causes

- The leading cause of this incident was the incapacity of diver B to control the free ascent.
- A contributing cause was that diver B could not find the ascent line.
- The availability of a single boat only, which had to wait for other divers to complete their decompression, made it impossible for the quick transportation of diver B to reach advanced care.

Error typology

The error committed by diver B was skill-based in that they could not correctly manage a free ascent. This error was likely aggravated by high anxiety that impaired correct and logical decision-making.

Lessons learned

- The buddy system should be enforced, and the divers should be aware of each other's position, especially in poor visibility situations, to avoid being separated.
- Impromptu teams should be avoided, especially for demanding dives.
- No one should be rushed into challenging dives without enough time to build proper experience.
- Anxiety-prone individuals should seek counseling about being involved in complex diving activities under stressful circumstances.

- When multiple divers are involved in deep dives requiring decompression stops, an emergency plan for transporting a potentially injured diver should be prepared, considering the need to assist other divers engaged in decompression.

Lost in a cave

This incident involved three cave divers who became temporarily lost in a cave due to some navigational errors. Although the divers safely exited the cave, this incident could have had fatal consequences. A description of the situation, an analysis of the causes, and what we can learn from the incident follow.

Situation leading to the incident

A cave was being explored, with new branches progressively surveyed by cave divers.

The maximum water depth was about 24 meters (80 ft), and the penetration length was around 300 meters (1,000 ft). The water temperature was 15–18°C (low 60s°F). The visibility was fairly good in the first section, worsening toward the end of the cave due to silt accumulation.

The passages in the cave were large, narrowing toward the end of the explored section.

Two cave divers (A and B) had been invited by one of the divers involved in the exploration (diver C) to dive within a newly surveyed section. Divers A and B have already dived into the cave, but they have never been into the new section.

The divers were equipped with double cylinders with manifold (closed during the dive to have two independent cylinders) plus side cylinders to be carried through the dive.

The rule of thirds and all the other standard safety procedures for cave diving were strictly observed.

A temporary continuous guide-line was present in the cave from the entrance to the end of the section currently in exploration.

A briefing preceded the dive with planning of dive time, estimated gas consumption, turning point, and lost-line procedures. It was decided that diver C would lead, with divers B and A following during the ingress phase, exiting in reverse order.

The incident

The penetration was uneventful, with the team following the guide-line until inside the newly explored section, which had reduced visibility and was narrowing.

Once the end of the guide-line was reached, diver C signaled the others to turn around to start the exit phase of the dive. All the divers were well within the planned air reserve.

Given that a very low ceiling characterized this cave section, the divers had agreed to simply turn around, reversing their order during the exit phase, with diver A becoming the leading diver, diver B in the middle, and diver C closing out the group.

Diver A followed the guide-line for a few minutes until it abruptly ended. There was no sign indicating a breach or rupture of the line. It was simply tied off to a rock. The divers were still inside the cave and nowhere near the exit.

Diver A started a "lost line" search with no result. During the search, the divers noted an open surface above them and decided to surface. The team emerged in what was a subterranean lake inside the cave.

At this point, diver C, the one who was involved in the survey of the new section, understood the mistake: the team had missed a T junction and followed a line leading deeper inside the cave instead of the one toward the exit.

Plenty of breathable air was in the cavity hosting the lake, and it was also possible to climb to some dry parts. One option was to send one diver with multiple redundancy cylinders and lights to look for the correct exit route and call for rescue. Following diver C's reassurance that they were sure of their position in the cave, the team decided to dive together in search of the missed junction with diver C leading.

The junction was successfully located, and the divers managed to exit the cave without further problems and with plenty of air reserve.

It was a lucky escape from an extremely dangerous situation that could have caused multiple fatalities.

The chain of events

Predisposing circumstances

- Diver C, although involved in the exploration of the new section of the cave, did not participate in the survey of the branch leading to the lake and therefore did not have perfect knowledge of the line disposition.
- Diver A, leading the team during the exit, did not have experience in diving in the new section.
- The presence of a T junction was never mentioned during the briefing.

- The T junction was very low on the floor of the cave, and there were no arrows pointing toward the exit.
- Visibility was reduced.

Initiating circumstances

- Diver A, now leading the team during the exit phase, missed the T junction.
- The divers did not notice any incongruence between the depth and shape of the section they were diving in compared to the one they had entered before.
- Even if diver C did realize the mistake, they could not communicate with the rest of the team until they surfaced in the lake.

Aggravating circumstances

- Swimming in the wrong direction away from the exit in a cave is extremely dangerous, likely leading to being lost and an out-of-air situation.
- The absence of arrows along the exit line contributed to the loss of orientation.

Mitigating circumstances

- The divers had plenty of air reserve to breathe, well above the minimum needed for the planned dive.
- The application of the rule of thirds further enhanced the air contingency reserve.
- The divers were well-experienced and skilled, being able to calmly assess the situation and act accordingly.

Analysis of the incident

Why did the divers miss the junction?

- Diver A failed to see the T junction, likely because the visibility was reduced and especially because they were unaware of the existence of such a junction.
- Poor knowledge of the new area by divers A and B and reduced visibility contributed to the error and to the fact that they did not realize they were not swimming toward the exit.
- Diver C, closing out the group, did not advise the rest of the team on the missed junction, likely because they were not able to call for their attention or because they were also confused, having not been directly involved in the deployment of the line in this section of the cave during the exploration.
- The absence of arrows pointing to the exit was a serious safety breach by the divers who deployed the line.

Main causes

- The main cause of this incident was the placement of a poorly indicated T junction in the line.
- Allowing diver A, who had not dived in this section of the cave before, to be the leading diver during the exit phase was also a contributing cause.

Error typology

The error committed by diver A was a knowledge-based one. They did not have knowledge of the presence of a junction and also failed to recognize the junction when they swam through it.

A contributing factor was the slip error of the divers being focused on swimming along the return path and not realizing the different depth and morphology of the section of the cave they were in.

Diver C was also the victim of a slip error, forgetting to mention the existence of a T junction during the briefing.

A third type of error was a ruled-based one. While it is correct to revert the order of divers during the exit phase of a cave dive, it would have been better to have the most experienced diver (diver C) still as the leader in this situation.

Lessons learned

- This incident highlights the paramount importance of an accurate briefing. Should the presence of a T junction have been mentioned, there is no doubt that the divers would have been more attentive in looking for such a point during the exit phase.

- It is also important to be flexible in applying the rules. In this specific situation, the divers should not have simply reversed their position during the exit phase but should instead have shuffled positions, with diver C still leading the team, given that they had experience in diving in the newly explored section of the cave.

- The positive outcome of the incident was likely because there was a large availability of breathing gas reserve, and the divers could stop, assess the situation and act calmly and rationally. This highlights the relevance of accurate planning of gas consumption, mainly when operating in overhead environments. Moreover, training, experience, and skills are the cornerstones of safely managing an emergency.

Missed pre-dive checks

This incident involved an expert diver who missed a basic pre-dive check leading to a close call with a potentially fatal out-of-air situation.

Situation leading to the incident

A diver planned a deep dive (50 meters / 164 ft) using a double cylinder with manifold, two regulators, and a full-face mask in cold water (6°C / 43°F).

The full-face mask was connected to the left-side regulator; the right-side regulator had a standard second stage with a mouthpiece. Both regulators had a pressure gauge.

As extra equipment, the diver used a helmet with lights as part of training for specific procedures.

The diver was accustomed to diving with a twin-set with the manifold closed, alternating between the two regulators; because the diver planned to wear a full-face in this dive, the manifold was to be left open so the gas stored in both cylinders could be used.

During the pre-dive checks, the diver was distracted by local bystanders enquiring about the unusual set-up. Following this, the diver forgot to check the manifold, which was in a closed position.

The incident

The diver started the descent along a steep seafloor, breathing normally through the full-face mask.

A few minutes later, the diver, checking the pressure gauge connected with the full-face regulator, noticed a higher-than-usual gas usage. He took a mental note of this, ready to reduce the planned bottom time accordingly.

Once at the maximum depth, the diver rechecked the gauge, becoming aware that the remaining pressure was alarmingly low. Only at this point did he/she check the other gauge connected with the secondary regulator, observing that it still indicated a full cylinder. The diver realized that the manifold must have been closed and that they were using only one cylinder.

The diver then tried to open the manifold, an operation they were used to doing as part of the standard safety drills. Unfortunately, in this dive, they were using a thicker than usual undergarment that made it difficult to reach the manifold valve, which was also tightly closed. Despite several attempts, the diver was not able to open the manifold.

At this point, the diver decided to begin the ascent using the remaining gas left in the cylinder connected to the full-face before attempting the removal of the full-face and the switch to the standard regulator connected to the cylinder that was still full.

When the first cylinder ran out, the switch was completed successfully. However, it caused a sudden exposure of the diver's face to cold water, with potentially adverse effects such as the involuntary gasp reflex. It required quite a laborious procedure, including removing the helmet, retrieving the spare mask, donning and purging, and switching to the secondary regulator.

The chain of events

Predisposing circumstances

- The diver was used to diving using double cylinders with a closed manifold, alternating between the regulators. Using an open manifold was not their usual procedure.
- The standard setting-up of the double cylinders was with a closed manifold.
- The diver was distracted during the pre-dive checks and therefore missed the critical step of checking that the manifold was in an open position.

Initiating circumstances

- Because of the closed manifold, the diver used only one cylinder, thus strongly reducing the gas availability.
- The diver noticed a higher-than-usual gas usage but did not link this with a potentially closed manifold until late in the dive.

Aggravating circumstances

- Using a helmet above the full-face made removing the mask more complex.
- Using a bulkier-than-usual dive suit made it even more challenging to reach the manifold.
- Sudden exposure to cold water due to the full-face removal could have caused an involuntary gasp with potential inhalation of water.

Mitigating circumstances

- The diver had a spare mask so that even with the full-face removed, they could see underwater and surface safely.
- Full-face mask removal, mask replacement, and switching to alternate regulator were all part of the standard safety drills periodically tested. The diver could act even under the unavoidable stress of an emergency.

Analysis of the incident

Why did the diver miss the pre-dive check?

- The diver was distracted during the pre-dive checks.
- If the checking procedure is interrupted, it should be started repeatedly to avoid skipping a step.
- A written checklist could have prevented missing a critical step.

Main causes

- The leading cause of the incident was diving with a closed manifold that should have been open.
- Failure to assess the issue sooner in the dive was likely because the specific diving configuration used was not the one usually adopted.

Error typology

The diver committed a slip error when they failed to check the manifold due to a distraction during the pre-dive checks.

Lessons learned

- This incident highlights the importance of accurate pre-dive checks that should be performed meticulously and accurately, avoiding distractions.
- If the checks are interrupted, they should be restarted from the beginning to avoid missing crucial steps.
- The use of written checklists should be enforced, mainly when a new/unfamiliar configuration is used.
- A safety check performed at the beginning of the dive in shallow water, typically at 5 meters (15 ft), including emergency valve shut-off procedure, would have shown that the diver could not open the manifold. This highlights the importance of conducting a quick safety drill before each dive, especially when new gear / a new configuration is used.

Professional pressure

This case study focuses on the negative impact that professional pressure –the need to complete a dive, which is part of professional activities – has on safety considerations.

Situation leading to the incident

A team of three divers (A, B, C) had an operational target to take underwater measurements of a submerged device and work on the device to connect some of its parts. This last job required the use of a lift-bag.

Divers A and C were using double cylinders with manifold (left open during the dive); diver B had two independent cylinders in a back position. Diver B needed to alternate breathing from the two cylinders during the dive. The diver was very well-experienced in the use of this configuration. Moreover, the gear set-up was tested during a training dive. Cylinders were full to their nominal capacity. All the divers were wearing drysuits and gloves.

The divers were well-trained and with much experience in diving in the area and performing such operations.

A briefing preceded the dive with details of the operation. During the briefing, it was decided to complete the tasks (measurements and components connection) over two dives instead of in one longer dive as initially planned.

Maximum depth was about 15 meters (50 ft), and the planned dive time for the first dive was around 30 minutes; the second dive was planned to last up to 60 minutes. A safety stop was scheduled for the end of each dive. The water temperature was 13°C (55°F).

The diving platform was a research vessel, and the crew had much experience operating in the area and with divers. The vessel was to be "live," not moored but remaining close to the diving point using its power.

Weather conditions were deteriorating faster than forecasted, becoming marginal at the time of arrival at the operative area during the first dive. The main issue was a big rolling swell affecting both the onboard and diving operations, causing a strong stirring of sediment from the seafloor, leading to almost zero visibility and pushing the divers around.

The incident

Due to the very limited visibility and strong surge, the measurement operations required longer than estimated, and the bottom time for the first dive stretched from the planned 30 minutes to more than one hour.

Once surfaced, the divers climbed aboard the vessel, and at this point, they also had to replace the cylinders, which were more depleted than expected due to the longer dive time. All the divers used doubles with a manifold for the second dive.

The weather conditions further deteriorated, and diver B had difficulties due to being tired from sleep loss in the preceding nights caused by stomach pain. This ailment and a degree of seasickness were also tasking the endurance of diver B.

Despite feeling tired, seasick, and overall unwell, diver B, even when asked, declined to forfeit the second dive.

Due to the increased movement of the vessel, swapping cylinders was more laborious than usual; all the divers were rushing to be quickly back in the water, feeling the impact of seasickness.

No pre-dive checks were done as a team; each diver did their checks. No safety drill was planned once in the water either because of the sea status.

Once on the bottom, the divers started to attach the lift-bag and prepare the components of the device to be moved around.

At this point, diver C called for the attention of diver B, indicating that the pressure gauge was reading almost zero.

Diver B correctly guessed that the valve of the cylinder of diver C (connected to the SPG) was closed and managed to open it quickly. Diver B also checked that the other valve was correctly fully open.

Operations proceeded for about 30 minutes before the dive

leader called for termination due to the worsening environmental conditions on the seafloor and concerns about diver B who was not wearing gloves and could have issues with the cold.

The chain of events

Predisposing circumstances

- Deteriorating weather conditions were affecting both surface and submerged operations.
- No team pre-dive checks.
- Time pressure to finish the job.
- Impact of seasickness.

Initiating circumstances

- Diver C entered the water with the valve of one of the cylinders closed.

Aggravating circumstances

- Workload and poor environmental conditions prevented diver C from checking the gauge upon arrival on the bottom
- Very poor visibility strongly limited underwater communication between the divers.

Mitigating circumstances

- The shallow water setting would have permitted a relatively safe emergency ascent if diver C was unable to access their breathing gas.

- Diver B was able to identify and solve the problem quickly.
- The experience of the divers avoided the escalation of the situation and/or panic behavior.

Analysis of the incident

Why did diver C not have the cylinder open?
- Time pressure and difficult conditions onboard due to the sea status prevented correct team pre-dive cross-checking.
- Diver C was more focused on the technical details of the planned operation and likely performed partial, if any, pre-dive checks.

Leading causes of the incident

- No pre-dive checks.

Error typology

The kind of error committed by diver C is a latent error due to slip. They likely forgot to check the valve because some other activity rushed and interrupted the pre-dive checks. The error remained latent until well below water when diver B realized the valve was closed.

There was a failure in performing as a unit at the team level. Cross-checking pre-dive checks are a key safety factor, and they should not be forfeited.

Lessons learned

- The worsening of the weather conditions and the unfitness of one of the divers should have called for the termination of the operations at the end of the first dive.
- Professional pressure played a key role in the divers' behavior; no one was willing to call off the dive.
- Entering the water with the cylinder valve closed is a serious mistake that can have even fatal consequences.
- Pre-dive checks must be performed with full attention before each dive, and the divers should cross-check each other.

12. DIVING RISK ASSESSMENT STRUCTURE

Chapter highlights

A diving risk assessment is structured following a logical sequence of steps that includes the identification of realistic risks, quantifying their impact on the operation, and formulating mitigation procedures and strategies.

Risk management should aim to achieve ALARP status, reducing the risk to an "as low as reasonably practicable" level.

The main areas of risk assessment include the divers' fitness and safety, environmental hazards, and potential gear problems.

Even if it is impossible to develop a plan that includes all conceivable risks, a good assessment should cover the main and most probable risk factors and procedures for their avoidance or mitigation.

There are several possible diving risk assessment plans that can vary in terms of structure and layout; what is important is that the risks are clearly indicated and proper management procedures followed.

Introduction

There are no risk-free activities, but a threshold of acceptable risk must be identified to conduct safe operations. Scuba diving is a reasonably safe activity based on acceptable risk (1). Activities with low accident rates do not necessarily occur in a low-risk situation because it could be that a severe risk was identified. Still, proper avoidance strategies are implemented, mitigating or avoiding it (2). Scuba diving is an activity where avoiding serious risks results from good practice and applying effective standards.

In diving operations, risk can be divided into two main categories (3):

1. *Safety risk*: Affecting the health integrity of the diver; primarily related to medical issues, absence of appropriate emergency plans, and violation of safety standards.
2. *Commercial risk*: Relates to economic losses due to inappropriate insurance cover, lawsuits, and loss of reputation.

Developing a risk assessment for diving shares the same basic principles as any other risk assessment for dynamic and unforgiving environments where life-support systems are paramount for the operator's survival (4).

Elements of risk assessment

A complete risk assessment should consider the whole system, including divers, materials, and environment.

Divers

The divers are the elements that need the highest protection. Therefore, all the relevant hazards that could become a risk should be carefully identified, and appropriate risk-reduction strategies applied.

Team: For most commercial/professional diving activities, the diving team should be composed of no fewer than three individuals with a lead diver, a reserve diver, and a diver supervisor; a medical advisor is also suggested. The diving supervisor and the medical advisor can be the same person. Under specific circumstances, such as for dives in waters shallower than 9 meters and with current of less than 0.5 knots, the team may be reduced to two individuals (5).

The rationale of having two divers is that they can offer reciprocal help during normal operations and in an emergency. This same rationale is the basis for the "buddy system" standard in recreational diving. There are specific situations where the effectiveness of the buddy system is questionable. For example, when diving in extremely confined spaces where practical reciprocal help would be impaired due to the restriction of movement and in the presence of differential pressure hazards where if the flow catches a diver, it is almost impossible to free the diver unless the differential pressure can be reduced, requiring action outside the diving team.

The diver supervisor, who remains topside, will guarantee the overall safety of the operations and act as the main communication link between the divers and other personnel (6). The presence of a diver performing as liaison is important because they will know the diving procedures and needs.

In other circumstances, the team could be composed of two divers in the water working together and a third diver topside acting as a standby diver ready to be deployed if needed. The state of readiness of the standby diver can be decided based on the required response time. Sometimes, the diver should be fully dressed and ready to enter the water at any moment; in other circumstances, the diver could be only partially dressed. Evaluating the risks will help in deciding the needed readiness level of the standby diver.

Training and experience: The training level and effective experience of the divers about the tasks to be performed should be part of the risk assessment (6), (7), (8).

More complex or unusual diving operations may require rehearsing the procedures before the actual operational dive. This will improve proficiency and likely make evident potential issues that may cause risky situations during the dive. It is important to conduct the rehearsal under realistic but safe conditions. For example, the practice dives could be performed at shallower depth to minimize air consumption and inert-gas intake, thus allowing the divers to focus more on learning the needed procedures without the added stress of tightly controlling the diving parameters. The divers involved in the operations must have effective experience for the planned depth.

Divers count: All divers must be back onboard at the end of the operation. For this reason, an accounting system should be used. The passive count uses at least two individuals to count the divers independently; an active count uses roll calls, tagging, or signing. This latter is more time-consuming but ensures a more accurate count. If the counting shows someone is missing, the emergency plan for a lost diver must be activated (6). This system is essential when a large group of divers is involved in the operations, with teams alternating throughout the day. For example, this is a common situation for search and rescue and law enforcement divers who must survey a large area, requiring multiple dives and teams. On charter boats, the divers' count is also critical. Failures in this procedure have caused several situations of lost divers, as sometimes reported in the media.

Fitness and medical: The overall fitness of a diver can be considered to be composed of medical fitness, physical fitness, and mental fitness. The impact of each component should be carefully addressed in the risk management strategy. The divers must have a valid medical for fitness to dive (6), (7). The frequency of such medicals may vary, with yearly checks being one of the most common requisites (5), (7). An in-water test, including swimming, free diving, rescue towing, and treading water, is a good tool for identifying fitness problems (9). With aging divers, specific medical tests could be required to ensure fitness.

Scuba diving significantly impacts cardiovascular stress due to various factors, including peripheral vasoconstriction, increased workload, and breathing resistance (10). Hydrostatic pulmonary edema may occur suddenly while at depth when a diseased heart fails to respond to the increased circulatory demand. Several unexplained drownings may have been due to pulmonary edema (10).

Temporary medical situations like cold and flu should also be considered as part of the fitness risk assessment (8).

Proper equalization techniques and absence of any pathological conditions are key safety factors to minimize the risk of tympanic barotrauma. Even more important is to have free air circulation within the lungs because even a slight pressure differential (around 0.1 bar) may cause alveolar damage. For example, a panicked diver could hold his breath during the ascent leading to lung over-pressurization and likely damage (10).

There is no evidence of long-term physiological damage associated with sport or recreational scuba diving (10).

Environment

Heat stress: Being exposed to heat can increase the risk of physiological damage to fully dressed divers, and their status should be closely monitored in temperatures above 21°C (70°F). A diver wearing a drysuit exposed to moderately high temperatures may lose up to 500 ml of fluids each hour, leading to dehydration (9).

Acquaintance with the environment: The divers should be experienced and competent in diving in the operational environment (8). Even a very good diver could find themselves in difficulties if required to operate in a totally new environment. Adequate training should be provided to build experience in working under the conditions of the diving area.

Potential hazards: The specific potential hazards of the diving area and their impact on the safety of the operations should be addressed as part of the risk assessment. Some hazards could be temporary, such as underwater construction activities and acoustic emissions, or permanent, for example, strong tidal currents that routinely develop in the area. Other hazards could be generated by the activity that the divers have to perform. For example, the use of heavy tools, suction/jetting devices, or suspended loads. Polluted waters, cold, reduced visibility, and differential pressure are specific hazards that are analyzed in Chapter 7 of this book.

Diving gear and equipment

Scheduled maintenance and pre-dive checks should be routinely performed (8). The planned servicing intervals are to be considered the minimum. The time between servicing should be shortened if the gear is heavily used and/or exposed to harsh environments. If anomalies are identified during a pre-dive check, the gear should not be employed; instead, it should be marked as "not to be used" and sent to maintenance. Minor repairs can be performed in the field but only by experienced personnel.

Redundancy should be assured for the most critical elements, such as regulators and breathing gas supply. Each diver should have at least a primary and a secondary gas source, and the divers should also be skilled in gas-sharing procedures.

If other specific gear is needed, it should be ensured that each diver has understanding and experience in its usage. Attention should be given to equipment that may present physical hazards such as trapping, suction, cutting, and similar. If not all the divers have proper experience in handling the gear, the plan should clearly indicate who within the diving team is authorized to use it.

The specific risks should be clearly assessed within the overall diving plan and an ALARP approach should be followed to reduce the risk. If this is not possible due to lack of proper gear the operation should be postponed until appropriate equipment is available.

In Appendix A1 and A2 examples of a diving risk evaluation and diving risk assessment are provided.

Lessons learned

- The risk assessment should aim to reduce the overall risks to an ALARP level.
- The most important point of any diving plan should be the protection of the divers.
- The diving environment and the related hazards should be carefully assessed.
- The diving gear is a life-supporting resource, and its reliability is a key safety factor.
- The risk assessment structure should ensure that all the relevant risks have been considered.

References

1. **Richardson, D.** Dive safety and risk management: Never let your guard down. *SPURS.* 2004.

2. **Adams, J.** *Risk.* Abingdon : Routledge, 1995.

3. **Nimb, H.** Risk management in recreational diving: The PADI approach. *SPUMS.* 2004, Vol. 34, 2.

4. **HSA.** *Guidelines on risk assessment and safety statements.* Dublin, Ireland : HSA, 2006.

5. **Dutch Labour Inspectorate.** *The main occupational risks in the diving sector.* s.l. : Arbeidsinspectie, 2008.

6. **Relations, Minister for Education and Industrial.** *Recreational diving, recreational technical diving and snorkeling code of practice.* Brisbane, Australia : Queensland Government, 2011.

7. **The University of Melbourne.** *Scientific diving risk management procedure.* Melbourne, Australia : The University of Melbourne, 2014.

8. **Government of Western Australia.** *OSH newsletter for employers in the recreational diving industry.*

9. **DUI.** *Risk management through advanced technology for public safety divers.* s.l. : DUI, 2012.

10. **Germonpre, P.** The medical risks of underwater diving and their control. *International Sport Medicine Journal.* 2006, Vol. 7, 1.

13. MEDICAL FITNESS TO DIVE

Chapter highlights

Diving is a potentially hazardous activity that requires a level of medical fitness to be safely performed.

To assess the fitness level, personal details such as medical history and prescribed medications of divers should be considered.

Ensuring diving fitness is critical for divers' safety and overall risk management. Medical problems considered minor daily can pose an unacceptable risk in a submerged environment.

Some medical conditions, unfortunately, will permanently prevent the affected individuals from diving. Other circumstances will only temporarily prevent participation in diving activities.

Generally, the cardiovascular, respiratory, and nervous systems are more physiologically stressed during diving, requiring careful evaluation by physicians trained in dive medicine.

Consumption of specific medications may affect the physical and psychological state of the individual, making them unfit for diving.

A medical assessment for diving should be periodically performed to ensure that the individuals are still fit to dive. Any event that could affect such fitness should be promptly reported to the physician in charge of the medical assessment.

Introduction

Scuba diving is a much safer activity than is commonly believed by the public. The probability of a recreational dive fatality is 1.6×10^{-4} deaths/person-year, roughly one-fifth of the fatality rate for car accidents (1). Nevertheless, diving is still a potentially hazardous activity, and a high standard of medical fitness is required for all divers to ensure an acceptable risk profile for each dive. This is particularly true when environmental conditions, such as cold water, extreme depth, and prolonged submersion, increase the overall risk. This risk comprises a combination of human factors, such as behavior and underlying medical conditions, as well as non-human factors, such as equipment function and environmental conditions. These components are interconnected; changing one variable alters the effects on others and increases or decreases the overall risk profile associated with each dive activity. For example, cold water diving increases the risk of hypothermia and requires heavier and more specialized equipment. Cold conditions can exacerbate underlying medical conditions, and using more specialized equipment can increase the risk of its malfunction. Therefore, the risks of diving are significantly higher when diving in colder temperatures.

The requirements to safely participate in scuba diving are dynamic and, most importantly, vary depending on each activity's expected conditions and intended objectives. Recreational, scientific, commercial, and technical divers will encounter different conditions while participating in a dive, spend different amounts of time underwater, carry different types and quantities of equipment, and have different objectives to accomplish while underwater. Every kind of diver will also have their standards of fitness level, which heavily influences each of these factors.

Therefore, when assessing the fitness to dive in each of these types of divers, it is necessary to follow an approach that considers all of these human and non-human factors.

While non-human factors are important to consider when planning for a safe dive, all divers, particularly the dive supervisor, should be aware of the human factors, including medical history and any physical conditions. By ensuring that all divers are *medically fit to dive*, a diving officer can achieve a higher level of safety for all dive participants and increase efficiency in completing underwater tasks.

Medical fitness to dive requirements

Medical fitness to dive implies that the prospective or current diver has no known medical conditions that significantly limit their ability to participate in diving, jeopardize the safety of the diver or the team, or predispose the diver to occupational illness (2). Ensuring fitness to dive among scientific and commercial divers is vital to ensure the work safety of the diver, as well as other members of the team. Fitness to dive can often be an abstract concept, with multiple meanings for diving in varying conditions. While some medical issues may pose a minimal risk in one particular environment, these same ailments could significantly threaten the safety of the diver and their entire team under different environmental conditions. Therefore, establishing fitness to dive involves reviewing each diver's medical and dive history, obtaining dive physician consultation as needed, and carefully assessing the environmental conditions where the diving activity will occur.

Ensuring fitness to dive involves recognizing the often-complex relationship between human and non-human factors above and below water. Human factors, such as medical conditions (known and unknown), medication and substance use, physical fitness, and experience level, are characteristics specific to an individual (or individuals) engaged in diving activities. Non-human factors, such as equipment, environmental conditions, and proximity to emergency medical services, are not directly a characteristic of an individual but can significantly modify the effect of human factors, resulting in a spectrum of situational safety.

Generally speaking, requirements to ensure a safe diving environment will vary significantly depending on the goals set forth by a dive organization. For example, those engaged in recreational dive activities, at shallower depths, in warmer water, and using less complicated equipment, will experience fewer hurdles in establishing safe conditions than those sponsoring technical diving at significant depth and in extreme conditions.

Multiple organizations have their recommendations on standards for ensuring safe dive practices. These recommendations have been designed specifically for the anticipated dive activities specific to certain disciplines within diving. For example, for recreational divers, the organizations NAUI and PADI have standardized their requirements for safety in a screening tool that all new divers are subjected to. This consists of a questionnaire reviewing the medical and surgical history and other potential factors that would increase the risk of diving (3), (4). Any positive screening results require evaluation by a physician to ensure suitability for diving. For scientific and commercial divers, who will be spending longer periods underwater, and in potentially more hazardous conditions, more in-depth recommendations and standards exist. The American Academy of Underwater Sciences (AAUS) requires that divers are examined by a physician every 2–5 years for a complete physical exam, urinalysis, chest X-ray, and electrocardiogram (EKG) (5). Extracts from these statements can be found in Fig. 13.1.a and b. Even more stringent evaluation is required by commercial diving organizations, including screening for illicit drug use and risk stratification scores for the probability of severe medical events, such as heart attack or stroke.

NAUI WORLDWIDE

R·S·T·C
Recreational Scuba Training Council

UNDERSEA & HYPERBARIC MEDICAL SOCIETY

MEDICAL STATEMENT

Participant Record (Confidential Information)

Please read carefully before signing.

This is a statement in which you are informed of some potential risks involved in scuba diving and of the conduct required of you during the scuba training program. Your signature on this statement is required for you to participate in the scuba training program offered

by______________________________and
Instructor

______________________________located in the
Facility

city of________________, state/province of ____________.

Read this statement prior to signing it. You must complete this Medical Statement, which includes the medical questionnaire section, to enroll in the scuba training program. If you are a minor, you must have this Statement signed by a parent or guardian.

Diving is an exciting and demanding activity. When performed correctly, applying correct techniques, it is relatively safe. When established safety procedures are not followed, however, there are increased risks.

To scuba dive safely, you should not be extremely overweight or out of condition. Diving can be strenuous under certain conditions. Your respiratory and circulatory systems must be in good health. All body air spaces must be normal and healthy. A person with coronary disease, a current cold or congestion, epilepsy, a severe medical problem or who is under the influence of alcohol or drugs should not dive. If you have asthma, heart disease, other chronic medical conditions or you are taking medications on a regular basis, you should consult your doctor and the instructor before participating in this program, and on a regular basis thereafter upon completion. You will also learn from the instructor the important safety rules regarding breathing and equalization while scuba diving. Improper use of scuba equipment can result in serious injury. You must be thoroughly instructed in its use under direct supervision of a qualified instructor to use it safely.

If you have any additional questions regarding this Medical Statement or the Medical Questionnaire section, review them with your instructor before signing.

Divers Medical Questionnaire

To the Participant:

The purpose of this Medical Questionnaire is to find out if you should be examined by your doctor before participating in recreational diver training. A positive response to a question does not necessarily disqualify you from diving. A positive response means that there is a preexisting condition that may affect your safety while diving and you must seek the advice of your physician prior to engaging in dive activities.

Please answer the following questions on your past or present medical history with a **YES** or **NO**. If you are not sure, answer **YES**. If any of these items apply to you, we must request that you consult with a physician prior to participating in scuba diving. Your instructor will supply you with an RSTC Medical Statement and Guidelines for Recreational Scuba Diver's Physical Examination to take to your physician.

____ Could you be pregnant, or are you attempting to become pregnant?

____ Are you presently taking prescription medications? (with the exception of birth control or anti-malarial)

____ Are you over 45 years of age and can answer YES to one or more of the following?
- currently smoke a pipe, cigars or cigarettes
- have a high cholesterol level
- have a family history of heart attack or stroke
- are currently receiving medical care
- high blood pressure
- diabetes mellitus, even if controlled by diet alone

Have you ever had or do you currently have...

____ Asthma, or wheezing with breathing, or wheezing with exercise?

____ Frequent or severe attacks of hayfever or allergy?

____ Frequent colds, sinusitis or bronchitis?

____ Any form of lung disease?

____ Pneumothorax (collapsed lung)?

____ Other chest disease or chest surgery?

____ Behavioral health, mental or psychological problems (Panic attack, fear of closed or open spaces)?

____ Epilepsy, seizures, convulsions or take medications to prevent them?

____ Recurring complicated migraine headaches or take medications to prevent them?

____ Blackouts or fainting (full/partial loss of consciousness)?

____ Frequent or severe suffering from motion sickness (seasick, carsick, etc.)?

____ Dysentery or dehydration requiring medical intervention?

____ Any dive accidents or decompression sickness?

____ Inability to perform moderate exercise (example: walk 1.6 km/one mile within 12 mins.)?

____ Head injury with loss of consciousness in the past five years?

____ Recurrent back problems?

____ Back or spinal surgery?

____ Diabetes?

____ Back, arm or leg problems following surgery, injury or fracture?

____ High blood pressure or take medicine to control blood pressure?

____ Heart disease?

____ Heart attack?

____ Angina, heart surgery or blood vessel surgery?

____ Sinus surgery?

____ Ear disease or surgery, hearing loss or problems with balance?

____ Recurrent ear problems?

____ Bleeding or other blood disorders?

____ Hernia?

____ Ulcers or ulcer surgery ?

____ A colostomy or ileostomy?

____ Recreational drug use or treatment for, or alcoholism in the past five years?

The information I have provided about my medical history is accurate to the best of my knowledge. *I agree to accept responsibility for omissions regarding my failure to disclose any existing or past health condition.*

Signature | Date | Signature of Parent or Guardian | Date

Product #10001PHY — Page 1 of 6

Fig. 131.1.a. NAUI medical statement.

AAUS MEDICAL EVALUATION OF FITNESS FOR SCUBA DIVING REPORT

_____   _____
Name of Applicant (Print or Type)   Date of Medical Evaluation (Month/Day/Year)

To The Examining Physician: Scientific divers require periodic scuba diving medical examinations to assess their fitness to engage in diving with self-contained underwater breathing apparatus (scuba). Their answers on the Diving Medical History Form may indicate potential health or safety risks as noted. Scuba diving is an activity that puts unusual stress on the individual in several ways. Your evaluation is requested on this Medical Evaluation form. Your opinion on the applicant's medical fitness is requested. Scuba diving requires heavy exertion. The diver must be free of cardiovascular and respiratory disease (see references, following page). An absolute requirement is the ability of the lungs, middle ears and sinuses to equalize pressure. Any condition that risks the loss of consciousness should disqualify the applicant. Please proceed in accordance with the AAUS Medical Standards (Sec. 6.00). If you have questions about diving medicine, please consult with the Undersea Hyperbaric Medical Society or Divers Alert Network.

TESTS: THE FOLLOWING TESTS ARE <u>REQUIRED</u>:

DURING ALL INITIAL AND PERIODIC RE-EXAMS (UNDER AGE 40):
- Medical history
- Complete physical exam, with emphasis on neurological and otological components
- Urinalysis
- Any further tests deemed necessary by the physician

ADDITIONAL TESTS DURING FIRST EXAM OVER AGE 40 AND PERIODIC RE-EXAMS (OVER AGE 40):
- Chest x-ray (Required only during first exam over age 40)
- Resting EKG
- Assessment of coronary artery disease using Multiple-Risk-Factor Assessment[1] (age, lipid profile, blood pressure, diabetic screening, smoking)
  Note: Exercise stress testing may be indicated based on Multiple-Risk-Factor Assessment[2]

PHYSICIAN'S STATEMENT:

_____ 01 Diver **IS** medically qualified to dive for: _____2 years (over age 60)
                                                              _____3 years (age 40-59)
                                                              _____5 years (under age 40)

_____ 02 Diver **IS NOT** medically qualified to dive:_____Permanently____
Temporarily.

Fig. 131.1.b. AAUS medical statement..

While meeting these specific goals can serve as an anchor for ensuring dive safety, achieving adequate fitness to dive on a personal and institutional level is a continuous process, requiring frequent reassessment of the human and non-human factors contributing to overall dive safety. These must be reviewed regularly.

Medical risk management

Ensuring fitness to dive is a strategy focused on risk mitigation for the individuals participating in diving and the organization in charge of directing dive activities. Carefully reviewing a diver's medical history, performing any necessary testing, and educating the diver can substantially reduce the risk of adverse incidents. However, it cannot wholly mitigate all risks. There is an inherent danger when humans depend on compressed gas and an artificial breathing apparatus for their survival while underwater. Additionally, very few (if any) divers can be considered perfectly fit to dive; nearly all divers will have some underlying medical problem or risk-associated human factor that can increase the probability of adverse events occurring while diving, even if only by a small degree. Therefore, it is up to the diver and their organization to decide what level of risk is acceptable for their particular activity. The diver and the organization must not lose track of the other important aspects of dive safety to maintain a risk profile consistent with its intended purpose.

Medical conditions

All individuals who intend to enter the water as a scuba diver must have a thorough medical evaluation, regardless of their known medical history or planned dive activities. While many medical factors play a role in overall fitness to dive, identifying comorbidities or underlying medical conditions that can influence safety is one of the most important first steps. This should focus on conditions that may place the prospective diver at risk of decompression sickness (DCS), pulmonary barotrauma, respiratory distress, sensitivity to changes in pressure, or unexpected

loss of consciousness underwater (6). Often, these can be identified by placing extra focus on the pulmonary, otolaryngologic,
cardiac, and neurological systems. Underlying psychiatric factors should also be considered (7). Especially when cold water
diving is anticipated, prospective divers should be evaluated for
their ability to respond to cold stress and cope with likely future
stressful situations and emergencies (6). Individuals with a history of these problems should be evaluated by a physician. However, their presence and general underlying pathology should be
known by anyone overseeing a dive operation.

Many underlying medical conditions pose an unacceptably
high level of risk for the individual diver and other diving team
members and their goals. The risks from these illnesses, both
acute and chronic, cannot be mitigated through modifications to
the environment and medical care and therefore represent absolute contraindications to diving (see the following section for
more detail). Other medical conditions pose risks, particularly
in cold water; however, with proper equipment, medication, and
team planning, divers with these conditions can successfully participate in diving-related activities with an acceptable risk profile.

Illnesses that permanently prohibit diving

Prior stroke, transient ischemic attack, or intracranial hemorrhage

These illnesses most commonly occur in individuals who have
underlying cerebrovascular risk factors, such as chronically elevated blood pressure. By definition, individuals with a history of

stroke are at an extremely high risk of having additional strokes or intracranial hemorrhage, especially when subject to some of the stressors associated with diving (6), (8). If another stroke were to occur while diving, this episode would likely be fatal, as the diver would experience weakness and/or paralysis of some extremities and an alteration in their level of consciousness. Additionally, the classic symptoms of stroke, such as focal weakness or loss of sensation, are almost impossible to differentiate from DCS, delaying proper diagnosis and medical treatment.

Severe prior DCS with neurological sequelae

Individuals who have experienced DCS may have an increased likelihood of subsequent repeat episodes of DCS and, therefore, should be carefully evaluated by a dive physician before returning to diving. This is especially true in cases of type II DCS or episodes that result in end-organ dysfunction, such as the central nervous system (9). Those with permanent sequelae, such as loss of sensation or motor function of an extremity, should be disqualified from further diving, as their current lack of function would be difficult, if not impossible, to differentiate from recurrent DCS. Additionally, this loss of function would make carrying out safe diving techniques more difficult.

Recurrent episodes of syncope (sudden loss of consciousness)

Recurrent syncopal episodes are often due to underlying cardiac arrhythmia, structural diseases such as valvular problems, hypertrophic obstructive cardiomyopathy, or autonomic dysfunction. Usually, no clear cause for these episodes is found. Syncopal episodes can be provoked by moderate or strenuous cardiac activity. An episode of sudden loss of consciousness would place the diver at significant risk of drowning, especially if using the common demand valve regulator (6). Since these conditions increase the risk of losing consciousness underwater, these individuals should be disqualified from diving.

Cardiac dysrhythmias – medication or implantable device dependence

Similar to the abovementioned risk of syncope, individuals who require antiarrhythmic medication have an increased likelihood of experiencing a sudden loss of consciousness, as these medications cannot prevent all dysrhythmias. Since these episodes will likely cause drowning and be fatal underwater, individuals with a history of cardiac dysrhythmias should be excluded from diving. Additionally, implantable cardiac pacemakers or defibrillators carry even greater risk when diving in cold water; these devices have been shown to have decreased reliability in cold environments (10).

Exertional angina left ventricular dysfunction due to prior myocardial infarction and congestive heart failure.

Individuals with these conditions are typically older and have many additional comorbidities that would make diving hazardous. Nonetheless, with a history of left ventricular dysfunction, a prospective diver would experience decreased exercise capacity that is needed to dive safely. Additionally, these conditions are strongly associated with an increased risk of recurrent myocardial infarction. Strenuous exercise is often required when diving, likely exacerbating existing symptoms and contributing to additional myocardial infarction.

History of cavitary lung lesions

Cavitary lung lesions caused by infectious diseases (such as tuberculosis or aspergillosis) or malignancy can leave behind a large empty space within the lung tissue, even after the primary disease has resolved. The presence of this cavity can increase the risk of pulmonary barotrauma and arterial gas embolism (AGE), as air-trapping may occur within them with changes in depth and pressure (6), (8). Therefore, the presence of these lesions should be considered an absolute contraindication to diving.

Prior spontaneous pneumothorax

Individuals with a history of spontaneous pneumothorax are frequently found to have small 'blebs' on the outer pleural surface of the lung. These are prone to rupture with the changes in pressure expected during diving and can cause pulmonary barotrauma or AGE (8). These individuals are likely to experience recurrence, even many years after their previous incident, and therefore should be disqualified from diving.

Recurrent small bowel obstruction

Recurrent small bowel obstructions often occur after abdominal surgeries due to adhesions that form within the abdominal cavity. While a history of abdominal surgery alone is not a contraindication to diving, individuals who have experienced obstructive disease have an increased risk of air trapping within a loop of the bowel, causing additional injury and possible hollow viscus perforation.

Open tympanic membrane perforation

A tympanic membrane perforation is a tear of the eardrum. It is a common injury in scuba diving that occurs due to failed middle-ear pressure equalization with changes in depth. Perforation usually heals on its own. However, diving should not be undertaken until this healing (or surgical repair) is complete. Water entering the middle ear decreases the likelihood of healing, increases the risk of infection, and can cause disabling vertigo due to cold stimulation of the inner ear (11). Following verified complete healing of the tympanic membrane, individuals may safely dive if they are given precautions regarding symptoms and are adequately supervised.

Pregnancy

Women who are pregnant or may become pregnant should avoid diving until after delivery. While studies have been unable to establish a significant correlation between diving and fetal abnormalities or pregnancy complications, it is likely that maternal diving does place an increased risk on the developing fetus (12). Given the changes in blood distribution associated with colder temperatures, diving in cold water may further increase these risks. Since diving is an avoidable risk for most women, the best advice is to avoid it once pregnancy has been identified.

Women who wish to return to diving following delivery should wait at least four weeks following normal vaginal delivery to allow for complete cervical closure and should wait eight weeks if they had a cesarean delivery (13). They should also be in adequate physical condition to resume strenuous activity, similar to guidelines suggested for other sports and activities.

Illnesses that raise concern and relative contraindications

Many other medical conditions will affect one's ability to safely participate in diving without necessarily preventing participation in the activity. However, the extent of this limitation depends on the severity of the disease or proper control with medication and/or lifestyle. They may require a diver to restrict their range of activities or take additional safety precautions. A dive physician should evaluate divers with these conditions before participating in organizational diving activities.

Seizure disorder

If a seizure occurs underwater, its associated loss of consciousness and subsequent postictal (unresponsive) period will put a diver at significant risk of drowning, similar to individuals with a syncope history, as described above. While using a full-face mask could theoretically reduce this risk, significant risk remains, as a seizing diver could experience other dive accidents, such as an uncontrolled ascent and involuntary breath-holding leading to potential lung damage during the ascent (14), (15). In the past, a history of two or more seizures in one's lifetime was considered an absolute contraindication to diving. However, this somewhat harsh restriction has been reconsidered in recent years.

There is scant epidemiological evidence to suggest that a history of seizure correlates with increased risk to scuba divers as long as divers do not require medication (15). Additionally, a history of febrile seizures in infancy, apneic spells, or seizures attributed to acute illnesses such as encephalitis and meningitis are thought to be unlikely to recur as long as a diver is not on controlling medication (8). Therefore, diving may be an acceptable activity for individuals who do not require medication for seizure prophylaxis. Guidelines vary on this; The Diving Diseases Research Centre (DDRC) states that if a person previously suffered from epilepsy but has been off medication without a seizure for at least five years, they may be fit to dive, while the European Diving Technology Committee guidelines for fitness to dive recommend that if a diver has been free of seizures for ten years without treatment, they may be fit to dive (2), (16).

Asthma and chronic obstructive pulmonary disease

Asthma is a respiratory disorder characterized by uncontrolled bronchoconstriction episodes, which can cause pulmonary obstruction, air trapping, and lung hyperinflation. Chronic

obstructive pulmonary disease (COPD), which is similarly characterized by bronchoconstriction and air trapping, can also pose
a major risk when breathing compressed gas through a demand
valve. Aspiration of cold water, as well as brisk exercise, can
trigger asthma and COPD attacks in many individuals. It was,
therefore, traditionally theorized that this significantly increased
risk for pulmonary barotrauma and bronchospasm made diving
unacceptably risky (6). However, epidemiological studies have
not demonstrated any link between mild asthma and increased
risk of pulmonary barotrauma or DCS (17). Divers can be
cleared by their dive physician if they are asymptomatic adults
with a childhood asthma history, have well-controlled asthma
with normal pulmonary function tests, or have not experienced
cold or exercise-induced wheezing (6).

Diabetes

While diabetes was once considered an absolute contraindication to safe participation in diving, diabetic divers have logged
countless safe dives. Therefore organizations such as DAN and
the DDRC have determined it to be an acceptable risk in certain
situations. The DDRC has found that divers with diabetes may
safely dive if they do not have associated retinopathy, peripheral
vascular disease, significant neuropathy, or coronary artery disease (18). DAN has also advised diabetic divers to avoid depths
below 30 meters (100 ft) due to possible confusion of nitrogen
narcosis with hypoglycemia, to limit dives to less than an hour
to allow for frequent blood sugar checks, and to avoid decompression stops or environments where quick access to the surface
is not possible (19). Additionally, dives in cold water could pre-

dispose these divers to hypoglycemia, exacerbating a significant underlying risk for diabetic divers (19). Therefore, dive planning should consider this and involve frequent blood glucose monitoring.

Other endocrine diseases

While diabetes is the most common chronic endocrine disease in the general adult population, additional endocrine illnesses exist which can compromise safety in cold water environments. Hypothyroidism and adrenal insufficiency result in decreased levels of circulating thyroid hormone and circulating cortisol, respectively. These conditions are associated with cold intolerance due to decreased heat production by the body, known as thermogenesis, predisposing prospective divers to hypothermia. These illnesses can also cause generalized weakness and, in extreme cases, dangerous drops in blood glucose. When adequate hormone replacement is done by medication administration, risks of cold intolerance and weakness are significantly decreased. Individuals with these medical conditions should only dive when their conditions have been stably controlled with medication for an extended period of time before their dive.

Patent foramen ovale

A patent foramen ovale (PFO) is a common condition (affecting up to 25% of the general population) and is a topic often mentioned when discussing fitness to dive. Its main importance is the possibility of causing a paradoxical gas embolism by the mechanism of venous blood (containing gas decompression bubbles) crossing from the right to left atrium during exertion (as well as during a strong Valsava maneuver), entering into the arterial circulation to cause an AGE. Additionally, some studies suggest that the presence of PFO could increase the risk of DCS (20), (21). Nonetheless, the incidence of DCS among divers with known PFO is still relatively low. Therefore routine screening for PFO is not indicated, except in divers with a history of severe or recurrent DCS (22).

Of note, a PFO should be differentiated from an atrial septal defect (ASD), which also allows for right to left intracardiac shunting, albeit to a greater degree. The presence of an ASD is an absolute contraindication to diving, as it dramatically increases risk of AGE (6).

Psychiatric diseases

Traditional fitness to dive surveillance focuses primarily on medical conditions and physical conditioning. However, there is increased awareness of psychiatric disorders that can significantly impact dive safety. Psychiatric conditions, particularly anxiety and panic attacks, can contribute to human error and should be assessed when divers are considered for underwater activity. All divers with a history of psychiatric illness should have had a recent evaluation by a trained psychiatric professional before engaging in diving (23).

Individuals with a history of panic disorder are at increased risk of panic attack while underwater, which can lead to uncontrolled ascents and poor decision making, which can impact dive safety for themselves and their team. While having a history of panic disorder was formerly an absolute contraindication to scuba diving, many guidelines have revised this to "untreated panic disorder" (24). Divers who are being treated for panic attacks may dive at an acceptable level of risk if their condition is well controlled with medications and/or non-pharmacological therapy, such as cognitive-behavioral therapy or mindfulness. Cold conditions and rough surface conditions can precipitate a panic attack, and divers with this history should be closely monitored whenever they enter the water, especially for the first time. Diving in tight spaces and overhead environments, such as below the ice or inside wrecks and caves, could increase the overall psychological stress. Individuals who have had adverse psychological reactions to such stressors should be excluded from diving.

Physical disabilities

A wide range of physical disabilities exists which may affect a diver's ability to safely participate in diving activities. While these may negatively affect mobility and dexterity, many disabilities may be less pronounced in the underwater environment, given the diminished effect of gravity on the body and heavy equipment. These effects vary depending on the mass and accessibility of equipment used. When cold environments necessitate heavier and bulkier equipment, the effect of physical handicaps may be magnified. Additionally, equipment that is both functional and protective in cold environments may be difficult to acquire or modify from existing gear. Individuals with special needs can still become proficient divers through specific training (for example, following the Handicapped Scuba Association standards) and gear configurations. A medical assessment should define the divers' capacity and limits to identify the best diving scenario for them.

Other medical factors that influence dive safety

Medication

Like underlying medical conditions, the use of medications by divers is quite common. In one UK study, over-the-counter drugs were taken by 57% of divers within six hours of their dive. Prescribed drugs were used by 23% of divers, and 10% reported the use of a cardiovascular medication (25).

Despite this high prevalence of medication use, very few studies have evaluated the effects of specific medications, or classes of medications, at depth. Therefore, it is ideal to have a physician knowledgeable in medicine and diving physiology to recommend specific drugs.

Some general recommendations do exist concerning more commonly used medications.

Antihistamines (such as diphenhydramine, promethazine, and chlorpheniramine) are used to treat allergies and respiratory illnesses. They may cause mouth and throat dryness or visual disturbances and sedation, which can inhibit a diver's cognition and reaction speed (26), (27). These medications may significantly impair the ability to perform essential tasks under stressful conditions (28).

Decongestants (such as pseudoephedrine, phenylephrine, and oxymetazoline) improve air flow through the nasal passages by constricting blood vessels in the nasal mucosa (26). As opposed to antihistamines, they cause central nervous system stimulation and can induce anxiety, tremor, weakness, and palpitations (26). When using these medications on longer dives, there is some risk of reverse block or air trapping and expansion within the middle ear. Additionally, the use of pseudoephedrine should be avoided when using enriched air due to the increased risk of oxygen toxicity (29).

Non-steroidal anti-inflammatory drugs (such as ibuprofen and naproxen) are some of the most commonly used medications in the world and temporarily relieve minor pain. While these have some mild side effects, such as gastric upset/heartburn, they may also mask early symptoms of DCS (26).

Motion sickness medications (such as antihistamine and scopolamine) are often used by divers to combat nausea and fatigue. These medications should be used cautiously, as they may induce the aforementioned visual disturbances and sedation and inhibit the ability to think and react quickly/appropriately (26), (29).

As mentioned before, there is little evidence regarding the effects of specific medications in the hyperbaric environment. Therefore, the following precautions should be taken (6):

1. Whenever possible, avoid all drugs when diving.
2. Any medication that impairs mental judgment or physical capacity should be carefully considered before being used when diving. If the medication is used, its expected benefits should outweigh the risks.
3. Never take a drug for the first time before diving.
4. Always consider whether the reason for taking a drug is itself a reason not to dive (for example, if nasal/sinus congestion is present, preventing adequate middle ear equalization, it is safer to cancel the dive rather than using decongestants).

5. Always consider the known side effects of a drug and whether they would be a problem when diving.

Recreational substance use

Similar to the usage of medication, ingestion of recreational drugs and alcohol is common among divers and significantly affects the ability to safely dive and perform other underwater activities. Nicotine, most commonly consumed through cigarette smoking, is decreasing in prevalence but is still used by many divers. Nicotine increases heart rate through sympathetic neural arousal, inducing coronary artery constriction and decreasing blood flow to the myocardium, the muscle cells of the heart (30). Additionally, cigarette smoking increases the amount of carbon monoxide in the blood, which can exaggerate the effects of hypoxia on the heart muscle. Smoking dramatically increases the risk of coronary artery disease, heart attack, and stroke, and divers are encouraged to quit smoking as soon as possible (30). Some training agencies (such as Global Underwater Explorers) will not allow smokers to attend their courses because of the adverse effect of cigarette smoking on a diver's health.

Alcohol is the most commonly used recreational substance among scuba divers. While alcohol can be safely consumed away from the water, its use dramatically increases the risk profile of diving. Due to the effects of nitrogen, divers are always at risk of developing confusion, decreased reaction time, impaired judgment, decreased coordination/dexterity, and loss of consciousness (31). These risks are severely increased when alcohol is combined with the activity (32). While this may seem intuitive, alcohol use can make dehydration more likely, a state that can predispose divers to the development of DCS (33). Additionally, alcohol increases the risk of hypothermia when diving in cold water. This is due to alcohol-induced dilation of the peripheral arteries, which diverts blood flow away from the core into the extremities, decreasing the amount of time required to develop hypothermia (33).

Other recreational drugs, such as cannabis, are less commonly used in proximity to diving. However, they do increase the risk of adverse events happening during a dive. Cannabis and other substances affect the ability to concentrate and perform cognitive tasks (34). Additionally, some reports have suggested that cannabis decreases tolerance to cold environments (34).

Dehydration

Due to multiple sensible and insensible causes, divers have an increased risk of developing dehydration before and during their dive activities. Scientific and technical diving requires carrying heavy equipment, often for prolonged periods and long distances, causing fluid loss by perspiration. During the dive, individuals breathe air with little humidity, increasing insensible fluid losses. When working in cold water specifically, the peripheral vasculature constricts, shifting blood volume to the core from the extremities in an effort to conserve heat. This reflex increases blood supply to the kidneys, which increases urine output, causing diuresis and further fluid loss.

For the average adult, approximately 60% of the total body weight is water, meaning that a 70 kg (150 lbs) adult is comprised of approximately 42 liters (11 gallons) of water. One-third of this fluid is located outside the cells and distributed within the intravascular and extravascular spaces (35). This quantity of free water expands and contracts with the body's ingestion and excretion of fluid. Mild dehydration (5% fluid loss) is associated with increased heart rate, decreased urine output, irritability, and drowsiness. Moderate dehydration (5–10% fluid loss) causes headache, dizziness, shortness of breath, and early neurological symptoms. Severe dehydration (10–20% fluid loss) results in severe neurological symptoms (such as hallucinations, delirium, and loss of consciousness), end-organ failure, and death. While mild dehydration can be treated with oral fluid and electrolyte replacement, moderate and severe dehydration require intravenous fluid administration and often hospitalization (36), (37).

These effects of dehydration significantly decrease the body's ability to shift blood flow from the periphery to the core, which can impair its ability to properly thermoregulate itself. While mild to moderate dehydration impairs only heat retention, severe dehydration can also prevent the body from conserving heat. Additionally, dehydration has been shown in animal models to significantly increase the risk of developing severe DCS and death, with a greater than double increased risk of DCS found among dehydrated pigs (38).

Medical exam

Medical evaluation of divers is an important process of identifying underlying medical conditions which may increase the risk of participating in diving activities. The most important examination is one that is done before diving, where the diver is screened before entering into high-risk conditions, such as cold water. Beyond this initial evaluation, routine reassessments must also be done after significant changes in health status, such as the development of new disease, or in routine time increments, as conditions may develop which contribute to overall risk. A doctor trained in dive medicine and familiar with the underwater conditions which divers will be entering into should always be consulted in order to ensure adequate identification of underlying conditions and proper risk mitigation steps.

Dive physicians may obtain additional testing for individuals who are seeking to safely learn to dive or re-enter the water after any change in health. This is particularly important if a diver will be entering cold water for the first time, as careful identification of underlying medical conditions which predispose a diver to danger in this unique environment will be required. In general, all divers should have a physical exam once per year, ideally by a physician who is familiar with dive medicine (23). Divers of advanced age and those with underlying medical conditions (such as those listed in the sections above) should have evaluations even more frequently (23).

A physician taking a meticulous medical history and using tools commonly available to general practitioners can successfully perform diver physical examination. Physicians will carefully assess any chronic complaints from the prospective diver and screen for a history of medical illness, medication use, and other substance ingestion. In addition to history and physical exams, specialized medical testing can be obtained. An EKG is a low-cost and easy to perform test which can identify any underlying cardiac dysrhythmias or predisposition to myocardial infarction. Pulmonary function tests, also known as spirometry, are performed to evaluate underlying asthma or COPD. Additionally, exercise tests while connected to a continuous EKG (known as a cardiac stress test) can be done to screen for underlying cardiac disease (Fig. 13.2). These tests are also done to ensure adequate exercise tolerance and are a valuable screening tool in detecting underlying medical conditions before they become problematic in the field.

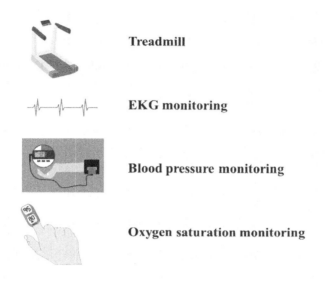

Fig. 13.2. Components of a cardiac stress test.

The diver must meet all necessary standards at the time of their medical examination in order to be considered fit to dive. If medical problems are identified, fitness status conditional to successful treatment can be granted (23). Restrictions on the type of diving, depth, time, environment, or duration of certification of fitness to dive may be imposed at the examining doctor's discretion. Dive supervisors should be aware of all findings to mitigate risk for the individual diver, the team, and the organization.

Lessons learned

- Diving generates stress on the human body.
- The cardiovascular and respiratory systems are the most affected.
- The psychological balance of the divers should also be considered.
- A medical assessment should carefully verify the presence of potential issues that prevent the divers from safely diving.
- Some medical conditions will permanently forbid diving activity; others could be only a temporary problem.

References

1. *Common factors in diving fatalities.* **DAN.** s.l. : DAN, 2010.

2. *Medical assessment of working divers: Fitness to dive standards of European Diving Technology Committee.* **Challenor, J.** 7, s.l. : European Diving Technology Committee, 2004, Occupational Medicine, Vol. 55.

3. **PADI.** *RSTC medical statement.* s.l. : PADI UHMS, 2006.

4. **NAUI.** *Medical statement.* s.l. : NAUI, 2022.

5. **AAUS.** *AAUS medical evaluation of fitness for scuba diving report.* s.l. : AAUS.

6. **Auerbach, P.S., Cushing, T.A. and Harris, N.S.** *Auerbach's wilderness medicine.* 7th edition. Amsterdam, The Netherlands : Elsevier Earth Sciences, 2017.

7. **Bates, M. et al.** Psychological fitness. *Military Medicine.* 2010, Vol. 175, pp. 21–38.

8. *Fitness to dive.* **Vorosmarti, J. and Linaweaver, P.G.** s.l. : 34th Undersea and Hyperbaric Medical Society Workshop, 1987.

9. **UHMS.** *UHMS best practice guidelines: Prevention and treatment of decompression sickness and arterial gas embolism.* s.l. : UHMS, 2011.

10. **Cloutier, J.M., Liu, S., Hiebert, B., Tam, J.W., Seifer, C.M.** Relationship of extreme cold weather and implantable cardioverter defibrillator shocks. *American Journal of Cardiology.* 2017, Vol. 120, 6.

11. **Daroff, B.** Vertigo. *American Family Physician.* 1977, Vol. 16, 4.

12. **St Leger Dowse, M., Gunby, A., Moncad, R., Fife, C., and Bryson, P.** Scuba diving and pregnancy: Can we determine safe limits? *Journal of Obstetrics and Gynecology.* 2006, Vol. 26, 6.

13. **DAN Medical Team.** *Return to diving after giving birth.* s.l. : DAN, 2016.

14. **Smart, D. and Lippmann, J.** Epilepsy, scuba diving and risk assessment: Near misses and the need for ongoing vigilance. *Diving and Hyperbaric Medicine.* 2013, Vol. 43, 1.

15. **Almeida Mdo, R., Bell, G.S. and Sander, J.W.** Epilepsy and recreational scuba diving: An absolute contraindication or can there be exceptions? A call for discussion. *Epilepsia.* 2007, Vol. 48, 5.

16. **DDRC Healthcare.** Can I dive with epilepsy? [Online] 12 30, 2019.

17. **Adir, Y. and Bove, A.A.** Can asthmatic subjects dive? *European Respiratory Review.* 2016, Vol. 25, 140.

18. **DDRC.** Diving and diabetes. *DDRC Healthcare.* [Online] [Cited: 6 11, 2016.]

19. *Guidelines to diabetes & recreational diving.* **Pollock, N.W. and Uguccioni, D.M.** Durham : s.n., 2005. Proceedings of the Undersea and Hyperbaric Medical Society/Divers Alert Network 2005 June 19 Workshop.

20. **Germonpré, P., Dendale, P., Unger, P. and Balestra, C.** Patent foramen ovale and decompression sickness in sports divers. *Journal of Applied Physiology.* 1985, Vol. 84, 5.

21. **Cross, S.J., Evans, S.A., Thomson, L.F., Lee, H.S., Jennings, K.P. and Shields, T.G.** Safety of subaqua diving with a patent foramen ovale. *BMJ.* 1992, Vol. 304, 6825.

22. **Bove, A.** Risk of decompression sickness with patent foramen ovale. *Undersea and Hyperbaric Medicine.* 1998, Vol. 25, 3.

23. **OSH.** The medical examination of divers. 2005.

24. **Colvard, D.F. and Colvard, L.Y.** A study of panic in recreational scuba divers. *The Undersea Journal.* 2003.

25. **Dowse, M.S., Cridge, C. and Smerdon, G.** The use of drugs by UK recreational divers: Prescribed and over-the-counter medications. *Diving and Hyperbaric Medicine.* 2011, Vol. 41, 1.

26. **DAN.** Over-the-counter medications. *DAN.* [Online] [Cited: 1 7, 2022.]

27. Diphenhydramine side effects. *Drugs.com.* [Online] [Cited: 1 7, 2022.]

28. **DAN.** DAN. *Motion sickness.* [Online] [Cited: 1 7, 2022.]

29. **Thalmann, E.D.** *Pseudoephedrine & enriched-air diving?* s.l. : DAN, 1999.

30. **DAN.** Medical nicotine and diving. *DAN.* [Online] [Cited: 1 7, 2022.]

31. **Clark, J.E.** Moving in extreme environments: Inert gas narcosis and underwater activities. *Extreme Physiology & Medicine.* 2015, Vol. 4, 1.

32. **Lee, J.** *Drinking and diving: Is it safe?* s.l. : DAN online, 2012.

33. **Brylske, A.** Alcohol, nicotine and divers: What you should know. *Dive Training Magazine.* 2003.

34. **DAN.** Cannabis and diving. *DAN.* [Online] [Cited: 1 7, 2003.]

35. **Tobias, A., Ballard, B.D. and Mohiuddin, S.S.** *Physiology, Water Balance.* s.l. : StatPearls, 2022.

36. Clinical practice guidelines: Dehydration. *Royal Children's Hospital, Melbourne.* [Online]

37. Dehydration and diving. *DIVER.* [Online] [Cited: 1 7, 2022.]

38. **Fahlman, A. and Dromsky, D.M.** Dehydration effects on the risk of severe decompression sickness in a swine model. *Aviation, Space, and Environmental Medicine.* 2006, Vol. 77, 2.

39. **Franklin, B.A., Berra, K. and Lavie, C.J.** Should I have an exercise stress test? *JAMA Cardiology.* 2016, Vol. 1, 9.

14. PLANNING FOR A SUCCESSFUL DIVE

Chapter highlights

Successful dives do not happen by chance. They result from carefully planned operations, wisely chosen divers, and identified goals.

A dive plan should provide all the essential information to safely and professionally complete operations. The operations' scope will dictate the plan's length and complexity.

The topics included in a dive plan should comprise goals and tasks, personnel involved, equipment needed, environmental considerations, and communication methods.

The plan should allow flexibility if a change in the conditions requires changes in the program. An alternative plan can often enable the team to continue with some operations, even under changed circumstances.

A step-by-step procedure can help manage more complex operations and be useful for less expert divers as guidance.

An emergency plan will identify the materials, personnel, and procedures needed for managing any situation that may threaten operations.

Introduction

Most divers know the saying, "plan your dive and dive your plan." Planning is at the core of safe and proficient diving, and enough time and resources should be allotted to this critical phase. A dive plan should include all the main variables involved in the underwater operations, including objectives, environmental conditions, tasks to be performed, roles of the personnel, equipment needed, step-by-step procedures, and emergency actions.

This does not necessarily mean that a dive plan must be a long and complex document; sometimes, just a few points suffice for successfully managing a dive. In other circumstances, such as when multiple dives with a broad scope of activities are to be performed, the plan will become more articulated.

Whatever the plan, it is important for the involved personnel to clearly understand the plan's elements and their role in it.

A dive plan is not "written in stone," meaning that if new conditions arise, it should be possible to modify the plan accordingly to suit the changed situation. A plan has to contain elements that allow for adjustments. If a plan changes, this change should be clearly stated and shared within the team.

Identify main objectives of the dive

The first step for a proficient dive is to clearly identify the objectives to be reached (1). This is even more important for dives related to working activity, where the goals are often agreed between the customer and the diver and are part of a formal contract.

The achievable objectives should be identified based on the following considerations:

- *Available resources*: Some objectives may require specific tools and equipment.

For example, suppose the main goal is to recover a deployed instrument. In that case, it could be necessary to use lift-bags or cranes involving topside support in addition to the standard diving gear.

- *Available divers*: The skills, experience, and number of available divers are crucial for assessing what kinds of goals are reasonably reachable. The skills and experience of the divers should be proportionate to the complexity of the operations, also taking into account the environmental conditions. Intuitively, more complex tasks will require more skilled and experienced divers. Still, even relatively simple tasks may become problematic if they have to be performed in more challenging environmental conditions, such as cold water or bad visibility.

For example, a team of divers who can safely operate in relatively shallow, clear, and warm waters could be unable (or unable safely) to achieve the planned goals in cold, deep waters with reduced visibility.

- *Available time*: The diving time is necessarily limited. It will be dictated by a combination of breathing gas duration, decompression limits, thermal exposure, and fatigue. For this reason, the divers need to have a reasonable estimate of the time they will need to fulfill any of the planned goals. A buffer should also be considered for unforeseen circumstances leading to delays in operations. In more complex procedures, the different objectives will likely need to be divided between multiple dives. In this case, if there is a specific sequence of operations to be performed, the divers should be clearly briefed on what task comes first and what follows.

For example, let's say a dive team is required to deploy a mooring system composed of helix anchors and sub-surface floats. The first step is to fix the anchors; once these are securely in place, the divers, in a following dive, will connect the rest of the system. An estimate of the time needed to place each anchor compared with the available dive time will indicate how many anchors can be deployed in each dive.

- *Available support crew*: Some goals may require additional personnel besides the divers to support the diving operations. This could include the boat crew, dive tenders, and standby divers. The plan should clearly identify the number and level of qualification needed for these extra support individuals.

  For example, if the goal is to retrieve a large, deployed instrument, it could be necessary to use a boat with a proper crane for lifting the instrument. In this case, an expert crane operator is needed.

Once all the objectives have been identified, they should be ranked in order of priority, with the more important being the object of primary attention and effort. Secondary objectives will be achieved only if time and/or resources allow. Sometimes a specific sequence is needed, with some goals completed before others. The diving team could operate together on each goal, or each diver could focus on a specific task. This will depend on the operations' structure and the divers' skills.

It is essential that all the primary and secondary objectives are clearly indicated in the diving plan and that the divers are briefed on the operation's goals, including their specific role in achieving the planned target. Other personnel should also know the tasks and the relevant procedures to reach them. In large operations, with multiple teams involved, this planning and briefing phase may require multiple days of meetings. Therefore, sufficient time should be allotted before the actual day of the dives.

Environmental and operational considerations

Diving environments vary, ranging from shallow, warm, and clear waters, such as tropical seas, to extremely deep, cold, and murky conditions. Therefore, the impact of the environmental conditions on the safety and proficiency of the divers is significant and should be assessed during the planning phase (1).

Dives that can be relatively easy to perform under good environmental conditions could become challenging in harsher conditions. For example, manipulative tasks are severely impaired when diving in cold water because of the unavoidable use of bulky gloves and the loss of dexterity associated with cold exposure. In this situation, the dive plan should consider splitting the tasks over multiple dives to limit cold exposure during each dive. Also, it could be wise to perform the most complex manipulative operations at the beginning of the dive when the impact of cold on the hands is still limited.

In some areas, strong currents may develop due to the tide. This may affect the divers, making underwater operations difficult or even impossible. Usually, a current speed of 1 kt is considered the upper limit for safe operations. In such environments, the diving plan should carefully assess the timing of the tides and associated currents to identify the best "window" to dive in slack water. It is to be noted that the actual starting time and strength of a current could be challenging to identify precisely, so a buffer should be built into the diving time. Planning a dive time that will come very close to the beginning of the tidal cycle and associated current is not prudent. Any small delay in the dive or any discrepancy between the forecasted current starting time and actual current development could put the operation and the divers at risk.

Another critical environmental consideration is the presence of contaminants in the water. The typology of pollutants should be assessed, and the best protection procedures should be implemented. Depending on the contamination's severity, these may vary from the use of a full-face and drysuit to a fully encapsulated diver. Diving in such waters and using specialized gear also require the divers to have specific training and experience. The diving plan should include what decontamination and prophylactic procedures are advisable and how these should be performed (2).

The presence of boat traffic is also a potential hazard that increases the divers' risk. This is particularly relevant when diving into areas such as ship lanes and harbors. The plan should include the procedures for signaling the presence of divers to the incoming boats, identifying boundaries that should not be crossed by the divers, and procedures for emergency ascent to avoid the most exposed sectors of the diving area. Another risk that should be addressed is the presence of strong acoustic emissions; these could be generated by sonar or by construction activities in the area, such as pylon driving. The plan should identify all the potential sources of such emissions and the appropriate mitigation strategies, such as advising the boats in the area not to use sonar in proximity of the diving zone or coordinating the dive operations with the construction works to avoid having divers in the water during the noisiest procedures.

Further environmental constraints include access to the diving area. The dive plan should indicate the procedure for entering and exiting the water and also identify if the access point is suitable for emergency rescue or if another egress zone should be considered for extricating an injured diver. Any submerged obstacle in the diving area should also be noted, especially if close to the entrance zone. If the divers use a boat as the diving platform, it should be specified whether the boat will be "live" or anchored during the operations. Operating from a "live" boat requires good coordination between the diving team and the crew, with particular attention to the position of the divers about specific hazards such as propellers, thruster, and any source of differential pressure generated by the boat. The recovery procedures for the divers should be indicated in the diving plan to be shared and discussed with the boat personnel.

In offshore settings, the plan should specify if "blue diving" procedures should be implemented and what specific marking and signaling devices are to be carried by the divers. The type and number of marking tools used will be defined based on the risk of the divers emerging far from the planned exit zone, therefore requiring a search by the support personnel. Each diver should generally carry at least one SMB; extra locating devices may include a signaling mirror, strobe-light, whistle, dye, and Personal Locator Beacon.

Team composition and roles

The team composition is a critical element of the dive plan. The divers should be chosen based on their experience and qualifications for the tasks.

It will be the least experienced/skilled member who dictates the actual level of proficiency of the team and the level of diving operations that can be safely performed (4).

Roles should be clearly stated for each team member. A team leader should be assigned; they will supervise, ensuring the dive develops by the plan. The leader will also switch to an alternate or emergency plan if needed due to operational or safety concerns. If a dive-buddy system is adopted, each diver should be paired with another, and they should be reciprocally responsible for each other during all phases of the dive.

Roles can be switched within a dive. For example, the diver who "opens" the team during the initial phase of the dive could be the one "closing" the group at the end of the dive. This inversion is common in cave diving when it is not advisable to shuffle positions at the end of the penetration. In this case, the first diver entering the cave will be the last when exiting. These role switches should be indicated in the dive plan to avoid misunderstanding and confusion during the dive.

In more complex operations, having several backup divers, in case one diver cannot fulfill the needed tasks, could be necessary. The roles of these divers should be indicated in the plan. The plan should also state whether exchanging just one diver or more is feasible or if the backup team can replace the whole team. Sometimes the latter solution is better in terms of proficiency, especially if the divers have only trained within their own team. Replacing the entire crew with the backup when one team member became unfit for the operations was standard procedure for the NASA Apollo missions because of the need to have astronauts well used to working together (4).

During the pre-dive briefing, the role of the divers should be reviewed, ensuring that each team member is well aware of their responsibilities and those of every other diver in the team. In some cases, the same task could be shared by multiple divers, building redundancy within the team. Once the roles have been agreed upon, they should be adhered to throughout the dive.

Equipment needed

The plan should indicate what diving gear is required and if any other specific tool is to be used during the diving operations. It should confirm (after checks are completed) that such gear is in working order and in a good state of maintenance.

Spare material should be available so that if something fails, it can be replaced in the field, allowing for the operations to continue. The number of spares is related to the complexity of the dive, the number of divers, and the available space and logistics on the diving platform.

One important point is to ensure that sufficient breathing gas is available and that each cylinder has been analyzed and labeled with its contents. It is also a good idea to verify the compatibility between cylinder valves and regulator first stages regarding the type of connection (DIN or Yoke/International).

A gear checklist should be integrated into the plan to help verify that all the needed gear is available and that all the material has been retrieved at the end of the operations. This list should be checked by the leading diver or by one individual specifically appointed to do so.

Some equipment to be shared between the divers, for example, full-face masks, regulators, and diving suits, may require specific cleaning and sterilization procedures between uses. In multi-day operations with the same team, assigning gear to each of the divers could be helpful. Each diver will be responsible for the assigned material and daily maintenance and cleaning.

Operative step-by-step plan

The dive plan should provide a reference for the sequence of tasks. This way, the divers will be guided through the operation's different stages, confirming that no step is missed.

Key steps that should be included are:

- Planned starting time of the dive.
- Ingress area and procedures.
- Safety check at surface and at depth (available gas, regulators check, computer/tables, no leaks, etc.).
- Planned maximum depth.
- Planned turn-around gas pressure and/or bottom time.
- Description of the specific operations and related procedures.
- Safety or decompression stops.
- Egress procedure.
- Emergency procedures.

The number of steps and, therefore, the length of the plan will depend on the complexity of the dive. The level of detail of the steps also relies on the experience of the divers. Student divers in their very first immersion will require a more detailed step-by-step description of the procedures than expert divers.

Contingency plan

Even the best dive plan can be compromised by some unforeseen event. As an example, a sudden change in weather conditions may make the planned diving area unsafe to reach or to operate within. For this reason, an alternative plan should be available.

A contingency plan will allow the team to refocus the operation on different targets that can still be achieved despite the change in conditions. The advantage of having this backup option is that it will still be possible to complete some valuable results instead of scrapping the whole operation, which would lead to loss of time, money, and resources.

The alternate goals could be targets planned for another dive that can now be done instead of the current dive that needs to be postponed, or they could have been secondary tasks that the new conditions now make primary.

For example, suppose the sea status does not allow diving in the intended location. In that case, the conditions at another site planned to be part of another dive may be acceptable.

The contingency plan could also require changes in the roles of the divers and the requirements in terms of material. For this reason, it is a good idea to discuss the alternative plan during the briefing so that the involved personnel are aware of the needed changes and ensure that the material is readily available.

The diving leader/supervisor should switch to the contingency plan based on all the available information. It should be immediately communicated to the rest of the team.

Emergency plan

An emergency plan covers the situation where a risky status has developed with potential material damage and personnel harm.

An emergency may manifest suddenly, and the time to react could be limited. For this reason, the procedures to be followed should be indicated in the plan, including what resources are available and the best way to activate the emergency response. All the involved personnel should be well acquainted with the plan to initiate it without delay.

Each plan will be tailored to the specific operation, but a few elements are shared between any emergency plan:

- *Conditions requiring the plan's activation*: It should clearly state what events will trigger the emergency response. For example, a "lost diver" situation will prompt a search operation.
- *Who is in charge of the plan*: The operations will be directed by a designated leader who will activate all the needed procedures. For example, the diving supervisor could be in charge of the plan. An "alternate leader" should also be identified if the "primary leader" becomes unavailable. This could be the case if the leader is involved in an emergency.
- *Roles*: The roles and duties of the personnel participating in the plan should be assigned so that each operator knows exactly what to do and how. For example, there could be designated first aiders with qualifications and experience.
- *Material resources*: The available resources and how to retrieve them should be indicated in the plan. For example, an oxygen kit should be available in a medical emergency.
- *Communication*: Define what kind of communication is available. For example, in offshore operations, communi-

cation could be possible via marine radio frequency and/ or satellite phone.

- *Transportation*: Identify a reliable plan for the medical evacuation of injured individuals. For example, this could include requesting a helicopter evacuation.
- *Follow-up*: Once the emergency has been resolved, appropriate follow-up procedures could include recording witnesses, securing the gear, debriefing the personnel involved, contacting the next of kin of the individuals affected by the emergency, and seeking legal advice. For example, if a diving accident occurs, the gear of the diver involved should be preserved untouched for the investigators.

A template for a basic diving plan is provided in Appendix A3.

Lessons learned

- A diving operation should follow a well-defined plan.
- The plan should include the goals and the required resources in terms of equipment and personnel.
- The plan should allow for some flexibility if the situation requires changes.
- An alternate plan could allow for continuing the operations even if the primary plan has to be scrapped.
- An emergency plan is needed to manage critical situations where a threat to the personnel or equipment develops.

References

1. **Dinsmore, D. and Bozanic, J.** *NOAA Diving Manual.* 5th edition. s.l. : NOAA, 2013.

2. **Barsky, S.** *Diving in high-risk environments.* 4th edition. Ventura, CA : Hammerhead Press, 2007.

3. **Lock, G.** *Under pressure.* 2019.

4. **NASA.** *Apollo 13 – Houston, we've got a problem.* Washington, DC : NASA, 1971. Document ID 19700021741.

APPENDICES

A1 – Risk evaluation example

Hazard	Low risk	Moderate risk	High risk
Weather	Calm weather	Worsening weather	Rough
Site exposure	Protected	Partially exposed	Totally exposed
Current	No current	< 0.5 kts	> 0.5 kts
Daylight availability	Start and finish in full daylight	Start before dawn – finish at dusk	Night operations
Water temperature	Warm (T > 20°C - 68°F)	Temperate (10°C < T <20°C - 50°F< T <68°F)	Cold (T < 10°C – 50°F)
Visibly	> 10 m – 32 ft	10 to 5 m 32 to 16 ft	< 5 m – 16 ft
Boat traffic	Minimal	Moderate	Heavy
Medical problems	EMS within 30 minutes	EMS 0.5 to 2 hours away	EMS more than 2 hours away
Deco plan	No deco	Limited deco	Long deco
Dive profile	Ideal profile	Square profile	Sawtooth profile
Dive depth	< 18 m – 60 ft	18 m – 30 m 60 ft – 100 ft	> 30 m – 100 ft
Dives/day	1 to 2 and shallow	2 to 3 and shallow	Multiple – deep
Out-of-gas	1/3 rule	50 bar / 500 psi reserve	All usable
Out-of-gas continued	Direct ascent available	Direct ascent possible but not preferred	Direct ascent impossible
Entanglement	Good visibility, limited use of lines, skilled divers using reels	Reduced visibility, multiple lines in water	Bad visibility, multiple lines in water
Task-related	Use of cameras, slates, reels, tapes	Use of small tools, light lifting	Use of heavy tools, heavy lifting, pneumatic systems

Buddy separation	Good visibility, good communication, roles planned and followed	Reduced visibility, loss of SA	Bad/zero visibility
Separation from boat	No current, clear weather, calm sea	Current, reduced visibility, waves	Strong current, bad visibility, large waves

Operations falling into the high-risk zone may require modification to the initial plan, extra action, or, if the risk is not manageable, may have to be postponed or canceled.

A2 – Diving risk assessment example

Hazard	Impacted	Risk	Primary mitigation strategy	Further mitigation
Illness/injury	All	Low	• Report to the diving supervisor. • Dive only when fit.	• The operations may need to be suspended.
Slips/trips/falls	All	Low	• Move carefully on deck. • Divers must not walk donning fins.	• Help from topside personnel during kitting-up and de-kitting.
Falling cylinders	All	Low	• Secure cylinders. • If possible, lay cylinders down flat.	• Provide first-aid if injury occurs. • Designed storage area.
Ear damage	Divers	Medium	• Equalize. • Do not dive with a cold/ear/sinuses problem.	• Assistance in water by dive buddy. • Apply appropriate first aid.
Nitrogen Narcosis	Divers	Medium	• Limit depth. • Be aware of first symptoms/signs.	• Dive buddy assistance. • Reduce inert gas in mix (Nitrox, Trimix).
DCI	Divers	Medium	• Conservative dive planning. • Follow no-deco profiles. • Ascend slowly.	• Provide oxygen at surface. • Monitor vital signs. • Transport to hyperbaric facility.
Rapid ascent	Divers	High	• Buoyancy control. • Check ascent speed.	• Provide oxygen at surface. • Immediate medical assistance.
Out of gas	Divers	High	• Use appropriate gas-management procedures. • Use redundant regulators/gas supply.	• Gas sharing with dive buddy. • Stage cylinders at deco-station.
Injuries with boat propeller	Divers	Medium	• Maintain communication with the boat crew. • Engine is off or in neutral when divers are in water.	• Use protected propellers or jet systems. • Entrance/exit far from propellers.
Other boats	Divers	Medium	• Have the diving flag and/or alfa flag exposed. • Use SMB if not surfacing along a shot/anchor-line.	• Boat crew on watch. • Communicate with approaching boats.
Injuries during entry/exit	Divers	Low	• Use appropriate entry techniques. • A solid divers' ladder to be used.	• Boat supervisor to brief on specific entry/exit procedures.

Hazard	Impacted	Risk	Primary mitigation strategy	Further mitigation
Low visibility	Divers	Medium	• Maintain close buddy contact. • Consider using reference lines. • Limit swimming distance.	• Review lost-buddy procedures. • Use a buddy-line. • Use tether diving.
Currents Drifting	Divers	Medium	• Use shot-line. • All divers to carry SMB. • Swim close to the bottom if possible.	• Maintain a lookout by topside personnel. • Have a tender ready for deployment. • Do not dive if current above 1 kt.
Entanglement	Divers	Medium	• Carry appropriate cutting tools. • Use streamlined equipment. • Be skilled in the use of reels.	• Add extra attention when diving in low-visibility water. • Be careful when handling ropes/lines.
Cold water Hypothermia	Divers	Medium	• Use appropriate exposure protection suit (drysuit preferred) to match conditions. • Consider reducing dive times. • Monitor divers for signs of cold. • Ensure all divers are aware of the signal to indicate chill.	• Consider aborting the dive and keep the diver warm and out of the wind on the boat. • Be prepared for mild hypothermia rewarming. • Provide heated shelter.
Cold air/ wind chill Hypothermia	Topside personnel	Medium	• Use appropriate exposure protection suit. • Consider wind-chill factor. • Limit exposure.	• Check the evolution of weather conditions. • Provide heated shelter.
Cold water/ air Equipment failure	Divers	Low	• Use cold-water regulators (sealed first stage). • Avoid breathing the regulators at the surface. • Store the gear in insulated containers.	• Review out-of-gas scenarios. • Be ready to abort the dive. • Limit use of purge buttons/inflators.
Diving equipment malfunction	Divers	Low	• Pre-dive checks. • Good equipment maintenance. • Redundant gas supply.	• Abort dive. • Diving buddy assistance. • Spare gear.

A3 – Dive plan example

Date: 01/02/2022	Location: Long Reef	Project: Video survey #A007

Divers	Certification	1st Aid	O₂	Signature
Joe Diver *	Dive Instructor – Scientific Diver	YES	YES	
Helen Deep	Dive Master – Scientific Diver	YES	YES	
Mike Tide	Advanced diver – Scientific Diver in training	YES	NO	
Lucy Wave	Advanced diver – Scientific Diver in training	YES	YES	

* Dive leader

Other personnel	Role – duties
Tony Helm	Skipper
Rose Compass	First Mate
Tim Rig	Deckhand

Equipment*		
Type of equipment		Supplied by
Drysuit	4	Personal
Regulators	4	Divers' locker – personal
Dive computers	4	Personal
BCD	4	Divers' locker
Cylinders	8	Divers' locker
Oxygen kit	1	Boat
SMB	4	Divers' locker
Weight system	4	Divers' locker
Divers recall system	1	Boat
First aid kit	1	Boat
Dive flag	1	Boat
Video camera	2	Science lab

* All gear checked to be in working order and serviced

Breathing gas		
Air	Nitrox O$_2$% 32	Trimix O$_2$% He%
Dive tables/computers/decompression software		
Specify table	Specify computer	Specify software

Type of diving* (check all that apply)		Diving mode
Near-shore	Night diving	Scuba
Offshore	Current	Tethered scuba
Blue water	Surf zone	Surface-supply/Hookah
Overhead environment	Repetitive dive	Full-face and comms
Cold water (< 10°C – 50°F)	Decompression dive	Rebreather

* some diving environments/modes require specific training. Verify that the divers have the required certification/experience.

Local environment characteristics	
Weather forecast	To be checked 72–48–24 hours before dive day
Current	Check tidal charts
Boat traffic	Monitoring CH 16 and lookout
Visibility	Consider bottom composition and weather conditions
Access	From boat platform and divers' ladder
Procedures	
Describe dive schedule (depth, time), planned operations, tools to be used, diving team composition, and duties.	
Specific hazards	
Identify potential hazards and mitigation procedures.	
Emergency contacts	
DAN number	
Local decompression chamber	
EMS	
Diving Safety Officer	

A4 – Mathematical elements of decompression models

Decompression models are based on theoretical tissues, often called compartments, that are in-gassing (absorbing) or off-gassing (releasing) inert gas in function of the ambient pressure, the partial pressure of the gas in the breathing mix, and dive time. For the gas kinetic, the gases are considered to interact with a liquid.

In this section, we will see some basics of physics and mathematics behind the decompression models.

For further details, the reader should refer to the excellent book "The Physics of Scuba Diving" by Marlow Anderson. Nottingham University Press. Nottingham, UK, 2011

Basic physics laws controlling decompression.

Dalton's Law: At a given temperature and volume in a mixture of non-reacting gases, each constituent exerts the same pressure as it would if it were the only gas in the same volume. This pressure is called the "partial pressure" of the gas.

The magnitude of the partial pressure of a gas is linked to the percent of this gas within the mix and the ambient pressure.

For example, nitrogen represents 79% of atmospheric gases; therefore, its partial pressure at sea level (ambient pressure of 1 atm equivalent to 33 fsw) is 0.79 atm (26 fsw). During a dive, with the increasing ambient pressure, N_2 partial pressure will increase proportionally, playing a key role in the in-gassing of this inert gas in the tissues.

Henry's law: The rate a gas dissolves in a liquid is proportional to its partial pressure and solubility constant.

As for the interaction with inert gas, the body tissues are considered "liquid." This means that all the rest being equal, gases with higher partial pressure will dissolve more in the tissues.

Exponential function

The process of gas intake and off-gassing follows what is defined as an exponential function. This function can be identified in several natural processes, including bacteria growth and radioactive decay.

An exponential function comprises a "base" and an "exponent."

It can be expressed as $y = b^x$, where b is the base, and x is the exponent. Fast-changing values characterize it, making the function graph steeper as the exponent value increases after a threshold.

A common base is the number "e," which is the number of Euler. It's an infinite number and can be expressed as:

$$e = \lim_{n \to \infty} \left(1 + \frac{1}{n}\right)^n$$

We consider the first few decimals for practical applications so that e = 2.71828. An example of such a function is $y = e^x$ (Fig. A.1)

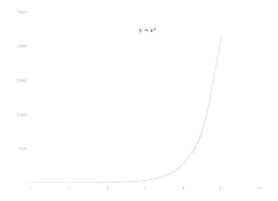

Fig. A. 1. Graph of an exponential growth function

Exponential growth

Let's consider the following function:

$P(t) = P_0 e^{kt}$ P_0 is a constant giving the initial value of the function
        k is a constant affecting the rate of growth of the function

For example, we will calculate the time the function will have doubled its value given an initial value of P_0 and the growing factor k.

$P(t) = P_0 e^{kt} = 2P_0$
$e^{kt} = 2$
$kt = \ln(e^{kt}) = \ln2$ $\ln2 = 0.6931$
$kt = 0.6931$
$t = 0.6931/k$

If we consider a growing factor of 0.5 and as temporal unit minutes, the function will have doubled its value after about 1.4 minutes. A higher growing factor leads to a shorter doubling time. In this example, if we consider a growing factor of 1, the doubling time will be about 0.7 minutes, which is half the one for the original growing factor. For a growing factor of 1 (growing rate 100%), the total growth rate of the exponential function is exactly P itself.

Exponential decay

The function controlling exponential decay is the same type as the one controlling exponential growth but with a negative exponent.

$P(t) = P_0 e^{-kt}$

In this case, over time, the value of the function decreases close to zero (Fig. A.2.)

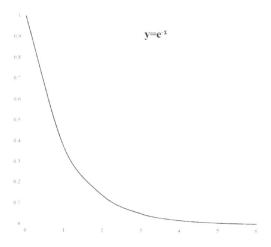

Fig. A. 2. Graph of an exponential decay function

Half-time

In the exponential decay function, the half-time, or half-life, indicates the time at which the value of the function will be halved. For example, in radioactive decay, this time indicates when half of the original element is changed in its decay product.

As an example of half-time, we consider the following function:

$P(t) = P_0 e^{-3t}$
In this function, the base is e, and the exponent (k) is 3
We want to identify the time t at which $P(t) = \frac{1}{2} P_0$
$\frac{1}{2} P_0 = P_0 e^{-3t}$
$\frac{1}{2} = e^{-3t}$

Calculating the logarithm of both components of the equation, we have:

$$\ln(1/2) = \ln(e^{-3t})$$

The logarithm can be expressed as a product between the base's logarithm and the exponent's logarithm. Because $\ln(e)$ is 1 by definition, we have:

$$\ln(1/2) = \ln(e) \times -3t = 1 \times -3t$$
$$\ln(1/2) = -3t$$

The logarithm of a fraction can be expressed as the difference between the logarithm of the numerator and the logarithm of the denominator; the logarithm of 1 is 0 by definition, therefore:

$$\ln(1/2) = \ln(1) - \ln(2) = 0 - \ln(2) = -0.6931 = -3t$$
$$-3t = -0.6931 \rightarrow t = 0.6931/3 = 2.31$$

This exponential decay function will reach half of its original value at a time $t = 2.31$

More in general, we can say that half-time and exponent k are linked by the equation:

$$k = \ln(2)/\text{half-time}$$

Partial pressure of inert gas in the tissue

The dissolution of inert gas into the tissues can be compared to the dissolution into a liquid; its tension (that is, its partial pressure as a dissolved gas in the tissue) will determine the inert gas load of the tissue.

The partial pressure (tension) of the dissolved gas (P_t) in the tissue at a given time t can be calculated from the following equation:

$$P_t = P_a + (P_0 - P_a) \, e^{-kt}$$

P_a is the partial pressure of the gas in the breathing mix.
P_0 is the initial tension of the gas in the tissue.
k is the growth rate of the function.

k is linked to the half-life of the tissue:
$k = \ln2/T$ T is the half-life of the tissue.

Pa is linked to the concentration of the inert gas in the breathing mix and to the ambient (absolute) pressure.

If $P_a > P_0$, then the tissue is in-gassing inert gas.
If Pa < P_0, then the tissue is off-gassing inert gas.

For example, we consider a diver starting a dive at sea level and breathing air as the mix (N_2 = 79%). His body is considered saturated at sea level.

P_0 = 0.79 atm. (equivalent to 26 fsw)

This is the initial partial pressure of nitrogen in the tissues in equilibrium with the atmospheric partial pressure at sea level.

If the diver descends to 66 fsw, the hydrostatic partial pressure of nitrogen will increase by 0.79 × 66 = 52 fsw equivalent pressure. Therefore, the total Pa of nitrogen will be the original sea level pressure plus the hydrostatic increase: 26 + 52 = 78 fsw equivalent pressure.

$$P_t = 78 + (26 - 78)\ e^{-kt} = 78 - 52e^{-kt}$$

This function approaches the ambient pressure (in this case, 78 fsw) over time. If this pressure is greater than the initial pressure, the diver is on-gassing; if the ambient pressure is less than the initial pressure, then the diver is off-gassing nitrogen.

Haldane decompression model

In Haldane's decompression model, the on-gassing and off-gassing of nitrogen are controlled by a series of tissues (five in the initial formulation of the model) of different half-times.

Considering the change in tissue tension as an exponential function, we have:

$$k = \ln(2)/\text{Half-time}$$

Considering Pa as the ambient nitrogen pressure, when a tissue reaches this value, it is considered saturated, and no further in-gassing will happen.

$$P(t) = Pa + (P_0 - Pa)\ e^{-kt}$$

After six half-times, $P(t)$ will be within

$$1 - (\tfrac{1}{2})^6 = \tfrac{63}{64} = 98.4\% \text{ of Pa}$$

For the original 5 compartments of the Haldane model (half-time in minutes), the relative k values are indicated in table TA.1.

Compartment half-time	k value
5	ln(2)/5 = 0.1386
10	ln(2)/10 = 0.0693
20	ln(2)/20 = 0.0347
40	ln(2)/40 = 0.0173
75	ln(2)/75 = 0.0092

Tab. TA.1. k values for the five Haldane compartments.

For example, consider the P_{N2} in the 75 minutes compartment after 30 minutes of dive at 60 fsw.

$Pt = Pa + (P_0 - Pa) \ e^{-kt}$

$P_0 = 0.79 \times 33 = 26$ fsw (initial N_2 tension in the compartment)

$Pa = 0.79 \times (60 + 33) = 0.79 \times 93 = 73$ fsw (N_2 pressure at depth)

93 fsw is given by the hydrostatic (60 fsw) plus atmospheric pressure at surface (33 fsw)

$Pt = 73 + (26 - 73) \ e^{-kt} \rightarrow Pt = 73 - 47e^{-kt}$

For the compartment considered (75 minutes half-time), k = 0.0092

$P_{30} = 73 - 47e^{-0.0092 \times 30} = 73 - 47 \times 0.76 = 37$ fsw

After 30 minutes of dive at 60 fsw, the 75-minutes compartment will have a P_{N2} equivalent to 37 fsw.

The load on the considered compartment is only 24% of the full saturation because:

$$1 - 0.76 = 0.24$$

The same differential equation applies to off-gassing. For example, consider a diver whose 20 minutes compartment (k = 0.0347) has a nitrogen load equivalent to 43 fsw. The diver ascents directly to the surface (ambient pressure equivalent to 33 fsw). What is the nitrogen load after eight minutes?

In this case:

$P_0 = 43$ fsw   initial N_2 load

$Pa = 26$ fsw (33×0.79) ambient N_2 partial pressure at surface

$Pt = Pa + (P_0 - Pa)\ e^{-kt}$

$P_8 = 26 + (43 - 26)\ e^{-0.0347 \times 8} = 26 + 17e^{-0.2776} = 39$ fsw.

Off-gassing reduces the diver's nitrogen load from 43 to 39 fsw.

Haldane deco-stops

In Haldane's model, decompression stops at 10ft increments are considered not to overcome the ratio between the inert gas's compartment tension and ambient pressure.

Following this model, during a deco stop, the tissues will off-gassing until their residual P_{N2} is below a critical value to safely ascend to the next shallower stop without violating the 2 to 1 ratio.

Calculating the time needed at each stop for the off-gassing is possible using the following equations:

P_0 = nitrogen load (tension) of the given tissue

Pa = nitrogen ambient partial pressure in the breathing mix

Pm = maximum nitrogen load (tension) to safely ascend to the next stop

$k = \ln 2/T$ $\qquad\qquad$ T = half-time of the considered tissue

$Pm = Pa + (P_0 - Pa)\, e^{-kt}$

$Pm - Pa = (P_0 - Pa)\, e^{-kt}$

$(Pm - Pa) / (P_0 - Pa) = e^{-kt}$

$\ln\left[(Pm - Pa) / (P_0 - Pa)\right] = -kt$

$t = -\ \ln\left[(Pm - Pa) / (P_0 - Pa)\right]$

$t = \ \ln\left[(P_0 - Pa) / (P_m - Pa)\right]$ *

$t = \ \ln\left[(P_0 - Pa) / (P_m - Pa)\right]$ **(1)**

* from the rule: $-\ln A = \ln A^{-1} = \ln (1/A)$

Equation 1 correlates the compartment's half-time with the needed decompression time at a given depth considering the inert gas ambient pressure and tissue tension.

Example:

A diver descends to 60 fsw and stays for 60 minutes. The breathing gas is air (N_2 79%).

Total ambient pressure at 60 fsw is 60 + 33 = 93 fsw. P_a at this depth is 0.79 × 93 = 73 fsw

The dive starts from sea level at ambient pressure of 33 fsw, and P_0 is 0.79 × 33 = 26 fsw

For the calculation, we consider the 20 minutes compartment with k = 0.0347

$$Pt = Pa + (P_0 - Pa)\,e^{-kt}$$

$$P_{60} = 73 + (26 - 33)\,e^{-0.0347 \times 60} = 68 \text{ fsw}$$

This is the inert gas tension within the 20 minutes compartment at the end of the bottom time.

Using the same equation, we can calculate the tension within all 5 compartments (Tab. TA.2)

Compartment half-time	N_2 load
5	73
10	73
20	68
40	57
75	46

Tab. TA.2 Nitrogen tension in the 5 compartments after 60 minutes dive at 60 fsw

After 60 minutes, the 5 and 10 compartments are saturated (60 minutes is 12 times the half-time of the 5 minutes compartment and 6 times the half-time of the 10 minutes compartment).

The diver starts the ascent to the surface where the partial pressure of nitrogen is 26 fsw. Four of the five compartments have a load of more than double this pressure; therefore, the 2 to 1 ratio is violated, and the divers need to stop for off-gassing before safely reaching the surface.

In this dive, the "controlling compartment" is the 5 minutes with the highest nitrogen load (the 10 minutes also has the same load).

Considering the 2 to 1 ratio, the diver can ascend to a depth where Pa is ≤ 73/2 = 37 fsw. The total nitrogen pressure at this depth is 37/0.79 = 47 fsw. This is equivalent to an actual water depth of 47 − 33 = 14 fsw.

Because Haldane's stops are calculated every 20 fsw, the first stop for this dive is at 20 fsw until Pa drops to a safe level to ascend to the next stop at 10 fsw.

To calculate the length of the stop at 20 ft, we can apply the following formula:

$$t = \frac{T}{ln2} \times \ln\left(\frac{P0 - Pa}{Pm - Pa}\right) \qquad \textbf{(2)}$$

Pa = (20ft + 33ft) × 0.79 = 42 fsw

This is the nitrogen partial pressure in the breathing gas at the 20 ft stop.

Pa = (10ft + 33ft) × 0.79 = 34 fsw

This is the nitrogen partial pressure in the breathing gas at the 10 ft stop.

Pm ≤ 2 × 34 = 68 fsw

Maximum N_2 load to safely ascend from 20ft to 10ft.

P_0 for the 5 minutes tissue is 73 fsw (see Tab. A.2).

Applying formula **2,** we can calculate the deco-time at 20ft

$$t = \frac{5}{\ln 2} \times \ln \left(\frac{73-42}{68-42}\right) = 1.4 \text{ minutes}$$

We can calculate the deco-time for the 10 minutes tissue similarly; the value is 2.4 minutes.

At 20 ft, the diver stops for 3 minutes allowing the 5 and 10-minute tissues to off-gas below their safety limits. The other tissues will also off-gas because Pa (42 fsw) is less than the one in each tissue.

Considering the formula $Pt = Pa + (P_0 - Pa) \, e^{-kt}$ for the 10-minutes tissue after 3 minutes at 20ft, we have:

$$P_3 = 42 + (73 - 42) \, e^{-0.693 \times 3} = 67 \text{ fsw}$$

To ascend directly to the surface, the nitrogen partial pressure in the five compartments must be no more than twice the N_2 pressure at sea level ($2 \times 0.79 \times 33 = 52$ fsw).

We can calculate the required deco stops by applying formula 2 to the tissues above such limit.

With the passing of time, the "controlling tissue" (the one controlling the decompression schedule) changes following the new saturation, or supersaturation, level of the tissues.

In general, for a diver to ascend to d feet, the tissue load (Pm) must be:

$$Pm \leq 2 \times 0.79 \times (33 + d) = 52 + 1.58d \text{ fsw}$$

This shows that the maximum nitrogen load to ascend to a given depth safely is a linear function of such depth.

M – values

The original US-Navy dive table considered six compartments with half-lives of 5, 10, 20, 40, 80, and 120 minutes.

The M-values are the maximum allowable over tension in each compartment (Pm) considering a surface PN_2 of 26 fsw equivalent (0.79 × 33).

The M-values have been calculated by gathering empirical data from a large number of dives (Table TA.3)

Half-life (minutes)	M-values (Pm)	Ratio (Pm/26)
5	104	4.00
10	88	3.38
20	72	2.77
40	58	2.23
80	52	2.00
120	51	1.96

Tab. TA.3 Original US-Navy M-values.

For the classic Haldane theory, Pm would be constant at 52 fsw, and the ratio would be 2 for any compartment.

The US-Navy tables are less conservative for the first 4 compartments and at least as conservative as Haldane for the last 2 compartments.

The direct ascent is possible when the tissues are loaded to no more than the corresponding M-value. We are in a no-deco-stop situation.

For example, consider a dive to 80 ft. breathing air (N_2 79%). We want to know how long we can stay at such depth without needing a deco stop.

Pa = 0.79 × (33 + 80) = 89 fsw

For the 5-minute compartment, the M-value is > 89, so it will not affect deco-stop needs.

For the 10-minute compartment, the M-value is 88, and we have to consider the following:

$$t = \frac{T}{ln2} \times \ln \left(\frac{Po-Pa}{Pm-Pa}\right)$$

t = maximum time at depth without exceeding the M-value of the tissue (for the 10-minute compartment, it is 88).

T = half-time of the tissue (in this case, 10 minutes)

Po = 26 fsw (partial pressure of nitrogen at sea level on resurfacing)

Pa = 89 fsw (partial pressure of nitrogen at depth)

Pm = 88 fsw (M-value for the 10-minute tissue).

The formula provides a maximum time at depth (t) of 59.7 minutes for the 10-minute tissue.

Extending the calculation to the other tissues, the shortest time (37.74 minutes) belongs to the 20-minute tissue. This is the "controlling tissue" for an 80 ft dive.

Changes in the M-values of the tissues will affect the maximum allowable time at any given depth for a no-deco dive.

The US-Navy also compiles decompression tables where the M-values are modified to obtain more conservative values.

Repetitive dives

After a reasonably long surface interval, the slowest compartment (half-time 120 minutes) will have the most residual nitrogen to be tracked to assess the overall residual nitrogen in the body.

This information is encoded in the US-Navy tables as the "pressure group letter."

Once at sea-level pressure, any compartment will be totally off-gassed after six times its half-life. For the 120-minute compartment, this equals 12 hours. For this reason, repetitive dives are defined as dives occurring within a 12-hours interval.

The minimum surface interval (10 minutes for the US-Navy tables) indicates that dives that follow each other within this time are considered a single (longer) dive regarding nitrogen intake.

The US-Navy tables consider the "total air pressure A_t" in the 120-minute compartment as:

$$A_t = Aa + (A_0 - Aa)e^{-kt}$$

Aa = Ambient total pressure

A_0 = initial load in the compartment

k = ln2/120 = 0.00578 for the 120-minute compartment

The pressure groups are defined by intervals of total air pressure in the 120-minute compartment for 2 fsw steps from 33 to 63 fsw (Tab. TA.4)

Letter	Total pressure	Letter	Total pressure	Letter	Total pressure
A	33 – 35 fsw	F	43 – 45 fsw	K	53 – 55 fsw
B	35- 37 fsw	G	45 – 47 fsw	L	55 – 57 fsw
C	37 – 39 fsw	H	47 – 49 fsw	M	57 – 59 fsw
D	39 – 41 fsw	I	49 – 51 fsw	N	59 – 61 fsw
E	41 – 43 fsw	J	51 – 53 fsw	O	61 – 63 fsw

Tab. TA.4 – US-Navy pressure groups defined by intervals of total air pressure.

As an example, consider a dive at 35 ft starting from a totally desaturated tissue (Tab. TA.5):

A_0 = 33 fsw (saturation at surface ambient pressure)

Aa = 35 + 33 = 68 fsw (total pressure at depth)

k = ln2/120 = 0.00578 (considering the 120-minute compartment)

A_t = 68 + (33 − 68)e^{-kt} = 68 − 35$e^{-0.00578t}$

t	A_t	Letter
5	34	A
15	36	B
25	38	C
40	40	D
50	42	E
60	43	F
80	46	G
100	48	H
120	51	I
140	52	J
160	54	K
190	56	L
220	58	M
270	61	N
310	62	O

Tab. TA.5 – Group letters for the total air pressure for the time periods given in the 35-foot row of the US-Navy Table 3.

Residual nitrogen time

It is the time required for a diver with no previous tissue loads who dives at a given depth to have their total air pressure in the 120-minute compartment rise to the interval corresponding to the letter designation.

For a 25-minute dive at 40 ft, we have:

$$A_t = Aa + (A_0 - Aa)e^{-kt}$$

$$A_{25} = 33 + 40 + (33 - (33 + 40))e^{-0.00578 \times 25} = 73 - 40^{-0.00578 \times 25} =$$
$$73 - 34.6 = 38.4$$

This value defines group C in the US-Navy tables. It means a diver with no previous nitrogen load spending 25 minutes at 40ft will have a final nitrogen load equivalent to a C group.

The US-Navy group letter designation

$A_t = Aa + (A_0 - Aa)e^{-kt}$ can be used to compile the US-Navy table letter designation groups considering 5-minute increments for any of the depths in the US-Navy Table 3. We have to consider the 120-minute tissue for the calculations (k = ln2/120 = 0.00578).

Fast compartments control deep dives. Because the tables are generated considering the slower 120-minute compartment, shallower dives to the NDLs lead to pressure groups further in the alphabet than deep dives to the NDLs.

Divers on deep dives run out of NDL in the fast compartments before building enough N_2 in the 120-minute compartment to increase their group letter. This creates the triangular shape at the bottom of US-Navy Table 3.

Altitude diving

At increased altitude, the atmospheric pressure is reduced following the exponential function:

$P_h = e^{-0.0000383h}$

P_h = pressure in atmosphere

h = altitude in feet

For this reason, the difference between the underwater pressure and the pressure at the surface is enhanced when diving at altitude.

The consequence is that the depth to consider for the inert gas calculations when diving at altitude is deeper than the actual one.

$D = d/e^{-\alpha}$

D = equivalent depth (ft)

d = actual depth (ft)

$\alpha = 0.0000383h$

h = altitude (ft)

For high altitude, the difference becomes relevant.

For example, consider a dive at an altitude of 5,000 ft (1,500 m). The atmospheric pressure will be:

$P_{5,000} = e^{-0.0000383 \times 5,000} = 0.83$ atm.

If we dive at a depth d at this altitude, it will be equivalent to a dive at a depth $D = d/0.83 = 1.2d$

That is a 20% difference.

Diving at altitude causes the tissues to be over-saturated compared to the new ambient pressure. To reduce the risk of DCI, the divers should wait for the 120-minute compartment to be in equilibrium with the new ambient pressure. This means waiting for 12 hours at altitude before diving.

If we dive before 12 hours, we should consider the tissues having some residual nitrogen. For example, we consider a dive at an altitude of 4,000 ft. At this altitude, the atmospheric pressure is:

$$P_{4,000} = e^{-0.0000383 \times 4,000} = 0.86 \text{ atm.}$$

The total pressure load is equivalent to 33/0.86 = 38.6 fsw. At sea level, this pressure is equivalent to a pressure group C (Tab. TA.4).

If the divers dive at 55ft for 40 minutes, this is equivalent to 64 ft at sea level, rounded to 70 ft on the US-Navy table. The RNT for this depth, starting from group C, is 15 minutes. The ESDT is, therefore, 40 + 15 = 55 minutes, exceeding the NDL for this depth.

Flying after diving

The normal pressurization in a commercial aircraft is to an altitude of 8,000 ft (2,400 m), which is 74% of 1 atm. Flying therefore exposed divers to reduced ambient pressure.

Theoretically, 12 hours surface interval should suffice for the total off-gassing of the 120-minute compartment and, therefore, of the whole body.

It seems that even slower compartments (up to 635-minute) should be considered when flying. Mostly if multiple dives and/ or multiple days of diving have been performed.

As a general consensus to mitigate DCI risk, 24 hours of surface time before flying is suggested.

Reverse profiles

In a direct profile (deepest phase first), some fast tissues could already be off-gassing when ascending at shallower depths. All the compartments will be on-gassing in a reverse profile (shallow phase first). Consider the following example:

First dive at 100 ft for 15 minutes, followed by a dive at 50 ft for 15 minutes.

$Pa = (33 + 100) \times 0{,}79 = 106$ fsw
$P_0 = 33 \times 0.79 = 26$ fsw

In a direct profile, we can calculate the nitrogen loads (see the section "Partial pressure of inert gas in the tissue" for the calculation) as in the following table (TA.6).

Tissue	5	10	20	40	80	120
100 ft	95	77	58	44	36	33
50 ft	69	70	61	49	39	35

TA.6 – Nitrogen tension within the compartments during a direct profile.

At 50 ft depth, the 5-minute and 10-minute compartments are off-gassing (the tension is reduced from the values at 100 ft to the ones at 50 ft).

In a reverse profile, the tension values are in the following table (TA.7).

Tissue	5	10	20	40	80	120
50 ft	61	52	42	35	31	29
100 ft	100	86	68	51	40	36

TA.7 – Nitrogen tension within the compartments during a direct profile.

In this case, all the compartments are on-gassing. The tissues will have a larger nitrogen load after a reverse profile than after a direct profile.

For this reason, it is more convenient to follow a direct profile when diving to minimize nitrogen loads and optimize the available dive time.

Depth	NDL	A	B	C	D	E	F	G	H	I	J	K	L	M	N	O
10	NL	60	120	210	300	797	*									
15	NL	35	70	110	160	225	350	452	*							
20	NL	25	50	75	100	135	180	240	325	390	917	*				
25	595	20	35	55	75	100	125	160	195	245	315	361	540	595		
30	405	15	30	45	60	75	95	120	145	170	205	250	310	344	405	
35	310	5	15	25	40	50	60	70	80	100	140	160	190	220	270	310
40	200	5	15	25	30	40	50	70	80	100	110	130	150	170	200	
50	100	10	15	25	30	40	50	60	70	80	90	100				
60	60	10	15	20	25	30	40	50	55	60						
70	50	5	10	15	20	30	35	40	45	50						
80	40	5	10	15	20	25	30	35	40							
90	30	5	10	12	15	20	25	30								
100	25	5	7	10	15	20	22	25								
110	20	5	10	13	15	20										
120	15	5	10	12	15											
130	10	5	8	10												
140	10	5	7	10												
150	5	5														
160	5	5														
170	5	5														
180	5	5														
190	5	5														

US-Navy Table 3. Depth in feet. Time in minutes. For demonstration purposes only.

ACKNOWLEDGMENTS

Writing a book is a challenging task; it requires time, attention, and endurance.

Seldom can a book be written without some help and support from others.

I wish to thank, first and foremost, Brian Strickland, M.D. He was extremely helpful in reviewing the medical facets of the book, and his chapter on medical fitness is an essential addition to the topic of risk management for diving operations.

Ed O'Brien, Dive Operations Manager for the Woods Hole Oceanographic Institution, not only encouraged me in writing the book but by working with him, I gained invaluable first-hand experience on most of the operations and topics described in the book.

Kim Malkoski and Joe Fellows provided constructive feedback to the book draft based on their experience as professional divers.

I also acknowledge the International Academy of Underwater Sciences and Techniques, of which I'm a member, for allowing the use of their prestigious logo.

Thanks to Dive System and Alessandro Grasso for the stunning cover picture.

Miss Taylor Gramkowski is the author of my bio picture. She did an excellent job despite the subject.

The technical part of a book is no less critical than the authorship for its success. I had the pleasure of working with two true professionals. Tom Bedford edited the manuscript, providing essential suggestions and reviewing its extended bibliography. Paul Baillie-Lane did a terrific job with the page design, typesetting, and book cover design.

As the author, any errors that remain are my sole responsibility.

Made in the USA
Middletown, DE
27 October 2023

41305540R00283